T0334760

ARCHITECT
OF
EVANGELICALISM

ARCHITECT

Essential Essays of

OF

Carl F. H. Henry

EVANGELICALISM

LEXHAM PRESS

Architect of Evangelicalism: Essential Essays of Carl F. H. Henry
Best of *Christianity Today*

Copyright 2019 Christianity Today International

Lexham Press, 1313 Commercial St., Bellingham, WA 98225
LexhamPress.com

Print ISBN 9781683593362
Digital ISBN 9781683593379

Lexham Editorial: Elliot Ritzema, Danielle Thevenaz
Cover Design: Lydia Dahl
Typesetting: ProjectLuz.com

CONTENTS

Foreword

If there was ever a time for us to think along with Carl F. H. Henry, now is the time. In glancing through the contents of this book, I was frankly amazed at the number of times Henry touched on themes that we wrestle with today. What most interests me is his ongoing efforts to help evangelicals engage the public square and to do so in a way that was true to the complexity of pursuing justice and the truth of Scripture.

I came of age intellectually in what might be called the post-Henry years. That's how it seemed to me at least, given the circle of evangelicals I was in. Henry was seen as a man for another time. He was too rationalistic. He drew lines a little finely. And he was too assured of himself.

What I've discovered in the last decade or so is this: He indeed was rationalistic, but given the Twitteresque and emotional way we carry on theological and political debate these days, we could use a jolting dose of rationalism again.

He was indeed a man for his own times, like all of us are. But unlike most of us, I believe the quality of his thought will bring wisdom to the later generations who take the trouble to read him.

He was indeed assured, and perhaps sometimes of himself. But what mostly bleeds through his words is a fierce devotion to

Jesus Christ and biblical truth. Anyone who displays that type of passion is going to be accused of being "too assured" now and then.

When another Karl, Karl Barth, visited America in 1962, he spoke in Washington, DC. Carl Henry was in the audience, and during the question and answer session, he stood, identified himself, and asked a question. Henry relates the moment in his autobiography:

> "The question, Dr. Barth, concerns the historical factuality of the resurrection of Jesus." I pointed to the press table and noted the presence of leading reporters. ... If these journalists had their present duties in the time of Jesus, I asked, was the resurrection of such a nature that covering some aspect of it would have fallen into their area of responsibility? "Was it news," I asked, "in the sense that the man in the street understands news?"

Henry was trying to see if Barth was committed to the historicity of the resurrection.

I'm sure what was going through Barth's mind was his previous interactions with editors of *Christianity Today*. Some questions had been submitted to Barth through Geoffrey Bromiley, translator of Barth's *Dogmatics,* but Barth refused to answer their queries. He likened them to an inquisition, saying, "These people have already had their so-called orthodoxy for a long time. They are closed to anything else."[1]

Henry continues,

> Barth became angry. Pointing at me, and recalling my identification, he asked: "Did you say Christianity *Today* or Christianity *Yesterday*?" The audience—largely

---

1. Karl Barth, *Letters 1961–1968* (Grand Rapids: Eerdmans, 1981), 7.

nonevangelical professors and clergy—roared with delight. When countered unexpectedly in this way, one often reaches for a Scripture verse. So I replied, assuredly out of biblical context, *"Yesterday, today, and forever."*[2]

Carl Henry at his assured best!

To the degree that Henry was merely self-assured, he'd be the first to eschew pride. We live in a time, however, when some of the most fundamental truths of the gospel are questioned and doubted and debated afresh. If only there were more intellectuals of Henry's caliber who had the assurance to affirm publicly and without shame the truth of the gospel yesterday, today, and forever.

Mark Galli

Editor in Chief, *Christianity Today*

---

2. Carl F. H. Henry, *Confessions of a Theologian: An Autobiography* (Waco, TX: Word, 1986), 211.

Introduction

On December 7, 2003, Carl F. H. Henry, the intellectual giant of the evangelical movement, was called home by our Lord at the age of ninety. Born the eldest of eight children on January 22, 1913, to German immigrant parents in New York City, Henry's life reflected much of broader American life in the twentieth century. Following high school, Henry was focused on a career in journalism. He served as a reporter for the *New York Herald Tribune* and the *New York Daily News*, and covered a section of Long Island for *The New York Times*.

It was through his experience as a journalist that he came in touch with the Oxford Group, and at twenty he encountered the truth of the Christian gospel and trusted in Jesus Christ. After he heard Wheaton College president J. Oliver Buswell deliver a persuasive defense of the Christian faith, he left his promising journalism career to enroll at Wheaton in 1935. While there, the young Henry made friends with Billy Graham and studied with philosopher Gordon Clark. He also met his future wife Helga Bender; they would marry in 1940 and have two children. Henry went on to complete his BA and MA at Wheaton, earn an MDiv and ThD at Northern Baptist Seminary, and later a PhD in philosophy with Edgar Brightman at Boston University.

Growing Influence and
Christianity Today

After teaching from 1942 to 1947 at Northern Baptist Seminary, he was invited by visionaries Charles E. Fuller and Harold J. Ockenga to join the faculty of the new Fuller Theological Seminary in Pasadena, California. Henry emerged as a key leader of the new seminary, serving as dean of the faculty and coordinator of the annual Rose Bowl Sunrise Service. In the same year he went to Fuller, Henry published his first significant book, *The Uneasy Conscience of Modern Fundamentalism.* The prophetic message of this work, combined with the new platform at Fuller, paved the way for Henry to become "the architect of evangelicalism." The themes expounded in *Uneasy Conscience* proleptically pointed to the emphases that characterized Henry's life and writings for the next several decades.

Less than a decade after his move to Pasadena, Henry in 1956 accepted the invitation to serve as founding editor of *Christianity Today* (*CT*). Henry's background in journalism as well as his grow-ing reputation as an academic leader and evangelical statesman made him the ideal person to lead the *CT* project as envisioned by Graham and Ockenga. From his post as editor, he solidified his leadership within American Christianity, climaxing with the chairmanship of the World Congress on Evangelism in Berlin in 1966.

This book represents the best of Henry's contributions to the pages of *CT*, laying out themes that are also regularly found in the fifty books that Henry authored or edited. Throughout his writ-ings, Henry convictionally articulated an unflinching commit-ment to the centrality of the gospel and the authority of Scripture while calling for serious engagement with the culture and the pressing issues of the day. Henry's irenic spirit enabled him to interact with others in an engaging way while holding unapologetically to the truthfulness of historic Christianity.

Evangelical Distinctives

The nearly three dozen essays found in this volume represent in an exemplary fashion what can be called "the evangelical mind." Part I offers eight essays that characterize various aspects of evangelicalism. Evangelicals are men and women who love Jesus Christ, love the Bible, and love the gospel message. Evangelicalism is a cross-denominational movement that emphasizes classical Protestant theology, which is best understood as a culturally engaged, historically shaped response to an empty and despairing mainline liberalism on the one hand and a doomed reactionary fundamentalism on the other. Evangelicals are heirs of the Reformation from the sixteenth century; of Puritanism and Pietism from the seventeenth century; of the eighteenth and nineteenth century revivalists and awakening movements; and particularly of the post-fundamentalists coming out of the twentieth century's modernist-fundamentalist controversies. In the first section of this volume, readers will see how Henry time and again focused on central core beliefs, stressing the importance of cooperation, scholarship, and cultural engagement with an emphasis on confessional beliefs and Christian unity.

Part II focuses on evangelicals and modern theology. By the middle of the twentieth century mainline theology had lost its compass, if not its soul, while fundamentalism had grown hardline, harsh, and isolationist. Henry stressed the importance of biblical inerrancy and authority to counter the emptiness of liberalism while calling for Christian unity and cultural engagement as an alternative to the irrelevance of fundamentalism. In order to avoid errors on the left and the right, Henry, in his journalistic approach to doing theology, invited his readers to center and ground their beliefs in Jesus Christ.

Evangelicalism, claimed Henry, exemplifies both a historical meaning and a ministry connectedness, but it also includes a truth claim, a theologically and historically shaped meaning. In the pages of *CT*, Henry never tired of contending that evangelicalism is more than an intellectual assent to creedal formulas, as important as that may be. It is more than a reaction to error and certainly more than a call to return to the past.

We cannot and must not miss the fact that evangelicals have focused on the authoritative Scripture and the gospel, as made known in the person and work of Jesus Christ. Evangelicals believe that salvation is by God's grace alone through faith in Jesus Christ. By grace believers are saved, kept, and empowered to live a life of service. At its heart, Henry maintained that evangelicalism is the affirmation of and genuine commitment to the central beliefs of orthodox Christianity, as these beliefs have been carefully and clearly articulated through the ages.

Evangelicalism in the World

Parts III and IV provide a vision for an evangelical educational model as well as a road map for faithful engagement with the culture. Henry rejected an anti-intellectual approach to the Christian faith. Rather, he prioritized the importance of the life of the mind, learning to think Christianly. He made a case for the place of rigorous academics, engaging all subject matter from the perspective of a Christian worldview. His vision for education displayed his own wide-ranging intellectual interests. Henry dreamed of a major evangelical research university in one of America's major cities that would engage the arts, the sciences, the humanities, the social sciences, and professional programs from the vantage point of God's natural and special revelation.

He longed for the next generation to recognize that truth counts, that there is indeed a historic faithful orthodoxy to be confessed and proclaimed.

Henry, years before many other evangelicals, saw the importance of cultural engagement and social ethics. He used the pages of *CT* to become the leading voice on these important issues among the growing movement, always wanting to wed evangelism with calls for racial reconciliation and social justice. Bringing together commitments to Christian worldview, active service, and global evangelism, Henry in his day also challenged the views of communism, Marxism, and fascism. He insisted that the evangelical movement must not be only otherworldly, but must remain culturally engaged.

He was quick to remind readers, however, that such engagement cannot be this-worldly only, for service apart from the gospel, while certainly helpful, is ultimately insufficient. Thus, instead of withdrawing from the world in a separatistic or legalistic fashion, as had been the tendency of fundamentalism, evangelicalism must be engaged in cooperative and collaborative educational, missional, and ethical efforts. Indeed, Henry trumpeted the call for Christian unity and cooperation both in mission and in shared core beliefs. Simultaneously, he reminded everyone of the biblical pattern for purity, holiness, and faithful Christian living. His vision for the evangelical world could be characterized as "partly hoping, partly fearing," as he lived between the tensions of his hopeful dreams and his fretful concerns for what he observed all around him.

Beyond the Christianity Today *Years*

Henry stepped down as *CT* editor in 1968 but continued to write a column called "Footnotes" between 1969 and 1977. The essays found throughout the pages of *CT* paved the way for Henry's magnum opus, the six-volume *God, Revelation, and Authority* (1976–1983), which in many ways represents a portrait of the evangelical mind. In this work, Henry presented a magisterial defense of historic Christianity while framing the issues of truth, propositional revelation, authority, and hermeneutics in a way that encouraged the faith once for all delivered to the saints (Jude 3) to be passed on to succeeding generations.

After leaving *CT*, Henry also returned to teaching, first at Eastern Baptist Theological Seminary and Trinity Evangelical Divinity School. He then served as lecturer-at-large for World Vision and Prison Fellowship, and was president of the Evangelical Theological Society and the American Theological Society. He delivered several of the most prestigious academic lectureships in the world, including the University of Edinburgh's famous Rutherford Lectures in 1989. That same year, Henry co-chaired, with Kenneth Kantzer, the Evangelical Affirmations Conference. For years he was affiliated with the Southern Baptist Convention and was for four decades a member of the Capitol Hill Baptist Church in Washington, DC, though most of his innumerable involvements took place outside of Baptist life.

Yet Henry's roles as author, editor, and lecturer only tell a portion of the story. Through his presence and leadership at key events throughout the second half of the twentieth century, cataloged by others as well as his own autobiographical reflections, Henry's influence was immense. Not only by his public writings, but through his prolific correspondence and mentoring of younger leaders, he influenced a generation to think Christianly about all of life. His penetrating insights into matters of culture and society provided the intellectual muscle to wrestle with key issues and challenges facing both church and society.

I had the privilege to know and learn from Carl F. H. Henry. Those who knew him well found him to be a devout believer and faithful disciple of Jesus Christ. Those who met him for the first time often stood in awe of his giant intellect. But soon, almost without exception, they became more impressed with his humility and gracious spirit. The essays in this volume reflect well his intellectual prowess and his gracious and irenic spirit, modeling in an exemplary way the characteristics of evangelicalism's intellectual and theological architect. Let us pray that the lessons available in this volume will serve well the evangelical movement in the twenty-first century as it struggles with similar issues and wrestles with the additional challenges of our day.

David S. Dockery
President, Trinity International University
and Trinity Evangelical Divinity School

Part I

DEFINING
EVANGELICALISM

Chapter 1

EVANGELICALS AND FUNDAMENTALS

A number of circumstances have transpired that call for review of the terms *evangelicalism* and *fundamentalism* in relation to the present theological situation. Several opposing schools of thought vie for use of the term *evangelical*. Appropriation of the word by those who do not hold to its biblical and historic content has caused some hesitancy on the part of those who hold to the doctrines of revealed Christianity, as to its proper use. They fear misunderstanding of their theological position.

Complication also results from the diverse connotations surrounding the term *fundamentalism* in various countries. Fundamentalism has a different savor in England and Australia than in the United States and Canada. Further confusion has been caused by criticism of the "fundamentalism" of Billy Graham by liberal and neo-orthodox leaders and the censure of the "modernism" of Mr. Graham by some fundamentalists. All this semantic confusion calls for clarification.

A growing preference for the term *evangelicalism* has developed within recent years in circles that keep to traditional doctrines held to be fundamental to Christian faith. This choice finds root in several important facts: first, the word is scriptural and has a well-defined historical content; second, the alternate, *fundamentalism*, has narrower content and has acquired unbiblical accretions.

In the New Testament the Greek *to euaggelion* (the evangel) is translated gospel, glad tidings. After the death of Christ the term signified the history of Christ and is the title prefixed to each of the four narratives of his birth, doctrine, miracles, death, resurrection and ascension. Further, the evangel signified the Christian revelation and was applied to the system of doctrines, ordinances and laws instituted by Christ. The evangel indicated more than a proclamation of pardon through faith and included all the teachings of Christ. Thus in the commission recorded in Mark the apostles were instructed "to go into all the world, and preach the gospel (the evangel) to every creature." That they were sent not only to proclaim pardon through Christ but to instruct men in all details of the Christian religion, is plain from the parallel passage in Matthew, "Go ye, therefore, and teach all nations ... teaching them to observe all things whatsoever I have commanded you." Moral precepts of the Sermon on the Mount must be included in the term *evangel*. Following biblical content, evangelicalism calls attention to the whole gospel as set forth in God's Holy Word.

Historically, the term *evangelical* follows the biblical content. *Webster's New International Dictionary* defines "evangelical" as "designating that party or school among the Protestants which holds that the essence of the gospel consists mainly in its doctrines of man's sinful condition and the need of salvation, the revelation of God's grace in Christ, the necessity of spiritual renovation and participation in the experience of redemption through faith." In accord with this definition the evangelical follows in the succession of Augustine, Wycliffe, Luther, Calvin, Knox, Wesley, Whitefield, Spurgeon, Hodge, Walther, Moody, Kuyper, Warfield, Machen and men of like caliber. These men, for the most part, not only proclaimed the great doctrines which concerned with salvation, but made the evangel apply to the whole of life. Spiritual and moral renovation receive emphasis as well as justification by faith.

The term *fundamentalism* does not possess biblical background nor has it gained the rich and well-defined content that history has endowed on evangelicalism. By this statement we do not disparage the contribution fundamentalism has made to the cause of Christianity. In the early part of the twentieth century the movement fought firmly and courageously for scriptural theology and the historic faith. Unashamedly fundamentalism clung to the supernaturalness and uniqueness of Christ and to the authority and inspiration of Scripture. Those who decry fundamentalism little realize that some liberals now speak of the supernatural Christ and the neo-orthodox leader, Karl Barth, defends the virgin birth. However, the word *fundamentalism* has an inherent weakness in that it cannot be biblically defined, and has an unpleasant connotation that cannot be blamed on the originators of the movement.

Because fundamentalism cannot be biblically defined, it cannot authoritatively define what is fundamental and what is not fundamental to Christianity. History associates it with five points that have become the *sine qua non* of the movement: the infallibility of the Bible, Christ's virgin birth, his substitutionary atonement, bodily resurrection and second coming. This reduction of vital doctrines has limited and circumscribed fundamentalism and reduced its effectiveness. The first World War caused some fundamentalists to focus their hope on the second coming and to exclude those who did not accept their interpretation. Unfortunately, extreme and weird prophetic interpretations became linked in the public mind with fundamentalism. The failure to employ the whole counsel of God in combating unbelief contributed to its ineffectiveness and placed the stamp of narrowness upon the name.

––––––––––––––––

At the inception of the movement in 1910 fundamentalists gave a place to the intellect and made plans for the establishment of a Christian university and Christian colleges. Later, men of lesser vision opposed education and nurtured an anti-intellectual spirit. In the debate against evolution extreme ridicule and vituperative personal invectives, rather than logic, became the custom. The charge of obscurantism was not entirely unearned. Not only in the fight against evolution, but in opposition to other matters, fundamentalists became involved in abusive personal attacks, rather than using the sword of the Spirit. Unyielding individualism of its leaders and their dictatorial spirit did not help the cause of orthodox Christianity.

Concentration on a few points of doctrine to the exclusion of ethics has also brought fundamentalism under discredit. Impression was given that ethics need only involve a spirit of negation—abstinence from externals such as smoking and card-playing. The more subtle and dangerous sins of the spirit and mind received scant attention. Failure to develop a system of Christian ethics for all phases of life proved harmful. Fundamentalism neglected to give biblical emphasis on true holiness in living and love among the brethren. Squabbles between

fundamentalist leaders on minor issues has given the movement
an unwholesome reputation and has made the term synonymous
with bitterness and pettiness of spirit.

———————

In all fairness it must be stated that some accretions have been
superimposed by unkindly and ignorant critics. Fanatic actions
and teachings of fringe groups have been attributed to the whole.
The handling of poisonous serpents by some sects (from a liter-
alistic interpretation of Mark 16:18) has been cited as illustrating
the literalism of fundamentalism. The dictation theory of inspiration has been unjustly foisted on the entire group. Unethical
practices of some radio broadcasters have been cited to reflect
the practice of all fundamentalists. These and many other unjust
accusations have added to its unsavory reputation in the eyes of
the public.

Evangelicals are turning away from the term *fundamentalism*
not because of any inclination to disavow traditional fundamentals of the Christian faith, but are prompted by its inadequate
scriptural content and its current earned and unearned disrepute. Moreover, the term lacks the appropriateness of the word
evangelicalism. Scripture gives content to the evangel and not the
exigency or crisis of the moment. The full-orbed gospel and the
whole counsel of God comes to view in its classical meaning. It
has a proud and noble succession in the history of the Christian
church. While certain periods of history have obscured its true
significance and foes have usurped its use, yet Scripture and history have made its import clear and its name dignified. Christians
who hold to traditional fundamentals of Christianity would be
guilty of grievous strategic error to accept a term not defined by
Scripture and of doubtful connotation or to meekly yield the

word *evangelicalism* to those who do not accept the content of the evangel revealed by Christ. Secular dictionaries, history and Scripture give strong witness that only those who maintain the fundamentals have the right to the term. In the midst of theological confusion evangelicals have a wonderful opportunity to live up to the scriptural and historical content of their name and proclaim the whole counsel of God.

Carl F. H. Henry, "Evangelicals and Fundamentals," *Christianity Today* 1, no. 24 (September 16, 1957): 20–21.

Chapter 2

THE EVANGELICAL RESPONSIBILITY

This appeared last in a series of articles published in June–July 1957 dealing with the question, "Dare We Renew the Modernist-Fundamentalist Controversy?" They were based on lectures Henry delivered at Northern Baptist Theological Seminary and Calvin College in May and June of that year and were later published under the title Evangelical Responsibility in Contemporary Theology *(Eerdmans, 1957).*

Ahigher spirit to quicken and to fulfill the theological fortunes of this century will require more than the displacement of modernism, more than the revision of neo-orthodoxy, more than the revival of fundamentalism. Recovery of apostolic perspective and dedication of the evangelical movement to biblical realities are foundational to this hope.

Exalt Biblical Theology

Evangelical theology has nothing to fear, and much to gain, from aligning itself earnestly with the current plea for a return to biblical theology. To measure this moving front of creative theology sympathetically, to understand its concern and courage and to name its weaknesses without depreciating its strength will best preserve relevant theological interaction with the contemporary debate.

The evangelical movement must make its very own the passionate concern for the reality of special divine revelation, for a theology of the Word of God, for attentive hearing of the witness of the Bible, for a return to biblical theology.

Positive Preaching

Rededication to positive and triumphant preaching is the evangelical pulpit's great need. The note of Christ's lordship over this dark century, of the victory of Christianity, has been obscured. If it be evangelical, preaching must enforce the living communication of the changeless realities of divine redemption. The minister whose pulpit does not become the life-giving center of his community fails in his major mission. Perspective on Christianity's current gains and final triumph will avoid a myopic and melancholy discipleship. The Christian pulpit must present the invisible and exalted Head of the body of Christ; linked to him this earthly colony of heaven moves to inevitable vindication and glory. The perplexing problems of our perverse social orders find their hopeful solution only in this regenerative union. Out of its spiritual power must spring the incentives to creative cultural contributions.

Enlarge Christian Living

The evangelical fellowship needs a fresh and pervading conception of the Christian life. Too long fundamentalists have swiftly referred the question, "What distinguishes Christian living?" to personal abstinence from dubious social externals. The Christian conscience, of course, will always need to justify outward behavior, in home, in vocation and in leisure. But Christian ethics probes deeper. It bares the invisible zone of personality wherein lurk pride, covetousness and hatred.

Unfortunately, fundamentalism minimized the exemplary Jesus in the sphere of personal ethics. The theme of Christ's oneness with God was developed so exclusively in terms of his deity that the import of his dependence upon God for all human nature was lost. The manhood of Jesus is essentially one with ours; its uniqueness is in the zone of sinlessness, not of humanness. His uncompromised devotion and dependence upon God, his sustained relationship of mutual love, embodied the ideal pattern of human life in perfect fellowship with God. In view of his unbroken union with God, his humanity holds a central significance for all humanity.

In this light, a new importance attaches to the Nazarene's learning of the Father's will in the course of obedient dependence. His struggle with temptation to magnificent victory over all the assaults of evil, his exemplary trust, his unwavering reliance on God even in the darkest hours, his interior calm of soul, the wellspring of love that flowed from his being—in all these experiences Christ models for us an ideal spiritual relationship with God. In Jesus of Nazareth, God is fully resident; in God, Jesus is fully at home. He lives out the "rest in God" that actualizes the "abiding" to which we are called.

Another way in which evangelicals need to move beyond the fundamentalist ethic is in comprehending the whole of the moral law in fuller exposition of love for God and neighbor, and in the larger experience of the Holy Spirit in New Testament terms of ethical virtue. Often quite legalistically, and with an absoluteness beyond New Testament authority, fundamentalism's doctrine of surrender, of rededication, has merely proscripted worldly practices, from which the believer was discouraged. Unemphasized, however, are the fruit of the Spirit and those many virtues which differentiate dedicated living in terms of biblical Christianity.

Social Concern

We need a new concern for the individual in the entirety of his Christian experience. He is a member of all life's communities, of faith, of the family, of labor, of the state, of culture. Christianity is by no means the social gospel of modernism, but is nonetheless vibrant with social implications as a religion of redemptive transformation. To express and continue the vitality of the gospel message, marriage and the home, labor and economics, politics and the state, culture and the arts, in fact, every sphere of life, must evidence the lordship of Christ.

Obviously, the social application of Christian theology is no easy task. For one thing, fundamentalism fails to elaborate principles and programs of Christian social action because it fails to recognize the relevance of the gospel to the sociocultural sphere. Modernism defines Christian social imperatives in secular terms and uses the Church to reorganize unregenerate humanity. Its social sensitivity gave modernism no license to neglect the imperative of personal regeneration. Evangelistic and missionary priorities, on the other hand, gave fundamentalism no license to conceal the imperative of Christian social ethics. Despite the perils, no evasion of responsibility for meaningfully relating the gospel to the pressing problems of modern life is tolerable.

The divine life is a "being in love," a social or a family fellowship in which personality expresses the outgoing, creative relationships of redemption. A worker by God's creation, man sees vocation as a divinely entrusted stewardship by which to demonstrate love to God and service to man. As divinely ordained, the state declares God's intention and the dignity of man's responsibility for preserving justice and repressing iniquity in a sinful order. This world challenges man to interpret literature, art, music, and other media in reference to eternal order and values.

Approach to Science

Evangelical confidence in the ontological significance of reason makes possible a positive, courageous approach to science. For more than a century and a half modern philosophy has regrettably minimized the role of reason. Kant disjoined it from the spiritual world. Darwin naturalized and constricted it within the physical world. Dewey allowed it only a pragmatic or an instrumental role. These speculations took a heavy toll in Christian circles. A segment of evangelical Christianity nonetheless maintained its insistence upon the Logos as integral to the Godhead, the universe as a rational-purposive order, and man's finite reason is related to the image of God.

Yet for more than a generation the evangelical attitude in scientific matters has been largely defensive. Evolutionary thought is met only obliquely. American fundamentalism often neglected scrutinizing its own position in the light of recent historical and scientific research. It even failed to buttress its convictions with rigorous theological supports.

Yet modernism, despite its eager pursuit of such revision, achieved no true correlation of Christianity and science. While modernism adjusted Christianity swiftly to the prevailing climate of technical conviction, its scientific respect was gained by a costly neglect of Christianity's import to science.

Today a new mood pervades the scientific sphere. That mood may not fully validate the evangelical view of nature, but it does at least deflate the presuppositions on which the older liberalism built its bias against the miraculous. The evangelical movement is now given a strategic opportunity to transcend its hesitant attitude toward scientific endeavor, and to stress the realities of a rational, purposive universe that coheres in the Logos as the agent in creation, preservation, redemption, sanctification and judgment.

The ramifications of revelation and reason are wider, however, than science, for they embrace all the disciplines of learning. The evangelical attitude toward education itself is involved. The day has vanished when all the levels of learning, from primary to university, were in the service of God. Christianity cannot long thrive in an atmosphere in which mass education is allowed to repress and impugn Christian confidence and conviction. Christianity must not withdraw from the sphere of education, but must infuse it with new spirit and life. Christianity need evade neither truth nor fact, for it offers an adequate view of the universe in which we are driven daily to decision and duty. In answer to the present secular perspective in public education, shall evangelicals establish private Christian schools? Or shall they rather work for eternal verities within the present public school order or perhaps even pursue both courses? One fact is certain: evangelical neglect of education will imply the irrelevance of historic Christianity to the pressing problems of the contemporary academic world.

Doctrine of the Church

The evangelical movement needs also the sustained study of the New Testament doctrine of the Church and a greater concern for the unity of regenerate believers. Its program for reflecting the unity of the body of Christ in contemporary history is inadequate in several regards.

Evangelical discussions of the unity of the Church are shaped to protest the ecumenical framework as a compromise to be avoided. Ecumenical Christianity blesses a cooperation broader than the New Testament fellowship; it needs to be reminded that not all union is sacred—that the more inclusive the union, the greater the danger of compromising and secularizing its Christian integrity. By contrast, the evangelical movement easily restricts cooperation more narrowly than does the Bible. It must learn that not all separation is expressive of Christian unity. The principle of separation itself may acquire an objectionable form and content, related more to divisive temper than to theological fidelity. In the face of the inclusive church movement, the evangelical spirit reacts too much toward independency. Through refusal to cooperate with believers whose theological conservatism and dedication to Christ are beyond question, evangelical Christianity is in danger of divisiveness and disruptiveness.

Sound Doctrine and New Life

Evangelical insistence that the unity of the body of Christ requires a basic doctrinal agreement and a regenerate membership is sound. The ecumenical temperament encourages the breakdown of denominational barriers at too great a price whenever it minimizes doctrinal positions. Interdenominationalism in our century has sprung from a peculiar assortment of motives. Fundamentalists stimulated denominational desertion through discontent with theologically inclusive programs ventured by liberal leadership in the established denominations. Such was not in actuality an antithesis to denominationalism, since denominational tenets were not called into question. Indeed, most evangelicals prefer to support New Testament programs within their own denominational lines, allowing interdenominational cooperation to spring from multidenominational dedication to common evangelical priorities. The compromise of priorities in denominational circles, however, led to interdenominationalism at the expense of denominationalism and quickened the sense of an extradenominational unity based on common doctrine and faith.

The liberal interdenominational urge had a different motivation, namely, a virtual depreciation of denominationalism as unworthy sectarianism insofar as any fixed creedal positions are affirmed. This exaltation of the experiential unity of the Church through the disparagement of doctrinal soundness is the great peril of ecumenical ecclesiology today. Its constant danger is the elevation of the concern for unity above the concern for truth.

Precision in Beliefs

Evangelical emphasis on an indispensable doctrinal basis for Church unity needs, however, to be defined with greater precision. Such concern accounts for evangelical uneasiness over the creedal vagrancy of the World Council of Churches whose nebulous emphasis is only on "Jesus Christ as Lord and Savior." Since the evangelical movement includes churches that are both creedal and noncreedal in heritage, a specific creedal unity has not been elaborated, although common theological tenets are listed. This evangelical listing of a doctrinal minimum raises difficulties for creedal churches, inasmuch as they consider no article of faith dispensable. To Reformed churchmen, evangelical formulas often appear open to objectionable development. They prefer a strict creedal fellowship, a restriction that excludes progress toward the unity of diverse evangelical elements. The evangelical failure to fully elaborate essential doctrines has resulted in fragmentation by granting priority to secondary emphases (in such matters as eschatology). Evangelical Christianity has been slow to establish study conferences in biblical doctrine, to encourage mutual growth and understanding. Ironically, study sessions on theological issues are now often associated with movements whose doctrinal depth and concern are widely questioned. The significance of Christian doctrine, its dispensability or indispensability, its definition as witness or revelation, the elements identified respectively as core and periphery—these are issues on which evangelical Christianity must be vocal.

Fellowship of Disciples

Evangelical Christianity too frequently limits the term "evangelical" to those identified with a limited number of movements. This needlessly stresses a sense of Christian minority and discourages cooperation and communication with unenlisted evangelicals. But the tensions of American church history in this turbulent century cannot be automatically superimposed upon all world evangelical communities. Ecumenical leadership in the Federal Council of Churches and its successor, the National Council of Churches, failed to reflect the viewpoint of that considerable genuinely evangelical segment of its constituency. In the World Council of Churches, leaders on the Continent also have often found themselves theologically far to the right of American spokesmen, and have found American evangelicals in the World Council disappointingly unvocal. Long before the establishment of organizations like the World Evangelical Fellowship, many European churches have approached the World Council in quest of an enlarging evangelical fellowship. Evangelical world alternatives to inclusive movements arose after most large historic denominations were already enlisted in the World Council. Does evangelical loyalty within these committed denominations necessarily depend upon public repudiation of the World Council, and upon entrance instead into minority movements quite withdrawn from the stream of influential theological discussion? Even the National Association of Evangelicals in the United States must accept the absence of Southern Baptists and Missouri Lutherans, whose antipathy for theological inclusivism keeps these denominations also outside the National Council. The question that obviously remains, of course, is whether an evangelical who prefers identification with the broader movements can justify his participation, if he knows his own spiritual heritage, except in the capacity of a New Testament witness? Must not a silent evangelical in this climate always ask himself whether the silence which once perhaps was golden, now, through a dulling of love for truth and neighbor, has become as sounding brass or tinkling cymbal. Indeed, must not the evangelical always and everywhere address this question to himself in whatever association he is placed?

Lack of evangelical communication across the lines of inclusive and exclusive movements is not wholly due to the exclusivists. Ecumenical enthusiasts have encouraged neither fellowship nor conversation with exclusivist evangelicals. This coldness contributed needlessly to the fundamentalist suspicion of all outside their own constituency, and did little to mitigate the incivility that some fundamentalists reserved for such individuals. The unity of the believing Church requires communication between evangelicals on a basis of mutual tolerance and respect.

Concern for Unity

Unfortunately for the evangelical cause, the concern for the unity of the Church is now largely associated in the public mind with the inclusive vision. The failure of evangelicals to hear what the Spirit says in the New Testament to the churches has created the void now being filled by inclusivist conceptions of unity. The evangelical church needs with new earnestness to seek unity in its fragmenting environment, needs to reflect to the disunited world and to the disunited nations the sacred unity of the body of Christ.

Although evangelicals have criticized the broad basis of ecumenical merger and unity, they have achieved in their own ranks few mergers on the theological-spiritual level. Without conceding that denominationalism is evil or that health increases in proportion to the reduction of denominations, may there not be evidence that evangelical Christianity is over denominationalized?

If doctrinal agreement enhances the deepest unity of believers, may we not expect progress in the elimination of unnecessary divisions by emphasizing the spiritual unity of the Church? Evangelical Christianity, if it takes seriously its own emphasis on the unity of the body, must show visible gains in demonstrating unity in church life.

Contemporary Christianity would gain if the discussion of ecclesiastical tolerance were set in a New Testament context. The scriptural respect for individual liberty in matters of religious belief must not obscure definite requirements for indentification with the body of Christian believers. The New Testament upholds specific doctrinal affirmations as indispensable to genuine Christian confession. In this biblical setting, divisiveness is depicted primarily as a theological question, not (as is usually the case today) as a matter of ecclesiastical attitude and relationship. The modernist tendency to link Christian love, tolerance and liberty with theological inclusivism is therefore discredited. Modernist pleas for religious tolerance and the caustic indictments of fundamentalist bigotry often were basically a strategic device for evading the question of doctrinal fidelity. This flaunting of tolerance, however, was discredited when inclusivist leaders suppressed or excluded evangelicals not sympathetic to the inclusive policy. The "tolerance plea" swiftly dismissed as divisive what was not clearly so in fact. Divisiveness meant disapproval of the inclusive policy, tolerance meant approval. But the New Testament does not support the view that devotion to Christian liberty and progress and to the peace and unity of Christ's Church is measured by the devaluation of doctrine in deference to an inclusive fellowship. From the biblical point of view, doctrinal belief is a Christian imperative, not a matter of indifference.

Whenever it professes a genuine regard for the scriptural point of view, the inclusive movement is driven to soul-searching in respect to doctrinal latitude and its own propaganda for organic church union. Within the World Council, in contrast with the National Council, exists a forum from which this ambiguity can be challenged. Evangelicals in this movement, if they bear an evangelical witness, must constantly call the Commission on Faith and Order to judge the theological and ecclesiastical question from the standpoint of Scripture.

The fact must not be ignored, however, that different evangelical conceptions of the visible Church are prevalent. Although historically the Christian churches have all insisted upon a minimal theological assent for admission to membership, Reformed churches share Calvin's view that even in the Church wheat and tares—professing and believing Christians—will dwell together until their final separation in the judgment. Baptist churches have traditionally placed greater emphasis on a regenerate membership and on a pure church. Even the disciplinary procedure of the more broadly conceived Reformed churches, however, considers church members flouting or indifferent to creedal standards as guilty as grave sin. Christian churches in the past stressed both a minimal requirement for membership and a maximal indulgence for avoidance of discipline or exclusion. But modernist leaders asserted the inevitability of doctrinal change. Heresy trials became an oddity in contemporary church history, not because of an absence of heresy, but because of the lack of zeal to prosecute heretics.

We dare not own any other authority over life and deed but the living God. We dare not own any other God than the righteous and merciful God revealed in Jesus Christ. We dare not own another Christ but Jesus of Nazareth, the Word become flesh who now by the Spirit is the exalted head of the body of believers. We dare not own any other Spirit than the Spirit who has breathed out Scripture through chosen men, that doubt may vanish about what

God is saying to the Church and to the world. We dare not own any other Scripture than this Book. Let other men proclaim another god, another Christ, another spirit, another book or word—that is their privilege and their peril. But if once again the spiritual life of our world is to rise above the rubble of paganism into which it is now decaying, it will be only through the dynamic of revelation, regeneration, and redemption, through the sacred message which once brought hope. We have a task to do, a task of apostolic awesomeness; let us rise to the doing. The hour for rescue is distressingly late.

Carl F. H. Henry, "Dare We Renew the Controversy? The Evangelical Responsibility," *Christianity Today* 1, no. 21 (July 22, 1957): 23–38.

Chapter 3

A PLEA FOR
EVANGELICAL UNITY

By contrast with the unification plans of the ecumenical movement, evangelicals often claim to enjoy the true unity of the Spirit. In a basic sense this is true. Yet the world is not impressed by mere assertion. In fact, evangelicals often seem to be one of the most divided and divisive forces in the ecclesiastical world even in their internal dealings. Splits, suspicions, wordy campaigns are common features. Squabbling about less essential matters seems to absorb the energy that should go to working together on essentials. And the tragedy is that the world both needs and would unquestionably be impressed and affected by a genuine manifestation of unity in spirit, purpose, and action on the part of evangelicalism. Indeed, it might be argued that such a manifestation is the only finally valid and effective criticism of modern ecumenism.

What should be the motivation of such unity? We must beware of secondary motives which may be right in their place but which in themselves are not enough. It is insufficient merely to seek to oppose to ecumenism a true counterpart. It is insufficient merely to think in terms of the strengthening of a cause. It is insufficient merely to desire the construction of a solid front against blatantly hostile forces like communism, materialism, liberalism, or resurgent Hinduism or Islam. It is insufficient merely to aim at a more efficient or economical evangelistic, missionary, educational, or social thrust. It is insufficient only to desire the creation of a stronger ecclesiastical or theological bloc.

The only motive that will really avail is a biblical one. To put it simply, Christ wills and prays for the unity of his people. This does not have to mean unification. On the other hand, it certainly cannot mean the dialectic of spiritual unity in actual conflict. It means unity manifested in united purpose and action. It means acceptance of a common mind and task. As this is the will of Christ for us, it must surely be our own will for ourselves. "Endeavouring to keep the unity of the Spirit in the bond of peace" is Paul's injunction (Eph. 4:3). "Be at peace among yourselves" is his command (1 Thess. 5:13). "Be of the same mind one toward another" is the direction of the inerrant and infallible Word (Rom. 12:16). If this is God's will, it must be also the will of the obedient disciple. No matter how loudly we proclaim our attachment to Scripture, we do it poor service, and gain ourselves little credence, if in our actions we flagrantly disregard the will of God therein revealed. Once the declared will of Jesus Christ is known, no other motive is needed. It is the delight and privilege of the sheep to hear and obey the Shepherd's voice.

On what basis? Is this just an ideal to be sought? Does spiritual unity lie in a world of mysticism and abstraction? Is the Lord's prayer for unity to be answered only in eternity? Does there run through the Bible a strain of Platonism, a rift between the ideal and the actual, which negates from the outset all attempts at manifestation of unity? If so, the manifest division of so many evangelicals might well be justifiable. God would be requiring the impossible—castles in the air without foundation.

In fact, however, there is no excuse. God has given us a solid basis. There is one God, one Christ, one Spirit. Faith into God means spiritual unity. There is thus one Bride, one Body. The members differ, whether in terms of individuals or churches. A uniform organization is not needed as the basis. But all are members of a Body which cannot but be one. There is one Word, one Baptism, one Cup. Externals may vary. The one Word may go forth in different tongues, the one Baptism or Cup may be administered under different rules of order. Even the one faith or doctrine may be expressed with some difference of formulation. Yet the Word of God is one and invariable. The Baptism and Cup of the Lord are the same. The One in whom faith is set never alters. Here in God, in the Word and work of God, is an unassailable basis of given unity. Here the people of God have to be one, whether they are prepared for it or not. Here the prayer of Jesus finds fulfillment in spite of our disobedience. Here we begin with what we are in the new life in Christ. Here we are enabled to be what we are, to put on the new man, to bring forth the fruit of the new life. Here we are given a solid and eternal basis on which to build.

But what are the prerequisites? The proper basis of unity is obviously the first. Apart from this, there can be only the fragile unity of common association and opinion. Are there any others? Secondarily, the unity of those who in the Spirit are building on this foundation implies at least three others. The unity must be that of those who do in fact look only to Jesus Christ and to none other. It must be a unity of those who follow the authoritative testimony to him in Holy Scripture. It must be a unity of those who are committed to the great task of world-wide evangelization which he has laid on his disciples.

Without a common looking to the Lord, a common confession of him as Savior, Lord, and God, a common knowledge of God in him, there is no building on the common basis and therefore no hope of unity. Faith in him, however, is not a leap in the dark. It is no blind or chance encounter. It is faith responding to a Word. And this Word is the authentic and authoritative record given concerning him. True faith in him is faith in the Jesus of Scripture who embraces both the so-called Jesus of history and the Christ of faith. It is faith enlightened and instructed and impelled by the written Word and its preaching and exposition. To the one basis belongs also the foundation of the apostles and prophets (Eph. 2:20). To build apart from Scripture is to build apart from Jesus Christ himself and therefore to destroy unity. Yet this faith is neither abstract nor ideal. It is busy and active. It is impelled as well as instructed. It is obedient. It accepts a task. It is given orders. It is endowed with the high privilege of ministry. It is given a Great Commission. Outside this Commission, we again pursue isolated and therefore divergent ends. We thus condemn ourselves to deviation and discord. The true faith which is loyal to the written Word, however, implies readiness for the Great Commission. The main prerequisites of unity in the Spirit are thus met.

What are the demands of unity? What does its manifestation require in us? How can we promote this expression of unity which is no mere matter of organization but our believing, living, and working together on a common basis? Some of the most urgent of these demands might be simply stated as follows:

It is demanded that we be oriented positively to the world-wide task of evangelism. There are subsidiary tasks of theology, pastoral care, discipline, and even administration. To make these autonomous, however, is to bring about that curving in on oneself which inevitably causes distortion and division. An unengaged force quickly becomes disaffected. Our vision is to be outward to the sin, ignorance, and error of the world. When energy is bent to this supreme task, there will be little to spare for inward wrangling. The converse is also true.

It is demanded that we be humble in relation to one another both in life and utterance. All that we have is received from God and through one another. All our truth is the truth of God's Word. We cannot boast of any attainment of our own. We have nothing about which to be self-righteous, whether in respect of purity of life or superiority of understanding. The infallibility of Scripture does not guarantee our own private infallibilities. We are all learners and teachers in the school of Christ and the Spirit. To remember this is to be safeguarded against the pride of the fancied master or doctor, who not only has nothing to learn but also imagines that his task is to judge rather than to edify. True humility before the Lord and his Word is one of the most potent bulwarks against the division which only too often bears marks of human arbitrariness and obduracy.

It is demanded that rebuke and correction be given and received in a spirit of meekness and with a view to edification. Errors occur as well as sins. They are not to be ignored or glossed over. We are to grow in knowledge as well as in righteousness. But the occurrence of sin or error is not to be the occasion for a display of self-righteousness or rancor. The rebuke and correction undertaken should be in the spirit of mutual helpfulness and with a lively sense of personal frailty. Meekness is not weakness. On the other hand there is no strength in discourtesy, belligerence, or angry pride. If firmness is needed, it should be that of speaking the truth in love which will evoke a response of love.

Finally, it is demanded that we have the mind of Christ, which is the mind of mercy and of love. Paul has much to say concerning this in Ephesians 4. All evangelical Christians and leaders might do well to make this chapter a regular feature in their biblical reading with a view to making it a more prominent feature in their biblical practice. It is of special applicability in times of tension. It gives us a final thesis and poses a final question. The problem of unity is simply the problem of how biblical we really are. It is by our attainment of the mind of Christ and therefore the practical unity of the Spirit that we show to the world our obedience to the Word which we proclaim. But if so, how biblical are we when it comes to doing and not merely to talking? Is Ephesians 4 reflected unmistakably in our utterances and actions, in our personal and church relationships, in our contacts with the world without, in our pursuance of the Great Task with which we have been entrusted? If so, and to the measure that this is so, we shall indeed enjoy and manifest the unity which is of the Holy Ghost.

Carl F. H. Henry, "A Plea for Evangelical Unity," *Christianity Today* 5, no. 12 (March 13, 1961): 24–25.

Chapter 4

EVANGELICALS IN THE SOCIAL STRUGGLE

Evangelical Christianity today confronts a "new theology," a "new evangelism," and a "new morality," each notably lacking in biblical content. A "new social ethics" has also emerged, and some ecumenical leaders mainly interested in politico-economic issues speak hopefully of a "new breed of evangelical" in this realm of activity. The red carpet rolls out when even a few evangelicals march at Selma, when they unite in organized picket protests and public demonstrations, when they join ecclesiastical pressure blocs on Capitol Hill or at the White House, or when they engineer resolutions on legislative matters through annual church meetings.

Since most evangelical churchmen traditionally have not mobilized their social concern in this way, non-evangelical sociologists are delighted over any and every such sign of apparent enlightenment. Moreover, they propagandize such church techniques as authentically Christian, and misrepresent evangelical non-participation as proof of social indifference in conservative Christian circles and as a lack of compassion. This favorite device of propagandists is effective among some evangelicals who desire to protect their genuine devotion to social concern from public misinterpretation. The claim that evangelicals as a whole are socially impotent, moreover, diverts attention from the long-range goals of social extremists by concentrating attention on existential involvement on an emergency basis.

That Christians are citizens of two worlds, that a divine mandate enjoins both their preaching of the Gospel and their promotion of social justice, that the lordship of Christ over all of life involves socio-cultural obligations, that Christians bear a political responsibility, are historic evangelical emphases. Evangelicals regard government and jurisprudence as strategic realms of vocational service to humanity. They stress that government exists for the sake of all citizens, not simply for certain favored groups, and that a just or good society preserves for all citizens equal rights before the law. This emphasis has equally critical implications for a society that seeks special privilege for one race above another and for any church that seeks partisan and sectarian benefits from government.

The heritage of evangelical Christianity includes both Jesus' sermon on the mount and his delineation of the Good Samaritan, and Paul's account of civil government as an agent of justice. Evangelical Christians recognized the moral claim of these scriptural elements long before Protestant liberalism distorted them into a rationalistic politico-economic perspective. The Evangelical Revival in eighteenth- and nineteenth-century Britain attested the devotion of believers, not only to the observance of public statutes, but also to the vigorous promotion of just laws. The seventh Earl of Shaftesbury headed the movement in Parliament that led in 1807 to the abolition of slavery in the British Empire. As a result of his own conversion Wilberforce led great reform programs, including child-labor laws. The Evangelical Revival placed evangelicals in the forefront of humanitarian concerns, not only for an end to the slave trade, but also for child labor laws, prison reforms, improved factory labor conditions, and much else in the sphere of social justice. It was evangelical social concern, in fact, that preserved the shape of Anglo-Saxon society from tragic revolutionary onslaught. An eminent church historian writes: "No branch indeed of the Western Church can be refused the honor of having assisted in the progress of humane ideas, and non-Christians have participated largely in the work of diffusing the modern spirit of kindness; but the credit of the inception of the movement belongs without doubt to that form of Protestantism which is distinguished by the importance it attaches to the doctrine of the Atonement. ... History shows that the thought of Christ on the Cross has been more potent than anything else in arousing a compassion for suffering and indignation at injustice. ... The later Evangelicalism, which saw in the death of Christ the means of free salvation for fallen humanity, caused its adherents to take the front rank as champions of the weak. ... Prison reform, the prohibition of the slave trade, the abolition of slavery, the Factory Acts, the protection of children, the crusade against cruelty to animals, are all the outcome of the great Evangelical revival of the eighteenth century. The humanitarian tendencies of the nineteenth century, which, it is but just to admit, all Christian communities have fostered, and which non-Christian philanthropists have vied with them in encouraging, are among the greatest triumphs of the power and influence of Christ" (F. J. Foakes-Jackson, "Christ in the Church: The Testimony of History," in H. B. Swete, *Cambridge Theological Essays*, New York, 1905, pp. 512–14).

Liberal Impact and Evangelical Reaction

For two generations liberal social ethics has been markedly influential in American public life in the areas of education, government, and labor. Liberal ecclesiastical reformers have only themselves to blame for the present lack of fixed governing principles in public policy, and for the declining spiritual influence of their churches in the private sector of national life. One theologian addicted to a radically secular version of Christianity—Professor William Hamilton of Colgate-Rochester Divinity School—tells us candidly that "we are well into the opening phase of the breakdown of organized religion in American life, well beyond the time when ecumenical dialogue or denominational mergers can be expected to arrest the breakdown" (*The Christian Scholar*, Spring, 1965). Professor Hamilton fails to recognize, however, that the modernist dilution of historic Christian theology was largely responsible for compromising the message and power of institutional Christianity. In no century of recent history have public structures been so directly influenced by American churchmen as they are in our time through the pressures of liberal social thought. Churchmen have increasingly manipulated the machinery of ecumenical Christianity in support of socio-economic objectives, including specific legislative proposals. Not even the breakdown of the League of Nations or the deformation of the United Nations, each endorsed as the world's best hope for peace, has encouraged "second thoughts" about the efficacy or legitimacy of the nature of their social activity.

This does not mean that evangelical Christians have reason to boast about social alertness on the explosive frontiers of public life. They were undeniably concerned with personal behavior in public social life, and with responsible community involvement in keeping with the standards and vocations of believers. To their further credit they realized that not an ethic of grace but rather an ethic of justice should govern social structures (including international relations, national government, and legal institutions generally). But evangelical Christians elaborated no Bible-based ethic impinging on the basis, method, and function of social structures and groups such as the state, labor movements and business corporations, minorities, and so on.

If excuses for neglect are in order, this may be the right place to note them. Evangelicals could plead, of course, that the "social gospeler's" neglect of God's good news of salvation for sinners imposed upon conservative Christianity the burden of biblical evangelism and missions throughout a perishing world—a staggering task indeed. Evangelical capability was decimated by liberal control of denominations, schools, and other ecclesiastical resources. But evangelical withdrawal from the arena of public life came mainly in reaction to the Protestant liberal attempts to achieve the Kingdom of God on earth through political and economic changes. The modernists so excluded supernatural redemptive facets of the Christian faith and so modified the proper content of the Christian ethic that, as evangelicals saw it, they had altered the very nature and mission of the Church. Evangelical Christianity reacted against the liberal Protestant concentration of effort in this area of concern by non-involvement, and this withdrawal yielded the field to the speculative theories of liberal churchmen and largely deprived evangelicals of an ethical witness in the mainstream of public life.

Fallacies of Liberal Ethics

Precisely what is objectionable in liberal social ethics from the evangelical viewpoint? This is no small matter, for criticism extends to presuppositions, methods, and goals.

The theological presuppositions of liberal social ethics are hostile to biblical theology. A generation ago the "social gospel" theologians deleted the wrath of God and dissolved his righteousness into benevolence or love; today the revolt has been extended. Dialectical and existential moralists surrender the objective being of God, while secular theologians disown his transcendence and, for that matter, his relevance as well. What passes for Christian social ethics in such circles dispenses with the supernatural essence of the Christian religion as foreign to problems of social justice and public righteousness. Evangelicals who insist on obedience to divinely revealed precepts, and who hold that redeemed men alone can truly fulfill the will of God and that only men of good will can enlarge the boundaries of God's Kingdom, are caricatured as "rationalists," despite the fact that Scripture specifically associates Jesus' mission with an era of good will on earth. Yet while existentialists reject the absolutes of a transcendent morality for an absolute of their own decision, thereby making each person his own church, and reject an ethics based on principles because they consider it impossible to achieve moral obedience by decree, they nonetheless agitate for laws to compel others to act in a predictable, principled way.

It may seem pedantic, if not picayune, in a secular society so perilously near doom, to surround the moral demand for *agape* with a complex of theological distinctions. After all, is not *agape* itself the central Christian moral motif? But the reply is simple: *"agape"* stripped of supernatural elements is no longer biblical *agape*. For biblical *agape* is first and foremost the love of God. Biblical *agape* is nowhere simply a matter of humanistic charity toward one's neighbors. "You shall love the Lord your God with all your heart, and with all your soul, and with all your mind, and your neighbor as yourself"—love them, as a well-phrased prayer reiterates, "with a pure heart, fervently." Although just laws are desirable and imperative, law has the power only of outward restraint; it lacks power to ensure outward obedience and inner conformity to its command. In the absence of moral men—of men willing to do the good—no body of law, however just, can ensure a good society. Authentic Christian ethics concerns what is done through a desire to do God's will, in obedience to his command; this is made possible only by spiritual regeneration. No other motivation can counter the selfish drives that haunt the noblest of unredeemed men and correct the faulty vision of an unredeemed society. The current existential appeal for everyman's "identification with others" naïvely presupposes that the "identifiers" are morally equipped with motivations unthwarted by selfishness. But universal love, even in diluted forms, is a requirement that far exceeds the capacity of unregenerate men; for a Jew to have loved Hitler must have posed a problem not unlike that involved in a Selma marcher's love for the governor of Alabama, or a Birmingham demonstrator's affection for the local sheriff. The modern devotion to mankind *in place of* God, on the premise of "the infinite worth of the individual," indicates the inability of some Western intellectuals to assimilate the basic lessons of recent history. They blandly overlook the power of evil in human nature and man's limitations in coping with it—witness not only the patent egoism of individuals and social collectivities and the barbarism of the dictators, but also the tragic fact of two world wars at the pinnacle of Western scientific development and the unresolved threat of imminent universal destruction. As George F. Thomas says, "man is neither infinite nor perfect, and his ideal ends are worthy of devotion only insofar as they are subordinated to the purpose of One who is both" (*Religious Philosophies of the West*, New York, Charles Scribner's Sons, 1965, p. 351).

The evangelical Christian mobilizes for social action in the spiritual context of transcendent justice, supernatural law, revealed principles, concern for God's will in human affairs, and love of God and man. Against ecclesiastical "young Turks" who propagandize the notion that social concerns cannot be expressed within the inherited theology, the evangelical contends that in so far as social concerns are authentically biblical, they can be adequately expressed and fulfilled only within scriptural theology. What the evangelical does in the social order, as in every other realm of life, he does as a matter of principled spiritual obedience to the Lord of life.

Differences in Goals

It is, moreover, a gross underestimation of differences in social action between evangelicals and non-evangelicals to imply that, beyond motivation, they agree wholly on goals and differ only in method. The liberal Protestant identification of Christian love with pacifism, then with socialism, even with Communism by some modernists in the recent past, is too fresh a memory to allow one to blunder into the notion that the Bible sanctions whatever social goals the liberal moralists endorse. Even the Communist hostility toward supernatural religion as an unscientific myth has moderated into tactical tolerance of religion as useful for promoting a social consciousness agreeable to the Soviet politico-economic ideology. Repudiation of private property, of the profit motive, and of inequality of wealth, and other Marxist ideals have been arbitrarily promoted by liberal social reformers in supposed devotion to the biblical vision of the Kingdom of God. Even their emphasis on equal rights has cheaply surrendered property rights as a fundamental human right, and also man's right to work apart from compulsory union membership.

Whenever the Church advances a political ideology or promotes partisan legislation, its ecclesiastical leaders are soon forced into the position of impugning the integrity of influential Christians who sincerely dissent from the official views. It should surprise nobody, therefore, that as the National Council of Churches comes under increasing fire, its spokesmen tend to demean critics of its political commitments as reactionary advocates of arrogant nationalism and of social, economic, and racial privilege.

Not a few goals approved by modern social theorists are wholly desirable, and evangelical differences in such cases concern the means of achieving these ends. Elimination of poverty, opportunity for employment, racial equality, and many other goals that stand at the heart of contemporary social agitation are not only acceptable but highly desirable. Evangelicals are not indifferent to the desirability of such objectives even if liberal social ethics mistakenly conceives the Kingdom of God as basically a politico-economic phenomenon and tends to dilute redemptive spiritual forces into sociological ingredients. In fact, as evangelicals see it, such features of social life are essential to a just and good society.

Evangelicals no less than liberals recognize social justice as an authentic Christian concern, despite serious differences over definition and content. If evangelicals came to stress evangelism above social concern, it was because of liberalism's skepticism over supernatural redemptive dynamisms and its pursuit of the Kingdom of God by sociological techniques only. Hence a sharp and costly disjunction arose, whereby many evangelicals made the mistake of relying on evangelism alone to preserve world order and many liberals made the mistake of relying wholly on socio-political action to solve world problems.

Conflict over Method

It would be naïve to argue from this, however, that liberals and evangelicals need each other for complementary emphases. Over and above differences of motivation and of goals stand the differences between evangelical and liberal ethics in respect to methodology. Most evangelicals reject outright the liberal methodology of social reform, in which more and more liberals call for a "new evangelism" that substitutes sociological for spiritual concerns. Just as in his theological view of God the liberal dissolves righteousness into love, so in the political order he dilutes social justice into compassion. This kind of merger not only destroys the biblical view of God on the one hand but also produces the welfare state on the other. This confounding of justice and love confuses what God expects of government with what he expects of the Church, and makes the state an instrument for legislating partisan and sectarian ideals upon society. Ideally the purpose of the state is to preserve justice, not to implement benevolence; ideally, the purpose of the Church is to preach the Gospel and to manifest unmerited, compassionate love.

Many sociologists and political scientists dislike this way of stating the case. But it is noteworthy that these particular disciplines are especially barren of evangelical perspectives; they tend to be theologically illiterate in respect both to eschatology and to a basic theology of justice. Current proposals to detach the Gospel from "right-wing" social reaction and current pleas for "political compassion" are rooted in leftist political ideology more often than in an authentic spiritual view of the role of government.

But in the present explosive era of history the problem of acting on an acceptable methodology is an urgent one for evangelicals. It is one thing to deplore ministerial marches and picket lines and well-publicized public pressures; but if evangelical conscience is to be a remedial and transforming social force, then evangelical convictions require articulate mobilization on their own account.

Evangelicals and Social Concern

Despite the present confusion caused by ecclesiastical intervention in political affairs, evangelicals have something socially relevant to say to both the secular man and the church man. The

Christian has social duties not simply as a Christian but as a man, and his sanctification therein does not come about automatically without pulpit instruction in sound scriptural principles. Evangelicals as a people consider themselves bound to the Word of God; for this reason they consider themselves a spiritual people with a divine message for themselves and for others in regard to social action. Evangelicals acknowledge a divine call to identify themselves with others—not with social customs or social vices or social discontents, but rather with persons in their survival needs: physical and moral and spiritual. These survival needs include material help in destitution, social justice, and the redemption that is in Christ Jesus.

Surely evangelical Christianity has more to offer mankind than its unique message of salvation, even if that is its highest and holiest mission. While it rightly chides the liberal for regarding the world as a unity (rather than divided into unregenerate and regenerate), it also has a message for all men as members of one society. The Christian is not, by his church identification, isolated from humanity, or from involvement in the political and economic orders. Not only is he called to identify himself with society: he *is* identified, by the very fact of his humanity, and as a Christian he bears a double responsibility in relation to the social needs and goals of mankind. Social justice is a need of the individual, whose dignity as a person is at stake, and of society and culture, which would soon collapse without it. The evangelical knows that spiritual regeneration restores men to moral earnestness; but he also knows the moral presuppositions of a virile society, and he is obligated to proclaim the "whole counsel" of God. He may have no message for society that insures unrepentant mankind against final doom—nor even against catastrophic destruction in our own time, while its leaders insist upon arbitrary human authority at the expense of the lordship of Jesus

Christ. But he can and ought to use every platform of social involvement to promulgate the revealed moral principles that sustain a healthy society and that indict an unhealthy one. More than this, the evangelical Christian should be represented, in his personal convictions, on the frontiers of government and in the corporate processes of society. Convinced that the cooperation of godly men in the social and collective order can be decisively influential, he should be concerned about relations between nations and about minority rights. There is no reason at all why evangelical Christians should not engage energetically in projecting social structures that promote the interests of justice in every public realm; in fact, they have every legitimate sanction for social involvement.

Of course the Church is to be ruled distinctively by an ethic of grace. But the Church is also in a world that is to be ruled by justice, an ethic of justice that does not *per se* require regenerate social structures. In this context, a positive ethic and corrective principles enunciated on the broad world scene by regenerate believers who are engaged in the social struggle can have decisive influence. Such an ethic will include (1) the Church's faithful exposition of divinely revealed standards of human justice as the only basis for a stable society and as the criteria by which the world will be finally judged; and (2) the Christian's energetic promotion and support of just laws as the formal hallmark of a good society. When Christian believers become thus involved in the struggle for justice, the world may recognize in a new way the presence of regenerate realities; noting the community of twice-born men that sees the restoration of sinners to fellowship with God and to holiness as the aim of the Gospel, the world may even recognize the validity of regenerate structures through their moral impact.

Any Christian engaged in the pursuit of social justice is painfully aware that, in a tragic world of fallen men, government decisions often involve a choice between greater and lesser evils rather than between absolutes of good and evil, and that only the Church of Christ can witness to a manifestation of absolute good in history. He will, however, avoid both the liberal error of "absolutizing relatives," as if these were identical with the will of God, and also the fundamentalist temptation to consider any gain short of the absolute ideal in history as worthless or unworthy.

Law and Gospel

But evangelicals must not perpetuate the liberal Protestant failure to distinguish between the social concerns of *Law* and the social concerns of *Gospel.* In law and justice—that is, the province of government—all men are obliged to support man's God-given rights as universally due to human beings whatever their race, color, or creed. The evangelical knows that no improvement can be made on a government that assures every man his rights, and that limits the freedom of citizens where and when it intrudes upon the rights of others. Evangelicals do not view government as an instrument of benevolence or compassion, since love is preferential and shows favor or partiality. Constantly pressing the question, "Don't you care?" liberals enlist support for legislating programs of benevolence. Such an appeal to "compassion" in support of legislative programs commits a twofold error, however: it diverts government from an ideal preservation of equal human rights before the law, and it shifts to the state a responsibility for compassion or benevolence that belongs properly to the Church. By concentrating on government to achieve the goals of both state and Church in a "benevolent partnership," liberalism reflects a reliance on political techniques in society to the neglect of the redemptive dynamisms inherent in Christianity. This reliance on political techniques to achieve ecclesiastical objectives means the loss of a genuine supernatural grounding of ethical concerns, the loss of the Church as Church in society, the loss of the redemptive evangel in deference to secular solvents of social malformity, and the loss of evangelical loyalties in the congregation.

What distinguishes evangelical Christianity is its refusal to impose sectarian obligations upon government, upon government which then employs compulsion to enforce a program of benevolence that individual citizens might or might not approve. Even if they did approve, they might consider the provision of such benevolences moral only if performed voluntarily; or they might consider it immoral to use taxation to compel others to do what they do not think to be right. While liberals justify their breaking of laws that appear unjust on the grounds of sensitivity to conscience, they nonetheless promote other laws that some persons regard as preferential and unjust.

To the evangelical Christian, the best alternative to the "welfare" state is the just state, and the best alternative to political demonstrations is civil obedience. The evangelical champions and strives for just legislation, and for obedience to law and respect for judicial process rather than for directly coerced action. The evangelical sponsors a principled ethic whose course is determined by divinely revealed moral principles. Much of contemporary liberal social action is not a matter of obeying laws; rather, it is a case of everyone's being on his existential own. Dialectical-existential ethics cannot indicate in advance what the moral agent ought to do, and looks upon any structured objective ethics as mere rationalism.

The evangelical holds that all persons are divinely obligated by the Scriptures to love their neighbors. While progress has been slow in the area of race tensions, nonetheless there has been progress. Yet even evangelical believers fall short of their highest moral aspirations, and laws are necessary to hold just social standards before Christians and non-Christians alike. All citizens should strive to replace discriminatory laws by non-discriminatory laws. The evangelical recognizes, however, that without public enthusiasm only moral earnestness vouchsafed by spiritual conviction and renewal assures the necessary devotion to right that guarantees social fulfillment. While the glory of ancient Rome was its genius for universal law, through its lack of heart for righteousness the Roman Empire sank into oblivion. The problem of racial discrimination can be permanently met only by Christian behavior that faces up to the ugliness of bias, the evils of immorality and delinquency, and the whole complex of problems that surrounds race feeling. The predilection for public issues over personal holiness in liberal social ethics is all the more disconcerting in view of this fact. Although liberal churchmen will throw their energies behind a public health program, they tend to remain silent about many of the personal vices; such concerns are left to the "purity nuts."

The history of Christian mission in the world makes it clear that evangelicals were interested in education, hospitals, care for the aged, and many current social concerns long before modern secular theory was ever born. Evangelicals were active in social work not only in the slums of America but also on distant mission fields a full century before the rise of modern welfare programs. To this day, rescue missions all across the land reflect a long-standing inner-city missionary concern for people in material and spiritual poverty. Evangelicals have not been as active as they need to be in the social arena; on the other hand, they have been far more active than they are sometimes said to have been.

The weakness of public demonstrations as the approved means of Christian social action is its limitation and externalization of Christian concern. It is arbitrary to imply that only those who demonstrate at a given point manifest authentic social concern. Moreover, since local demonstrations gain national significance through radio and television, the implications of massive civil disobedience are the more distressing. Ecclesiastical demonstrators who never persuade observers to become disciples of Jesus Christ ought to ask how effectively Christian is such amorphous "witness by demonstration." The motivations for demonstrating are internal, and apart from verbal interpretation might equally well be sub-Christian, non-Christian, or anti-Christian. As a matter of fact, Jews and humanists resent a Christian interpretation of their demonstrating. If authentic social concern demanded the ecumenical chartering of planes to officially designated out-of-town points, it would require a large expense account to enable everybody to travel to somebody else's home town "to identify." If every supporter of an item of disputed legislation had to march to Capitol Hill, if every Christian citizen had to put in a personal appearance to let legislators know what laws he thought God specially wanted, what would tourist-jammed Washington be like then? If the representative role of congressmen were superseded by the group pressures of ministers, the whole machinery of American government would soon collapse. The question remains, moreover, Whose conscience answers for whom? These clergy are received by congressmen, not on the premise that they speak only for themselves, but as voices for their churches. No one disputes a clergyman's right as an individual to picket or demonstrate anywhere he wishes (the right of conscience is a Protestant principle). It is unlikely, however, that pastors can wholly detach themselves from responsibilities to their congregations. When prominent churchmen parade as Reverend Church, moreover, they are simply encouraging future counter-demonstrations at 475 Riverside Drive or the Witherspoon Building.

What many socially sensitive ministers especially deplore is the implication left by the well-publicized minority of marchers that non-marchers are lacking or inferior in social concern. "I don't mind another minister's marching if he must relieve his conscience that way," said one Washington minister, "but I don't see why my social concern—never before questioned—should now be in doubt because I didn't engage in this form of exhibitionism." In Copenhagen, when Evangelist Billy Graham opened his crusade, a heckler interrupted him with the cry: "Why didn't you march in Selma?" But Graham had been integrating meetings in the South long before some of the marchers had become existentialized and, moreover, had done so in the context of biblical Christianity. It is a neat propaganda device to imply that evangelical social concern is immobile because it does not conform to liberal methods—it merely proves that political propagandism is a technique in which liberal ecclesiastical leaders have become adept. In some ecclesiastical circles, the defense of this one controversial method of action has apparently justified the repudiation of all theological grounds of social concern.

Evangelical Distinctives

When evangelicals manifest social concern, they do so first by proclaiming the supernatural revelation of God and the historical resurrection of Jesus Christ. Thus they emphasize the transcendent basis of justice and the divine basis of the Gospel. They declare both the standards by which Almighty God will judge the human race and the redemption from sin unto holiness that is to be found in Jesus Christ. They affirm God's institution of civil government to preserve justice and order, and the Church as a spiritual fellowship of redeemed men who esteem their neighbors in holy love and dedicate themselves to social righteousness.

The evangelical Christian's social concern is first directed towards the family as the basic unit of society. He finds a hollow ring in the social passion for "one world" that simultaneously lacks indignation over divorce, infidelity, and vagrancy in the home. Because liberalism fails to see society as a macrocosm of the family, it is bankrupt to build a new society. Liberalism changes ideological loyalties and social perspectives every generation; evangelical Christianity treasures the family bound to the changeless will of God and to the apostolic faith. Hence evangelical Christianity regards the Sunday school, the prayer meeting, and the family in the church as a cohesive social unit that reflects in miniature the ideal social order. No new era of brotherliness and peace is likely to emerge in the absence of a new race of men. Evangelicals consider alliances of nations uncommitted to transcendent justice to be as futile a foundation for future mutuality as premarital promiscuity. As evangelical Christians see it, the vision of One World, or of United Nations, that is built on geographical representation rather than on principial agreement is as socially unpromising as is a lawless home that neglects the commandments of God. Walter Lippmann has somewhere said: "We ourselves were so sure that at long last a generation had arisen, keen and eager to put this disorderly earth to right ... and fit to do it. ... We meant so well, we tried so hard, and look what we have made of it. We can only muddle into muddle. What is required is a new kind of man."

Evangelical Christianity finds the most natural avenue for social witness beyond the family circle in the world of work when it is viewed as a divine calling. How sadly liberal Christianity, during its past-generation domination of ecclesiastical life, has failed in the organized church's social witness is nowhere more apparent than here. Almost all political leaders of the race-torn states are church members; Alabama's Governor Wallace belongs to the Methodist Church, which is in the forefront of liberal social action programs. Almost all congressmen are church members. Either the religious social activists have failed miserably in inspiring churchmen in political life to view their vocations as avenues for the advancement of social justice, or an elite ecclesiastical cadre is pressuring leaders to conform their political judgments to the partisan preferences of a special bloc of churchmen—or perhaps both are true. Since everyone lives in a world of labor and economics, evangelical Christianity emphasizes that man's work is a divinely appointed realm in which man is to glorify God and invest his talents for the good of his fellows; it is not only a means of livelihood but also an avenue of service.

This concept of divine vocation, of work as a calling, has all but vanished from the work-a-day world at the very time in modern history when liberal social action commissions have conspired with the labor unions in their skyrocketing material benefits. Meanwhile evangelical Protestants have organized a Christian Medical Society, Christian Business Men's Committee, Christian Professional Women's Club, Christian Law Society, Christian Teachers Association, Officers Christian Union in the Armed Forces—even a Christian Labor Union—in order to emphasize the spiritual responsibilities of vocation. It must be conceded that many of these Christian organizations serve mainly an evangelistic role, or one of vocational fellowship; only a beginning has been made in the equally urgent task of shaping an ethic for the social structures in which these groups operate. Beyond fulfilling person-to-person Christian opportunities, such agencies have an opportunity to supply guidance to both Christian and non-Christian on what is implied in a specified social order in the way of justice.

Evangelical Christians consider this recognition of the priestly nature of daily work to be more basic to social renewal than is a reshuffle of economic features that locates the fundamental flaws of society in man's environment rather than in man himself and his works. The importance of just laws is not in dispute, since civil government is divinely designed as a coercive force to restrain evil, preserve order, and promote justice in a fallen and sinful society. Because there is no assurance that all men will repent and seek the will of God, and because even Christian believers must contend with the remnants of sin, just laws are indispensable in human history, and God's common grace in the lives of men everywhere matches conscience with law in the interest of social preservation. But evangelical Christianity is not so infatuated with the external power of coercion as to exaggerate its potentialities, nor so skeptical of the spiritual powers of regeneration as to minimize its possibilities. Precisely because law does not contain the power to compel obedience, evangelical Christianity recognizes that a good society turns upon the presence of good men—of regenerated sinners whose minds and hearts are effectively bound to the revealed will of God—and upon their ability under God to influence humanity to aspire to enduring values.

Although society at large has seldom been overwhelmed by the Church's proclaiming the Gospel from the pulpit, the obedient fulfillment of the Great Commission has called new disciples one by one into the circle of regenerate humanity. The voice of the Church in society has been conspicuously weaker whenever the pulpit of proclamation has been forsaken for mass pressures upon the public through the adoption of resolutions, the promotion of legislation, and the organization of demonstrations. Whenever the institutional church seeks public influence by mounting a socio-political platform, she raises more fundamental doubts about the authenticity and uniqueness of the Church than about the social aberrations against which she protests.

To evangelical Christianity, history at its best is the lengthened shadow of influential men, not the compulsive grip of impersonal environmental forces. A change of environmental forces will not transform bad men into good men—let alone into a good society. But transformed men will rise above a bad environment and will not long be lacking in a determination to alter it.

At the present time, involvement in the race problem is the crucial test of devotion to social justice. Of the evangelical Christian's love for men of all races the long-standing missionary effort leaves no doubt; from Adoniram Judson and David Livingstone to Hudson Taylor and Paul Carlson, the story is one of evangelical sacrifice of creature comforts, even of life itself, that men of every land and color might share the blessings of redemption. In mid-twentieth-century America, humanism and liberalism and evangelicalism alike were slow to protest political discrimination against the Negro, although evangelical missionaries have deplored the incongruities of segregation. Regrettably, the Negro's plight became for some liberal reformers an opportunity for promoting social revolution, and for some conservative reactionaries an occasion for perpetuating segregation and discrimination. Evangelical Christianity has a burden for social renewal but no penchant for revolution or reaction. Because it champions the redemptive realities inherent in the Christian religion, evangelical Christianity will in the long run vindicate the judgment that the Negro is not only politically an equal but also spiritually a brother.

Some Governing Principles

A new breed of evangelical? Yes, indeed! But not because evangelicals are switching from proclamation of the good tidings to pronouncements, picketing, and politicking as sacred means of legislating Christian sentiment on earth. Rather, evangelicals are a new breed because redemptive religion seeks first and foremost a new race of men, new creatures in Christ. Whenever Christians lose that motivation, they surrender more than their

New Testament distinctiveness; they forfeit the New Testament evangel as well.

In summary, evangelicals face the social predicament today with four controlling convictions:

1. The Christian Church's distinctive dynamic for social transformation is personal regeneration by the Holy Spirit, and the proclamation of this divine offer of redemption is the Church's prime task.

    In the twentieth century the ecumenical movement has failed most conspicuously in its mission to the world by relying on political and sociological forces, and by neglecting spiritual dynamisms.

2. While the corporate or institutional church has no divine mandate, jurisdiction, or special competence for approving legislative proposals or political parties and persons, the pulpit is responsible for proclaiming divinely revealed principles of social justice as a part of the whole counsel of God.

3. The most natural transition from private to social action occurs in the world of daily work, in view of the Christian's need to consecrate his labor to the glory of God and to the service of mankind.

4. As citizens of two worlds, individual church members have the sacred duty to extend God's purpose of redemption through the Church, and also to extend God's purpose of justice and order through civil government. Christians are to distinguish themselves by civil obedience except where this conflicts with the commandments of God, and are to use every

political opportunity to support and promote just laws, to protest social injustice, and to serve their fellow men.

Carl F. H. Henry, "Evangelicals in the Social Struggle," *Christianity Today* 10, no. 1 (October 8, 1965): 3–11.

Chapter 5

WHO ARE THE EVANGELICALS?

Defining an "evangelical" is becoming no less difficult in America than defining a Jew in Israel. Americans have traditionally used the term in a more specific sense than many Europeans, for whom it early served to commend Reformation Christianity for its call to personal faith in contrast with the Romish emphasis on sacraments. Protestant churches thus became widely known as evangelical.

But many European "evangelical" churches compromised the ancient creeds and historical doctrinal affirmations of Christianity as modernistic theology—influenced by Kant, Hegel, Schleiermacher, Ritschl, and Troeltsch—captured the fancy of Protestant intellectuals. A generation ago in England the "liberal evangelicals" emerged with one foot insecurely in each of the rival options. More recently, Karl Barth, who anathematized modernism as heresy, used the title *Evangelical Theology: An Introduction* for an exposition of his own dialectical neo-orthodox alternative.

Ecumenical syncretists, eager for a world church whose unity they sought in social activism rather than in creedal consensus, chafed under what they considered an artificial American cor-relation of Christianity with the term *evangelical*. Some ecu-menists popularized the designation *conservative evangelical* to depict the outlook of evangelist Billy Graham, the positions taken by *Christianity Today*, and the stance of agencies like the Evangelical Foreign Missions Association or the National Association of Evangelicals. This label spared such enterprises the odious overtones that modernistic polemicists had attached to the term *fundamentalism*, while it enabled ecumenists in their other associations to retain the term *evangelical* for those whose doctrinal loyalties lay elsewhere.

The term *conservative evangelical* was minted after earlier efforts by some ecumenists to chide American evangelicals for having supposedly misappropriated a venerable religious term for partisan and factious purposes. This maneuver was remark-able for several reasons. In the thirties, before the emergence of the National Association of Evangelicals, the Federal Council of Churches was so predominantly non-evangelical in its theo-logical sympathies that the term *evangelical* was hardly one it sought for itself. Moreover, the theological commitments and evangelistic emphases of the rising American evangelical move-ments were anticipated in Germany and England by evangelical alliances with similar concerns.

In contrast to the modernist versions of Christianity, or to lib-eral religion, the evangelicals emphasized their alignment with doctrinal positions recovered by the Protestant Reformers and their devotion to an authentic biblical faith. Theological syncre-tists who accused Bible-believing Christians of deforming the term *evangelical* seemed to be rewriting church history on mod-ernistic presuppositions.

Evangelical has several notable advantages over *funda-mentalist* as a description of New Testament commitments.

Fundamentalism has been stigmatized by its modernistic foes until not even the devil would envy the label, and the mood and mentality of some fundamentalist polemicists has helped to fasten the caricature on the movement. In its beginnings early in this century, the fundamentalist vanguard emerged to challenge the Christian legitimacy of Protestant liberalism. The five-fold fundamentalist test swiftly exposed the semantic subtlety and evasiveness of many modernists; for example, "virgin birth" was more precise than "supernatural origin," and "bodily resurrection" less ambiguous than "life after death."

Although the fundamentalist credo served such polemical purposes well, when these distinctives became almost the sole provender of some pulpits, the laity became theologically undernourished. To the forefront of pulpit proclamation fundamentalists increasingly elevated emphases that, though they are significant in the total context of Christian faith, do not stand in the forefront of apostolic preaching. Here one thinks not only of the virgin birth but also of biblical inerrancy—themes that stress the *how* more than the *what* and *why* of the Incarnation and of the inspiration of the Word of God. The point is not that the New Testament lacks all basis for these emphases; indeed, the very first Gospel opens with a birth narrative. Nevertheless these emphases are not conspicuous in apostolic proclamation. Indeed, where dispensationalism left its mark upon fundamentalist circles, the millennium also gained kerygmatic prominence.

It may be said, of course, that the Bible has its insistent fundamentals no less than its central evangel; the kerygma is broadly identifiable as what the Bible teaches, and apostolic doctrine supplies its authoritative orientation. Yet the term *evangelical* has a firm basis in the language of the New Testament, and in his earliest writings the Apostle Paul succinctly states the core of "the evangel." If Christian commentators have long regarded

Romans 3:21–26 as the gist of the Gospel, in view of the notewor-thy declaration of Christ's propitiatory death for sinners, they have also emphasized that the Apostle in 1 Corinthians 15:3 and 4 transmits to his readers as the essence of the Christian evangel what he identifies as the earliest missionary preaching voiced in the Christian churches: "I delivered to you as of first importance what I also received, that Christ died for our sins in accordance with the Scriptures, that he was buried, that he was raised on the third day in accordance with the Scriptures ..."

There can hardly be any doubt about what Paul here consid-ers central and indispensable to the evangel, and to authentic evangelical faith. He expressly states three considerations: first, the death of Jesus of Nazareth in the place of sinners; second, the bodily resurrection (on the third day) of the slain and buried Jesus; and finally, the teaching of the sacred Scriptures.

The most striking aspect of the Apostle's declaration lies not in the uncompromising centrality he accords the resurrection of the Crucified One—decisively important as this historical devel-opment is—but rather in his twofold emphasis on the authorita-tive Scriptures. Repetitiously he affirms that the events of the crucifixion-resurrection weekend are to be biblically compre-hended; he twice invokes the Scriptures to frame the single men-tion of Jesus' substitutionary death for sinners and of his bodily resurrection.

In line with this New Testament representation, evangelical Christianity is distinguishable by its forefront proclamation of good news—forgiveness and new spiritual life available to sinners solely on the ground of Jesus' death and resurrection—and dis-tinguishable beyond that by the scripturally based and biblically controlled character of its message. Evangelical Christianity is properly suspicious of every effort to reconstruct the heritage of Christian faith that gives low visibility to the authority of Scripture. Its unabashed epistemic emphasis falls on what the Bible says.

Carl F. H. Henry, "Footnotes: Who Are the Evangelicals?," *Christianity Today* 16, no. 9 (February 4, 1972): 23–24.

Chapter 6

EVANGELICALS AND THE BIBLE

What evangelicals say about God, Christ's life and work, and man's present predicament and future hope, they say on the authority of the Bible. Insofar as religious knowledge is trustworthy, it derives not from subjective intuition, personal experience, or metaphysical speculation, but from divine revelation, and more specifically, the prophetic-apostolic Scriptures.

Modernist theology drove a wedge between God and the Bible, little realizing that the devaluation of Scripture involved also the discounting of God. Forsaking the miraculous—in deference to evolutionary immanentism—modernists approved only Scripture snippets compatible with their experimental theory, and scoffed at all claims for the Bible as a specially authoritative Book. Christians, they stressed, recognize only one absolute authority: God experienced personally in devotion to Jesus Christ.

This high-sounding appeal did not, however, supply a convincing reply or alternative to the evangelical commitment. Evangelical Christianity has never espoused two ultimate authorities. It considers the authority of the Bible no basis whatever for rejecting God's authority; rather, it invokes divine authority for its commitment to an authoritative Scripture.

Evangelical Christians affirm one final authority only, the Living God. This is theological shorthand for their insistence that the final authority is solely the Living God incarnate in Jesus of Nazareth. That, in turn, is but an abbreviated way of affirming that the only ultimate authority is the Living God incarnate in Jesus Christ, whom Christians acknowledge to be Divine Lord and Savior by the Holy Spirit. In conclusion, this is a summary phrasing for the full evangelical formula: the supreme authority in doctrine and morals is the Living God, incarnate in Jesus Christ, acknowledged as Lord by the Holy Spirit, whose special inspiration makes the scriptural writings the epistemic source of trustworthy knowledge of God and his will and word for man.

The world-church, projected by modernists as a fulcrum for social action amid doctrinal diversity, has fallen into much the same frustration as the United Nations, to which humanists looked as the hope of the world. The Christian churches are now more polarized and divided than at any other time in the present century, and the most conspicuous achievement of the ecumenical movement has been the substitution of larger denominational groupings for smaller ones. Worst of all, theological confusion is now so rife in many ecumenical seminaries that students are taking a rain-check on theological commitments since momentarily current views may become passé before they begin their own pulpit ministries. Many younger churchmen are simply opting for Marxism as a social ethic.

Many evangelical spokesmen had warned that the modernist erosion of an authoritative Bible would lead to the erosion also of an authoritative God, and to modernism's deflation into humanism. Once it became evident that modernism lacked any objective basis for its attempted reformulation of the doctrine of

God, modernism itself was eclipsed as a commanding influence in twentieth-century theology. The churches were deployed from the preaching of the Gospel to the promotion of socio-political change, and if persuasion and legislation would not achieve these goals, revolution would.

Mediating efforts to recover an authority of sorts for the Scriptures, by dialectical-existential theologians who deny the objective inspiration of the texts, have not held ground. These theories attracted some timid evangelicals ready to invoke the "leap of faith" as a solution for every major intellectual difficulty, yet not bright enough to see that the way into the superrational was exploited by every variety of mysticism. If the authority of the texts was to be defined solely as a development "if and as God speaks through them," the same claim might be made for Balaam's ass.

Among some evangelicals it seems to be becoming faddish to affirm that the Bible is authoritative while neglecting questions of inspiration and canonicity and denying the inerrancy of Scripture. This strange mix of logic may confuse a supportive constituency, but seminarians are reluctant to speak of the fallibility and errancy of that to which they assign divine authority.

The serious evangelical is called upon not simply to subscribe during installation ceremonies to revered traditions but to pervasively and coherently expound the principle of religious authority whereby one intelligibly and consistently arrives at his doctrinal commitments. If one presupposes, for example, that the creation narratives in Genesis are at bottom simply an edited version of traditions prevalent throughout the ancient Semitic world, he merely begs the critically important question whether all conceptualities assigning meaning and worth to human life are mythological, or whether among the multitudinous explanations of man's significance and destiny, one has its basis in special divine revelation.

An evangelical who erodes all his energies contending for the inerrancy of the Bible and neglects to unsheaf its revelational content has, to be sure, a warped sense of evangelical duty. But no less tragic is the situation of the evangelical who insists that he champions the inspiration and authority of Scripture but who readily espouses critical concessions and eagerly adduces "biblical errors." Academic responsibility and professional integrity require such a one to furnish an objective criterion for distinguishing biblical truth from what are alleged to be scriptural errors, or else students will be encouraged to receive or reject the biblical materials merely on the basis of subjective preference.

Evangelicals should be on guard against historical overviews of Christianity that underplay the role of Scripture, or that present the Bible mainly in a context of debate over its inspiration or inerrancy. A special word of caution may be added about the canard that those who assert the inerrancy of the Bible tend to be loveless because they thereby question the Christian authenticity of others. The same distortion of motives might be associated with the evangelical affirmation of the sinlessness of Jesus of Nazareth, or any other doctrinal tenet. It is sheer nonsense to convert the proposition "The Bible is divinely inspired, authoritative, and inerrant" into the proposition that whoever affirms these truths should lovelessly cut off anyone who rejects them. What is fundamentally at stake in any academic discussion of the authority of the Bible is not protecting human considerations and relationships but the validity of biblical truth.

Carl F. H. Henry, "Footnotes: Evangelicals and the Bible," *Christianity Today* 16, no. 11 (March 3, 1972): 35–36.

Chapter 7

EVANGELICAL SUMMERTIME?

Do we really live in the "day of the evangelical"?

In some evangelical circles it is considered spiritually unpatriotic to voice doubt. Those not given to evangelical puffery are often considered cynics and personally out of touch with the remarkable spiritual breakthroughs that supposedly attest that an evangelical awakening is under way in America.

The national media depicted 1976 as "the year of the evangelical." The Gallup Poll reported the beginnings of religious revival in the United States. Evangelical Christianity displays ongoing visibility as a life-changing force; witness Charles Colson, Eldridge Cleaver, Graham Kerr (the "Galloping Gourmet"), and others. Conservative churches are growing, and evangelical seminaries are burgeoning with students. The White House now lodges an openly evangelical president who hesitates neither to carry a Bible nor to teach a Sunday-school class.

No one should underestimate the religious importance of these and other recent evangelical trends. The reemergence of evangelical Christianity to national prominence—in contrast to its subculture role a generation ago—is among the striking religious developments of the last quarter century. The dynamic Graham crusades, the penetration by *Christianity Today*, the steady growth of evangelical divinity centers, the impact of Campus Crusade for Christ and Inter-Varsity among students, the discipling ministry of Navigators, the Urbana conferences that channel young intellectuals to distant mission fields, and the emergence of conservative scholars in biblical studies are only some of the formative contributions to this phenomenon.

Among major trends in American religious life in the past two decades have surely been the evident deterioration of non-evangelical Protestantism (represented by ecumenical initiatives), the disarray of Roman Catholicism with its authority crisis, and the public reemergence of evangelical Christianity as a life-transforming power manifested both in vigorous local churches and in thousands of house groups.

Yet no objective observer of the American scene can stop there, for overarching all these trends is an increasing secularization of American society. Its stranglehold is reshaping the basic values of home and family, molding the mental and moral attitudes in schoolrooms and campuses, and maneuvering the mass media into a bold mirroring of the rampant permissiveness and relativism of our day. A little thought about this radical secularism ought to puncture, certainly temper, our evangelical euphoria over present-day American religion. Say what it may about incipient religious revival, the Gallup Poll overlooks the multiform and even contradictory character of religious phenomena; it does not evaluate the fact that belief in God and expectation of a brighter immortality exist side by side with astounding, soaring statistics of abortion, crime, divorce, drug addiction, gambling, prostitution, shoplifting, and so on.

It is exceedingly risky—in view of the secularization of American learning and life—for evangelicals to think they are now controlling the formative cultural forces in our society. It will do Christian witness little good to bask in the day of the evangelical if the deepening night of secularism increasingly overshadows an all too feeble light. Evangelical Christianity has not yet in fact very deeply penetrated the radically secular mentality evident in schoolroom and society today and reflected by the media.

Conservative religious forces tend to look cosmetically impressive because neo-Protestant ecumenism has declined and because evangelical enterprises are reclustering. In financially inflationary times, the geographical huddling of related enterprises has much merit for promoting institutional economy and achieving mutual goals. Establishment of the Graham Center at Wheaton College and relocation nearby of *Christianity Today* will doubtless strengthen regional agencies like the National Association of Evangelicals, Moody Bible Institute, Trinity Evangelical Divinity School, and numerous missions enterprises. The suburban Chicago area may become something like an evangelical heartland for the nation.

But such clustering also has its risks and liabilities, particularly if its motivation is protective rather than penetrative. To cluster agencies not especially distinguished for cultural penetration, and in some cases motivated by a desire to escape the inroads of non-evangelical influence, may through aseptic isolation nurture an unfortunate illusion of strength at the cost of neglect of the secular world.

In some respects one can sense a thawing climate for evangelical penetration. An anguished sense of personal emptiness engulfs multitudes who once thought that moral relativism was the route to personal fulfillment. The life-changing power of the Gospel seen in the astonishing transformation of erstwhile "ugly Americans," the spectacle of a Bible-carrying presidential family reassured by the vitalities of revealed religion, the churchgoing throngs whose homes are happy and whose lives are buoyant, cannot but provoke many emotionally frayed seekers to wonder whether they have overlooked an unsuspected treasure. The godly example of leaders in high places and of neighbors at the local level can stir the conscience of a relativistic age, evoking self-examination and a longing for better things. A television series like Alex Haley's *Roots*, for all its stereotyping, mirrors what a people do to themselves when a moral and spiritual heritage is perverted; it attests, too, the potential moral power of the media.

Impressive as they are, such factors stop far short of a cultural setting in which evangelical Christianity wields a shaping initiative. But they can be the first waves of a winsome argument that places its hearers on the defensive.

There are distressing signs, however, that personal ambition and internal conflict among evangelical frontiersmen may strip the term "evangelical" of the gains that in a single generation made it once more a bright symbol of religious hope. Will maneuvering on both the right and the left politicize and institutionalize the polemical differences that have recently been revived? Will we see an emerging era of evangelical controversy, or will evangelicals unite for spiritual awakening in our needy land?

Carl F. H. Henry, "Footnotes: Evangelical Summertime?," *Christianity Today* 21, no. 13 (April 1, 1977): 38–40.

Chapter 8

EVANGELICALS: OUT OF THE CLOSET BUT GOING NOWHERE?

Evangelicals have failed to penetrate the
public mood and conscience.

Are evangelical Christians facing an identity crisis at just
the time America is experiencing a religious awakening?

On one hand we see the extended impact of the Graham
crusades, burgeoning enrollments in evangelical colleges and
seminaries, and the cumulative influence of magazines like
Christianity Today. In addition, we see the stimulus provided by
the World Congress on Evangelism and the Lausanne Congress
on World Evangelization.

But on the other hand, will evangelical indecision and disagreement nullify these spectacular advances?

We can expect prophecies of such a fallout from certain quarters. Humanists and secularists consign biblical faith to cultural

obsolescence. Others see its decline as a corollary to a neo-Protestant renewal of ecumenical fortunes.

But prophecies of an approaching evangelical upheaval come also from within the so-called evangelical establishment. The editor emeritus of *Christianity Today*, for example, tells us in *The Battle for the Bible* that a massive revolt against biblical inerrancy is sheltered by evangelical colleges and seminaries, and that many institutions firmly committed at midcentury to a consistent evangelical faith now have theologically divided faculties and accommodate destructive critical views.

The controversy over the Bible will not go away. It seems, rather, to be building toward a day of institutional upheaval. On one hand, the new International Council on Biblical Inerrancy is preparing a massive program of literature on the subject of scriptural inerrancy. On the other hand, stung by innuendos about false evangelicals, a cadre of mediating scholars from various conservative campuses is preparing a major Bible commentary series that combines extensive biblical criticism with broad evangelical positions.

A second internal controversy surrounds the nature of legitimate evangelical social involvement. Some young evangelicals, critical of secular capitalism or of mounting militarism, have been alienated by a swift branding of their views as communist or socialist. They are turning for support outside the evangelical arena to avowed ecumenical leftists whose theological deficiencies they reject but whose social protest they share. Evangelical leaders themselves are increasingly divided to the point of controversy over the issue of evangelical social concern and political involvement. In the absence of powerful intellectual analysis by institutional leaders and other spokesmen who hold the reins of evangelical power, a restless vanguard tends to divide and subdivide into conflicting camps prone to question each other's biblical adequacy and even authenticity.

Advances Since the 1950s

This time of ferment is all the more foreboding because of the evangelical movement's remarkable growth and impact since midcentury. Unbiased observers of the religious scene agree that since 1950 evangelical Christianity has come out of the American churches and tabernacles onto the streets and into the marketplace with phenomenal energy, and it has moved notably beyond radio into television.

Much of this momentum from the subculture to cultural centers came initially through the countercultural Jesus movement, which has now passed its peak, but which made a public issue of many prevalent values. Thousands of high school, college, and university students came to personal faith in Christ despite the fact that radical secularism held center stage on most campuses. While ecumenical student work dwindled, evangelical collegians emerged as probably the most vigorous vanguard in the American religious arena, and they have entered conservative seminaries by the thousands to prepare for pastoral, missionary, and educational careers. Today denominations within the National Council of Churches sponsor less than 8 percent of the U.S. missionary task force.

American evangelicals meanwhile are intensifying their world missionary concern by focusing on the more than 16,000 subcultures where no Christian church yet exists. The charismatic movement has ventured into evangelism by daily television programs centered upon personal experience, along with a sometimes not-so-soft-sell promotion of tongues, multiplied miracles, and even fresh revelation. In the big American cities the churches that thrive tend to be evangelical ministries that involve outreach enlisting a dedicated laity.

The advance of evangelical interests since 1950, however, is not due solely to the young. Evangelical religion also has won a kind of cultural respect even among many Americans whose basic commitments are secular. Evangelical vocabulary has gained public acceptance and intelligibility, even if the mass media secularize and corrupt the terms; the *Washington Post,* for example, reported, "Down in the hollows of Briar Mountain (Virginia) ... the 'likker' business is being born again."

In the face of idleness and theft among employees, many employers welcome evangelical workers, whom they can trust to give an honest day's work and not to pilfer from their employers. In a day when problems of sex and drugs plague high school campuses, even some parents having no religious preferences are sending their children to Christian schools as a means of preserving family respectability.

The wave of interest in Asian cults (whether Zen, transcendental meditation, or others) has lent to evangelical Christianity a new aura of acceptability among parents who prefer that their teen-agers take up with the Jesus movement or with the charismatics rather than join the Moonies, because these evangelical movements promote love of family rather than alienation, and at least reflect the American religious heritage. Evangelical Christianity has gained wide public acceptance even in a secular society that hesitates to make a biblical religious commitment.

Advances More Apparent Than Real

But all this is far from being an effective evangelical penetration of public mood and conscience. A close look at politics, business education, and mass media shows this.

Admittedly, we have an evangelical in the White House—an evangelical with moral sensitivity, whose simple faith in the Bible sometimes motivates bold personal initiatives. But that devotion is not without a theological ambiguity that reflects the doctrinal imprecision found in many professedly evangelical churches where the end results are problematical. Nor is the presidency devoid of concern for personal image and political ambition. For all that, Carter has brought more spiritual lucidity to the White House than many of his predecessors, though his retinue leaves much to be desired.

We must also concede that competent evangelicals are found in the world of business, but their influence registers far more aggressively in personal evangelism than in moral analysis that shapes ideals in the world of economics.

Further, while we have evangelical professors in prestigious colleges, the most influential classroom thrust on mainstream campuses today comes from radically secular humanists who disown supernatural beliefs.

We also have evangelical personalities and programs in the mass media, but the main media mood reinforces the tide of contemporary permissiveness, giving the impression that biblical values are archaic.

Lack of wide-scale penetration of our society by evangelicals suggests that we need to implement two priorities. First, the evangelical movement must place worldly culture on the defensive. It will remain on the margin of national life and public conscience until it does this. Evangelicals need publicly to argue the case that present cultural commitments lead to a life that is neither wise, good, nor happy; that the biblical alternative can offer people and nations a profound vision of truth, fresh resources of moral and spiritual power and a devotion to justice and decency, and that it can give an aimless and declining society new direction and hope.

Second, no less do we need a well-formulated statement of evangelical goals in contemporary society, and an elaboration of strategy and tactics for moving beyond principles to policies and programs that enlist the movement's resources for specific objectives. This does not devalue the need for increased devotional life. Sustained prayer has gone out of many churches, and is all too meager in the frenetic home life of our century. Further, the great Bible conferences of a generation ago have all but vanished as evangelicals have channeled their energies into this or that cause. We must admit that no extension of evangelical influence will long survive the loss of devotional realities. But devotional vitality of itself will not compensate for the lack of orderly vision and cooperative engagement.

Destructive Trends

In the absence of such evangelical advance, the mounting signs of trouble within the evangelical movement are too disturbing to disregard.

1. Southern Baptists. This largest predominantly conservative denomination in the United States, with 13 million members, not only faces a decline in the number of baptisms, but is now also losing 1,000 pastors from the ministry annually. Further, biblical criticism and theological dilution in many seminaries and colleges have become a denominational issue. Forces either supporting or opposing biblical inerrancy vie for denominational leadership.

2. Authority. Evangelicals must cope with the possibility, according to Harold Lindsell, that not more than a handful of their interdenominational seminaries and colleges remain truly committed to full biblical authority. They must weigh the consequences of the theological dilution of their most prestigious divinity school, Fuller Theological Seminary, and of other evangelical enterprises.

3. Mass evangelism. The Graham crusades continue to garner the largest public display of evangelical cooperation. But they have yet to achieve their initially announced goal of permeating American churches with evangelistic vitality that restores the initiative of community evangelism to the local church. Moreover, the loss in follow-up of those making public decisions remains a matter of deep concern among sponsoring committees almost everywhere. Admittedly, this evangelistic thrust produced a greater evangelical impact during the past generation than any other single element. But it failed to penetrate the core of mainline World Council denominations. Methodists, for example, have lost more than one million members in the last 10 years; one member of the General Council of Ministries sees the prospect of losing another million in the next decade.

4. Mass media. TV and radio have been used most prominently by charismatic Christians who present the claims of the Bible mainly in terms of inner experience, but they tend to neglect a systematic presentation of Christian truth. Many listeners are confused by the proffered prospect of constant miracle and by the erroneous impression that tongues-speaking validates an authentic Christian experience.

5. Secular education. Public high school, college, and university classrooms remain predominantly committed to radically secular views of man and the world. Many campuses are more open to evangelical Christians not because of their theology, but because in today's proliferation of religious cults evangelicals seem less extreme. Their views are largely ignored in the current environment of naturalistic evolutionary assumptions about life and the world. The campus, along with television, tends to shape a natural climate of thought that places inherited Judeo-Christian values on the defensive. Parental influence that Protestant and Catholic Christians—and for that matter, orthodox Jews—exert on children in the home is swiftly challenged and eclipsed by community influences.

6. *Politics.* Evangelicals have no philosophy of social and political involvement; rather, they tend to be cynical about the role of law in society, and pay little attention to governing policies and specific programs that channel political power in support of social righteousness. We can trace this failure to four causes: a tendency to regard evangelism as the only morally significant force in national life; a stream of theology resigned to inevitable historical decline until Christ's return; a disposition to view world political power as ultimately in the service of Satan rather than God; and a broken confidence in divine providence in the life of the nations.

7. *Literature.* The surge of evangelical materials that brought a wide new market to religious publishing houses and bookstores seems to be leveling off. To be sure, *Christianity Today* is enjoying its highest circulation; its content now serves a broader range of lay readers while it seeks under editor Kenneth Kantzer to maintain the magazine's distinctive role as a thought-journal. Other magazines, like *Moody Monthly, Christian Herald,* and *Eternity,* continue to be widely read. But readers face rising subscription rates due to increased printing and postal costs. They also have less to spend due to inflation and to budget cutbacks rising from a simplified lifestyle. Bonuses often artificially balloon the number of subscribers by temporarily attracting readers with no real sympathy with for magazine.

Tyndale House Publishers, with large overruns of the Living Bible, has been forced to cancel its projected *Tyndale*

Encyclopedia of Christian Knowledge despite an extensive financial outlay. Other publishers have been caught with large overruns of volumes intended to exploit the "born again" motif. Publishing costs are driving up book prices; in inflationary times, scholars are beginning to show interest in books with permanent value. By contrast, for the most part lay theological interest tends to remain more at a popular than an instructional level.

Some book clubs thus simply reconcile themselves to a perpetual demand for accounts of spiritual rescue from a sordid life of drugs, crime, or sexual permissiveness.

Present Strengths That Justify Hope

Despite such lacks, one must not overlook the dramatic, even surprising penetration of evangelicals into areas of personal and public concern.

1. Humanitarian interest. A decade ago few dreamed that evangelicals would ever respond as compassionately to pleas concerning world hunger and poverty as to pleas for evangelism. But in 1978 Christians gave $58 million to World Vision International for famine relief, child care, and development; this equals the amount they gave to the Billy Graham Evangelistic Association for evangelistic purposes. Now the World Relief Corporation of the National Association of Evangelicals with 30,000 related churches is projecting a broadly similar humanitarian program under the aegis of World Evangelical Fellowship, Evangelical Foreign Missions Association, Interdenominational Foreign Mission Association, and the recently integrated Development Assistance Services. World Relief Corporation has already been sharing in the resettlement of refugees with a program that by the end of 1981 may involve one in five NAE churches. Yet for all their commendable funding of Graham Association enterprises and World Vision projects, America's 40 to 50 million evangelicals averaged less than a dollar per person to each organization.

2. Political interest. A vanguard of young evangelicals has entered the legal profession. Specializing in political science, they are gaining valuable experience at various levels of state and national government, and are increasingly giving leadership. For many evangelicals the right-to-life movement provides a one-issue banner under which to learn the public use of political power for registering moral conviction. But as a whole, evangelical interest in politics involves little more than pulpit exhortation and support of single issues and personalities.

3. Scholarship. An emerging network of evangelical scholars is increasingly gaining recognition in the world of liberal learning that has lost consensus concerning God, truth, and values. Many publishers are issuing scholarly Bible commentaries and major theological works (some are retailing at less than four cents a page); the public media are beginning to recognize these works.

Leading evangelical seminaries continue to funnel competent graduates into mainline universities for doctoral studies. These scholars are particularly moving into linguistic and Near Eastern disciplines, pursuits that nonevangelical scholars seem to be forsaking. Trinity Evangelical Divinity School alone has 26 graduates from its Old Testament department working on doctorates in European and American universities. Some evangelical colleges report a lessening of the Jesus movement outlook that dominated campuses for much of a decade; more reflective engagement is taking hold as courses in philosophy and theology once again command interest. But evangelicals have shaped no great nationally recognized university, and collegiate interests are correlated more and more with evangelistic enterprises than with comprehensive liberal arts learning.

4. Local evangelism. The phenomenon of lay witness for Christ that emerged during World War II has escalated through church growth movements. It has produced many evangelistic programs geared to involve every church member. While the National Council of Churches tried to capture lay activity for social change, evangelicals preserved it for evangelistic outreach. Here lay interest has been particularly valuable since clergymen number less than one out of every 200 American Christians, and thus find little opportunity for personal evangelism. Though even the most active programs for lay witness enlist only a minority of evangelical church members, they have brought remarkable evangelistic vitality to local congregations. Many churches consider lay witnessing the next major framework for evangelical advance.

Focus for the '80s: Beyond Present Gains to New Achievements

Such encouraging signs suggest the next steps the evangelical movement should take under the Holy Spirit's guidance. By these steps it can move into broader usefulness in the only world it can serve.

1. Missions: Beyond present missionary gains to untouched major groups. We need to reorient world missionary objectives in terms of geography and ideology. As Ralph Winter emphasizes, national Christians everywhere need help in reaching across cultural lines to the hidden peoples. Just as Wycliffe Bible Translators try to make Scripture available in every known dialect, so the missionary task force must try to evangelize not simply where churches already exist, but especially in cultures yet unreached.

But the call to deal with resistant groups leads us to a concern over resistant forces often linked to such groups. The Christian mission must appraise powerful forces that reorient the national and international loyalties of great masses of people. We must vigorously challenge pagan misstatements of the Western biblical heritage. These emerge in the radical secularism now creating the climate of major universities.

Marxist theologies of revolution and liberation pose another concern. We must patiently weigh the opportunities as well as the difficulties of Christian evangelism in Communist lands. Fully as important, we need accelerated spiritual engagements in the Muslim world, which sweeps more and more African and Asian nations into its orbit and is hostile to the very idea of religious freedom.

2. Discipleship: Beyond lay evangelism alone to responsible church membership. The church growth movement must stress this goal along with evangelism if it is to meet the requirements of biblical discipleship. As people discover their gifts and abilities, they should be given opportunity to use them. Ordinary men and women should help in local church life and leadership. The 1981 American Festival of Evangelism to be held in Kansas City will emphasize such a balance.

3. Apologetics: Beyond experiential emphasis alone to demonstrating that belief in Christ is intellectually credible. Some observers fear that present existential, experiential, and charismatic emphases may lead to an equally objectionable overcorrection in the form of arid orthodoxy. While that may be a possibility, it is not presently a threat. What must we do? We must stress something more than that Christianity is a faith; the intellectual world today grants that it is, and catalogues it with dozens of other religious faiths. The question today concerns the intellectual credibility of Christian commitment.

So evangelicals should present evidence and warrants that accompany faith in the self-revealing God and Savior of sinners. Christianity insists that reason is on the side of biblical teaching, that spiritual commitment does not ideally build on contradiction, and that all the reasons cited against faith in the living God are but rationalizations. The world needs to hear this claim and be confronted with its persuasive supports, particularly in an unreasoning and existentially-oriented age. It is noteworthy that the Society of Christian Philosophers has recently been formed with the American Philosophical Association.

4. Bible: Beyond controversy over the Bible to an unleashing of its authority. The Bible must come to new centrality in the churches, not as an object of controversy, but because of its comprehensive truth, transforming power, and stimulus to witness and world engagement. We must not allow present debate over inerrancy to conceal two equally important facts: First, no movement can hope to speak convincingly to the world if its leaders constantly question the integrity of its charter documents. Second, no movement will unleash the power of the Word in the public realm if it uses its energies only to defend scriptural authority and inerrancy. In a society that has lost intellectual discrimination and moral power, the Bible must be known not only for new translations but also for its abiding truth and life-giving power.

5. Public affairs: Beyond preaching on private affairs alone, to Bible exposition declaring that the Lord of nations holds society accountable and offers hope in public affairs. Evangelical churches renowned for forceful pulpit ministries are disconcertingly few. Evangelical proclamation, even what passes for Bible exposition, is inexcusably thin and powerless. While the great biblical realities are proclaimed, often they seem to be exhibited like archeological ruins unearthed from the ancient past.

Further, sermons apply biblical truth mainly through a plea for internal decision and existential response. They virtually ignore God's external activity amid the tumult of our times. But he is the God of nature and of nations, who works decisively in present-day history. Consequently, he addresses the mind and conscience of those outside the churches, too, and holds them accountable worldwide. Biblical truth becomes introverted when the pulpit does not show how it arches forward into our age, to speak to our society. The text is seldom allowed to open for public no less than private affairs a hopeful way into the future.

6. *Stewardship: Beyond generosity to voluntary sacrifice (without legalism) in the use of resources.* American evangelicalism is being spiritually thwarted by its affluence. No group of Christians has been more generous: few groups have more to learn about sacrifice.

Yet some are implying that only one lifestyle—one not too far above the poverty level—is authentically Christian. Others, equally extreme, concentrate only on the new birth and personal evangelism, totally ignoring economic issues. Some discussions appear legalistic, proposing graduated tithing or particular abstentions or negations. However, not one but a number of lifestyles are compatible with Christian conscience.

Yet, obviously, some lifestyles are clearly non-Christian if marked by greed, extravagance, self-gratification, or lack of compassion for the needy. It is probably safe to say that evangelical lifestyle in America today often compromises the biblical doctrine of stewardship, and needs to be adjusted in view of humanity's severe difficulties. Evangelicals too readily forget that many of our economic blessings are a fruit of biblical virtues and, therefore, as the gift of God are at his disposal and not simply something we have achieved by ourselves.

Many congregations are still much too building-oriented rather than people-oriented. Even so, homes and possessions could be used for spiritual ends to a much greater degree. If each of us added to his present commitments a sum equivalent to less than the cost of a tankful of gasoline, we would more than double evangelical giving for evangelism and humanitarian effort.

Inflation and shortages of energy are forcing changed patterns of living upon both Christians and non-Christians. The real test of spiritual commitment is in voluntary obedience to Christ rather than in obligation or necessity in altering one's lifestyle.

7. Pastoral concerns: Beyond general interest in counseling to practical church programs that cultivate emotional balance, psychological wholeness, and wholesome family relationships. Suppose a Christian under emotional stress walked into a Christian group. How could its members help him? Ordinary laymen should be able to minister to one another at least on an elementary level, through cell groups, for instance. And a church must find a way to put to work those to whom God has given counseling gifts, perhaps even using them to establish a clinic overseen by a specialist and offering help to those with somewhat more complex problems. All thoughtful help need not come from the pastor.

8. Ecumenism: Beyond a defensive attitude toward World Council of Churches ecumenism to vigorous advocacy of a convincing Bible ecumenism. Especially in these days of a moribund WCC, the declaration of biblical thinking is critical. This should be applied to practical areas so evangelicals can act in unity around a core of accepted biblical essentials while being magnanimously tolerant of secondary differences.

9. Summary: Beyond vast potential to orderly vision and coordinated strategy in accord with God's worldwide sovereignty. Seldom in history has the evangelical movement had such potential for world impact. It has resources in people, in possessions, and in established institutions and widely dispersed movements. These constitute a vast reservoir of spiritual hope and moral power. Yet what is often missing is a comprehensive sense of evangelical family, of unified mission and coordinated strategy, of the Spirit's overwhelming empowerment, of confidence that God and not earthly Caesars govern the daily fortunes of history.

Worse yet, life in the big inner cities seems daily to be turning more pagan, while evangelicals tend to withdraw to the fringes of involvement. Organizational complexes such as at Wheaton, Illinois, can easily spawn misleading impressions of prominence and priorities, even as modern ecumenism discovered at 475 Riverside Drive in New York.

Beyond the Visible to the Active

Our task remains that of lighting and salting an otherwise darkening and putrefying world. In a generation for which SALT has become an acronym for Soviet-American adjustments in a vicious arms race, and LIGHT is a phenomenon that scientists computerize in interplanetary correlations, even Christians easily forget that lighting and salting is their mission to the world.

We are not charged, of course, with launching millennial solutions—we are not in the business of shaping utopian programs. That is God's work, and not even he is presently engaged in that. But at this point in history, God has a purpose for both church and civil government. We control neither but are called to make responsible Christian choices and obedient commitments while we leave the rest to divine providence. That course will deliver us from both lethargy and social enthusiasm.

Each of us can exercise influence through lifestyle, through evangelistic engagement, through political participation. In many parts of the world lifestyle is not a matter of decision but of survival, and political policy is a matter of dictatorial determination and not of national option. We in America are free to demonstrate what the lordship of Christ implies for the whole of life, free to do so at a moment in history when such freedom is ebbing away. It is high time to realize that fulfilling Christ's mandate lies not in international talkathons. It lies, rather, in individual response to opportunities for decision and deed that crowd our calendars day after day after day.

Evangelicals seem to be in a holding pattern, sometimes approaching a long-awaited landing, then circling round and round a cooperative objective, even at times moving exasperatingly away from it. We perform a series of maneuvers whose outcome is complicated by gathering storms that may divert us to an unforeseen and unintended destination.

Major dialogues are being held, some polarized on the far right, some characterized by confusing pluralism, some concerned with institutional image and opportunity. All too few manifest a call to intellectually powerful analysis of the cultural crisis and the task it implies for vital evangelical impact.

Evangelical Christianity in our generation has come out of the closet. It has yet to discover what it means to come confrontationally and creatively into the culture.

Carl F. H. Henry, "Evangelicals: Out of the Closet but Going Nowhere?," *Christianity Today* 24, no. 1 (January 4, 1980): 16–22.

Part II

EVANGELICALS AND MODERN THEOLOGY

Chapter 9

REVELATION AND THE BIBLE

No theme is more worthy than the Word, whether the Incarnate Word or the Inspired Word. And surely renewed interest in special revelation is timely and necessary for our befuddled world of thought and action. We are all aware that in this century speculative idealism has passed its prime, naturalism has gained ascendancy, and Communism incorporates into modern history a world-life view resolutely anti-supernatural. It is indeed the good providence of God that we are once again permitted, even forced to, the biblical heritage of Western culture.

Emil Brunner has said, and I think rightly, that "the fate of the Bible is the fate of Christianity." When we interpret such expressions, we are all concerned to avoid both understatements and overstatements of the significance of the Bible. How shall we properly relate the Bible to divine revelation? This question continues to be a fundamental issue in modern theology. Karl Barth, for example, in *The Doctrine of the Word of God*, speaks of doing the Bible "a poor honor" by identifying revelation with the Book. On the other hand, evangelical Protestantism believes that despite the new emphasis on the Bible as "witness" to special revelation neither Barth nor Brunner nor neo-orthodox theologians generally honor Scripture as they ought. Meantime evangelicals are charged with exaggerating the role of the Bible—with making it a "paper Pope," with worshipping it, with allowing it to crowd out the authority of God, the authority of Jesus Christ. What shall we think and say of these matters?

We dare allow only one final authority in the Christian life. We dare acknowledge the authority of no other god than the living God who made heaven and earth and man in his image. We dare acknowledge only the authority of the living God incarnate in Jesus of Nazareth, the authority of the living God who regenerates and reigns in the life of believers by the Holy Spirit ("No one can say 'Jesus is Lord' except by the Holy Spirit," 1 Cor. 12:3 RSV). Must we not also acknowledge the living God, incarnate in Jesus Christ, renewing believers by the Holy Spirit, as the authoritative source of sacred Scripture, the divine rule of faith and practice ("All scripture is God-breathed, and is profitable ... that the man of God may be perfect, thoroughly furnished unto all good works," 2 Tim. 3:16)? To affirm the authority of Scripture neither undermines nor threatens the living God as final authority in the believer's life; but rather, like the recognition that the Spirit regenerates and rules, and that Jesus of Nazareth is Savior and Lord, it guarantees the removal of illegitimate aspirants or pretenders to his authority.

Thrust of Neo-Orthodoxy

To exhibit the divergent views I shall present the basic issue from two sides, noting first, that the neo-orthodox rival view fails to do justice to the status of the Bible as revelation; and second, that the evangelical view honors the revelation-status of the Bible.

The main premises of the neo-orthodox view of the Bible, as I see them, are (1) the Bible is the indispensable witness to special redemptive revelation; (2) no identity exists between the Bible, in its written form of words and sentences, and special revelation; (3) the Bible is the instrumental frame within which God personally encounters man and actualizes revelation in the form of dynamic response.

Instability of Liberalism

This view brought welcome relief to the problems that harassed Protestant liberalism for half a century. Remember that Wellhausen's post-evolutionary criticism had narrowed the traditional confidence in the infallibility of Scripture by excluding matters of science and history. The Bible was then considered reliable only in matters of faith and practice. Next, William Newton Clarke's *The Use of the Scriptures in Theology* (1905) yielded biblical theology and ethics to the critics as well as biblical science and history, but reserved "Christian theology," or the teaching of Jesus Christ, as reliable. British scholars took a further step. Since science and history were involved in Jesus' endorsement of creation, the patriarchs, Moses and the Law, English critics more and more accepted only the theological and moral teaching of Jesus. Contemporaries swiftly erased even this remainder, asserting Jesus' theological fallibility. Actual belief in Satan and demons was intolerable to the critical mind, and must therefore invalidate his theological integrity, while the feigned belief in them (as a concession to the times) would invalidate his moral integrity. Had not Jesus represented his whole ministry as the conquest of Satan and invoked his exorcism of demons to prove his supernatural mission? The critics could only infer his limited knowledge even of theological and moral truths. The Chicago school of "empirical theologians" argued that respect for the scientific method in theology disallows *in toto* any defense of Jesus' absoluteness and infallibility. Harry Emerson Fosdick's *The Modern Use of the Bible* (1924) championed only "abidingly valid" *experiences* in Jesus' life that could be normatively relived by us. Gerald Birney Smith took the final plunge in *Current Christian Thinking* (1928): We are to gain inspiration from Jesus, but it is our own experience that determines doctrine and a valid outlook on life.

This history of concession and retreat had one pervading theme, namely, that the Bible differs from other so-called sacred books only in degree; it contains the highest religious and ethical insights gleaned from universal divine revelation. Liberalism moved from the fallibility of the Bible to the fallibility of the God-man to the fallibility of the indwelling Spirit to the fallibility of everything except, perhaps, of contemporary criticism! The resulting confusion and chaos were therefore a propitious time for a view which recognized that the perplexing problem of religious knowledge could not be solved in so narrow, so artificial a framework. If that new view, moreover, could dissolve the need for identifying the Bible in part or whole as the Word of God—thus rising above the fatiguing and exasperating game of epistemological "blind man's bluff"—it could attract the liberal theologian and critic even while it disputed him.

Neo-Orthodoxy's New Look

Neo-orthodoxy sets out with a new look at controlling ideas of the nature and activity of God. It rejects liberalism's metaphysics of extreme divine immanence and accepts instead a reactionary doctrine of extreme divine transcendence. Furthermore, neo-orthodoxy rejects the post-Hegelian epistemology of extreme monistic realism that virtually identifies God's knowledge with man's knowledge. But its doctrine of subjectivity perpetuates the error of epistemological dualism, bridging the tension between eternity and time not conceptually but dialectically and/or existentially in dynamic faith-response. Gordon H. Clark traces this development of modern counter-thrust to the excesses of Hegelian rationalism in his book *Thales to Dewey*. He discloses the generous philosophical rather than biblical indebtedness of recent theories of God and revelation. One could say of the contemporary theology of revelation that its vocabulary is the vocabulary of Abraham, Isaac, and Jacob, but its plot is the plot of Kant and Kierkegaard, of Ebner and Buber.

Our immediate concern, however, is the role of the Bible in the new theology of the Word of God. Assuredly, the current interest in special revelation has stimulated fresh exploration of the Bible. As opposed to the old liberalism, neo-orthodoxy no longer gears Scripture to a naturalistic, evolutionary *development* of religious experience, nor demeans the Bible as a human interpretation of a *universal* divine activity. Instead, the Book's theological message is an authentic witness to God's unique self-disclosure in Jesus Christ.

Evading the Biblical Witness

Precisely this profession of neo-orthodoxy, however, to honor the Bible as a witness to special divine revelation, is an Achilles' heel. For the witness of the Bible does not conform to the dialectical and non-rational exposition of revelation affirmed by the contemporary theology of the Word of God. Because of this divergence, neo-orthodoxy ultimately must choose one of two alternatives: either the new theology must abandon its merely formal appeal to the Scriptures as witness to special divine revelation, or neo-orthodoxy must dissolve its antithetical exposition of revelation and reason.

If the inspiration and revelation-status of the Scriptures as depicted by neo-orthodox writers is set alongside the witness of the biblical writers, their conflict becomes apparent at once. Geoffrey W. Bromiley, translator of Karl Barth's *Church Dogmatics*, has long observed that whereas Barth emphasizes the "inspiringness" of Scripture, that is, its dynamic potency in religious experience, the Bible itself moves beyond this claim to assert the very "inspiredness" of the writings. The decisive reference here, of course, is 2 Timothy 3:16, "All scripture is inspired by God ..." This passage identifies Scripture itself as "God-breathed"; the writings themselves, as an end-product, are a unique product of divine activity. The divergence of crisis theology from the biblical witness is even more apparent in neo-orthodoxy's claim that divine revelation does not assume the form of concepts and words. This assertion runs so directly counter to the specific claim of the biblical writers that Emil Brunner, uneasy in the presence of the repetitious Old Testament formula "Thus saith the Lord ...," concessively called this prophetic ascription of words and statements to Deity "an Old Testament level of revelation" (*Revelation and Reason*, p. 122, n. 9).

One of Brunner's students, Paul King Jewett, has long since pointed out that to admit such propositions as revelation, whether low or high, breaks down the assumption that revelation is conceptually and verbally inexpressible, and unwittingly surrenders the thesis that divine revelation must take a form that impinges dialectically upon the mind of man. Not alone do the Old Testament prophets provide a biblical basis for identifying the inspired spoken and written word with the very Word of God; this selfsame identification is made by the New Testament apostles as well. Paul wrote that the Thessalonian converts "received the word of God which you heard from us ... not as the word of men but as what it really is, the word of God" (1 Thess. 2:13 RSV).

Peter declared that "no prophecy ever came by the impulse of man, but men moved by the Holy Spirit spoke from God" (2 Pet. 1:21 RSV). The writer to the Hebrews repeatedly ascribes to God what the prophets had spoken. One senses their uniform readiness to regard the sacred teaching as sharing the authority of divine revelation.

Certainly both the evangelists and apostles distinguish Jesus of Nazareth as the supreme and final revelation of God. Matthew records Peter's confession that he truly is the Christ, the Son of the living God (16:16). John writes that "no one has ever seen God; the only Son, who is in the bosom of the Father, he has made him known" (1:18 RSV). Paul finds the climax of the gospel in redemption personally secured by the death and resurrection of Jesus Christ (1 Cor. 15:1–4). But the New Testament writers never make this staggering fact of God's personal revelation in the flesh by Jesus Christ the occasion for depriving the inspired utterances of the sacred writers of a direct identity with divine revelation. In thus honoring the prophetic word as the veritable Word of God (cf. Paul's characterization of the Old Testament as "the oracles of God" in Romans 3:2), the disciples and apostles had the sacred example of their Master and Lord; he spoke of himself indeed as the one "the Father consecrated and sent into the world," yet he spoke at the same time of those "to whom the word of God came (and scripture cannot be broken)" (John 10:35).

Besides this validation of the divine authority of Scripture, Jesus' followers heard him ascribe absolute significance to his own words and commands uttered in their hearing. The dialectical theory, if true, would preclude any direct identification with divine revelation of the spoken words of Jesus, no less than of prophets and apostles. In line with its presuppositions neo-orthodoxy distinguishes constantly between the Word of God as revelation and the "pointers" to revelation or assertedly fallible human ideas and words. But this distinction will not bear the scrutiny of Jesus' teaching. For Jesus held men responsible not only for hearing his "word" (John 5:24), but for Moses' "writings" and his own "words" (5:47). Indeed, he specifically identifies his own words and commands with the Father's word: "The words that I say unto you I do not speak on my own authority; but the Father who dwells in me does his works. ... He who does not love me does not keep my words; and the word which you hear is not mine but the Father's who sent me. ... If you abide in me, and my words abide in you, ask whatever you will, and it shall be done for you. ... If you keep my commandments, you will abide in my love, just as I have kept my Father's commandments and abide in his love" (John 14:10, 24; 15:7, 10 RSV).

Integrity of Theology

All this may seem like a needless revival of marginal concerns in circles throbbing to modernist traditions. But the very integrity of theology is at stake. As a theology that professes to honor the biblical witness to revelation, neo-orthodoxy must face the fact that it does not really derive its doctrine of revelation from the witness of Scripture; it does not have an authentically biblical concern for the fundamentals of that doctrine.

The new theology may disparage identification of the Bible in whole or in part with revelation as a kind of bibliolatry, as dishonoring to the idea of revelation, or as injurious to faith. Yet several facts remain clear. The new theology cannot find support for its anxieties over the evil implications of the traditional view in the biblical witness itself. The Bible nowhere protests nor cautions against identifying Scripture with revelation, but rather approves and supports this turn. Whoever evades these verities in constructing a doctrine of revelation, however vocal his plea for biblical theology, shows greater concern to baptize biblical criticism with an orthodox justification than to confirm the central features of the scriptural view.

The neo-orthodox rejection of the Bible as revelation rests actually on rationalism rather than on reverence. To expel Scripture from the orbit of revelation itself to the sphere of witness, and subsequently to ignore that witness in forging a doctrine of revelation, reveals speculative rather than scriptural and spiritual motives. The devout considerations by which neo-orthodoxy ventures to support its maneuver are unpersuasive. A radical skepticism in metaphysics, a relational theology still tainted with the philosophical influence of Kant and Schleiermacher, determine its elaboration of divine revelation.

Whatever problems the evangelical view may create, it commendably upholds the inspiration and revelation-status of Scripture. This recognition keeps faith with the witness of Scripture itself, and with the historic Christian confidence in the Bible.

A Fairer Hearing

For many years misunderstood and often misrepresented, the evangelical view today seems to be evaluated more objectively and temperately. No doubt the evangelical position is still deplored in some circles as anti-intellectual, in much the same spirit as a generation ago some groups disparaged and dismissed original sin, the atonement and other realities that now once again are lively centers of theological interest. The recent volume *Fundamentalism and the Church* by Gabriel Hebert reveals that

---

Carl F. H. Henry, "Revelation and the Bible (Part I)," *Christianity Today* 2, no. 18 (June 9, 1958): 5–7.

the old innuendos about "bibliolatry" and "mechanical dictation" are not gone, but failure to stigmatize fundamentalism with
a mechanical and naive literalist view of inspiration is increasingly evident. Fundamentalists have long been unable to recognize their own view in such attacks, since they themselves reject
the formulas so frequently ascribed to them. One of their British
theologians, J. I. Packer, recently commented that the "dictation
theory" of the psychology of inspiration is "a complete hoax." He
insists that evangelical and Protestant theologians have never
held it; that there is no evidence to think that even the Church
Fathers used the "dictation" metaphor to explain the mode of
inspiration (*The Christian News Letter*, July, 1957, p. 37). Even its
larger outlines should dissolve complaints that the evangelical
view narrows revelation to the Bible, that it is anti-intellectual,
or that it is wholly disinterested in the bearing of the actual textual phenomena on the doctrine of Scripture.

Pivotal points of the evangelical view of revelation are:

1. The evangelical view distinguishes the personal
    Word of God, the *Logos Theou*, from the Word of God
    written, or the *Hrema Theou*. It affirms the priority
    of the personal or speaking Word over the spoken
    or written Word.

2. All revelation of God is revelation by the Logos.

3. This revelation is both general and special. God is
    revealed in nature, history and conscience, as well
    as in Scripture. The Bible witnesses to the reality of
    this general revelation (Ps. 19, Rom. 1:19 ff., 2:15 ff.).

4. Special revelation is itself broader than Scripture.
    While the Bible states all the essentials for salva-
    tion and spiritual maturity, the written record

has not always existed. Abraham received special revelation but we have no reason to think he had scriptures. While our Lord's spoken word was revelation, not all his teaching is recorded. Moreover, there is an eschatological fulfillment yet to come. For another reason special revelation must be considered broader than the Bible, which is shaped for a fallen race in need of salvation. Even by creation and before the fall, God specially revealed his will to man (Gen. 2:16). This fact indicates that even man's creatureliness, and not his subsequent sinfulness alone, involved this special dependency on God.

5. Special revelation includes God's redemptive events climaxed by the incarnation of the Logos, his atonement and resurrection. Without these great realities, special revelation is reduced to an inspired literature. What lifts Hebrew-Christian religion head and shoulders above the pagan religions is not simply its possession of "the oracles of God," but the dynamic related plot these writings record. The living climax of that plot is the Logos who makes all things, illumines man in the divine image, discloses himself as the secret center of nature and history, and by his triumph over sin and death rescues a doomed race.

6. These redemptive events do not stand before us without interpretation. Scripture gives the authentic sense or meaning of the divine saving acts. While the Bible mirrors both general and special revelation, and affirms that the incarnate Logos translates God into the world of flesh, the Bible also captures that revelation in intelligible language. Revelation

is dynamically broader than the Bible, but epistemologically Scripture gives us more of the revelation of the Logos than we would have without the Bible.

7. What then is the connection of the Bible and special revelation? According to the evangelical view, the Bible is a record of special revelation, and a witness to special revelation, if by the terms "record" and "witness" we do not mean the Bible is *only* a record and witness. Even to affirm that the Bible "contains" special revelation is quite acceptable if one intends no distinction between essence and content, but implies thereby, as does the Westminster Catechism, the unique inspiration of the whole of Scripture. For the evangelical view affirms that alongside the special divine revelation in saving acts, God's disclosure has taken the form also of truths and words. This revelation is communicated in a restricted canon of trustworthy writings, deeding fallen man an authentic exposition of God and his purposes. Scripture itself therefore is an integral part of God's redemptive activity, a special form of revelation, a unique mode of divine disclosure. It is, in truth, a decisive factor in God's redemptive activity, interpreting and unifying the whole series of redemptive deeds, and exhibiting their divine meaning and significance.

Whether one appeals to Augustine or Aquinas, to Luther or Calvin, he finds the selfsame confidence in this revelatory character of the Word written as characterized the biblical writers. The Bible is for them, as for evangelical theology generally, special revelation in a normative and trustworthy form. Its difference from other sacred books of the world religions is no mere matter of degree. Rather, a special activity of divine inspiration differentiates it in kind from every other literature. This explains why the Hebrew-Christion religion has characteristically identified itself with a canon of unique writings that fulfill a divine intention of communicating special revelation. This idea of a canon did not originate suddenly in the early Christian centuries, as if by accident or by human impulse; it was a conviction already cherished by Hebrew religion, and accredited to the Christian conscience by Jesus of Nazareth. What the spirit says to the churches is, for evangelical Christianity, what is written in the inspired books. The content of this special divine revelation is to be found by historical-grammatical exegesis.

Evangelical Landmarks

While a generation ago it was customary to disparage this view as anti-intellectualistic, today it is popular to despise it as rationalistic. This remarkable change in the militant mood of apologetics reflects, of course, some important facts about recent Protestant theology. One is its basic philosophic instability that lodged first in the mires of Hegelian rationalism, and then in the muck of post-Hegelian irrationalism. Another feature is its persistent failure to rise above the fictitious disjunction that Schleiermacher first impressed upon the history of Christian thought, namely, that divine revelation consists in impartation of life, not of doctrine. The Protestant Reformers were careful to guard the Christian heritage against such errors of rationalism, irrationalism and mysticism. To prevent Christianity's decline to mere metaphysics, they indeed stressed that the Holy Spirit alone gives life. But to prevent debasement of the Christian religion to formless mysticism or to speculative rationalism, the Reformers emphasized the Scriptures as the only trustworthy source of the knowledge of God and his purposes. These historic positions are still landmarks of the evangelical view.

Every exposition of revelation and inspiration stands in some larger context. The doctrine of Scripture necessarily implies a compatible and congenial doctrine of God; it cannot be isolated from actual dependence upon the nature and manifestation of God. Overarching the evangelical view is the cardinal fact of God's sovereignty in his being and activity, in his goodness and truth, and especially in his supremacy in the realm of truth as God of the Covenant. Unlike the irrationalistic metaphysics that surcharges the theology of Kierkegaard, Barth and Brunner, the evangelical doctrine postulates a view of God, of his image in man, of the divine renewal of that image coherent with the biblical representations of revelation.

God and His Image

The biblical delineation of revelation and reason does not hesitate to lodge the Logos unreservedly in the Godhead. Truth and goodness are not external criteria to which the Deity is answerable. Rather, truth and goodness are God's essence, so that his very nature itself defines rationality and morality. This concept we know to be basic in the Hebrew-Christian doctrine of God.

A rational God has ordered a rational universe in which rational creatures created in his image are to think his thoughts after him and to do them. This fact of a rational Creator maintains the unity of the general divine revelation in nature, history and man. That man bears the image of God by creation (Gen. 1:26), that he is uniquely lighted by the Logos (John 1:9), is one of Scripture's profoundest teachings about him. It supplies the setting also for some of the most intricate controversies in contemporary theology. Barth has had at least two theories of the *imago Dei* thus far, and Brunner at least three. It may be fruitful, by way of contrast, to consider a view currently advocated in evangelical circles as an alternative, since it transcends the tensions tearing many of the newer theories. The image of God in man constitutes man a spiritual-rational-moral agent. It includes therefore, at very least, the forms of reason and conscience, and the idea of God. What man knows, he knows through the law of contradiction, or he does not know. The laws of logic therefore belong to the *imago Dei*. This propels us directly into the analysis of the form and the content of reason. Recent generations largely accepted the view of Kant or of the evolutionists. Kant said that the form of reason is innate, but that experience supplies its content; the evolutionists said that experience supplies both form and content. The scriptural view requires a reference to the *imago Dei* for both the form and content of reason. Moreover, the Scriptures do not separate reason, conscience and worship as if these were independent considerations.

The *imago Dei* does include man's formal realization that truth and error, right and wrong, God and not-God are genuine distinctions. But the *imago Dei* is more than *formal*; it is *material* as well. The very forms of the *imago* (including the laws of logic; the essential unity of the ideas of truth and goodness and God) belong to its content. Man as sinner no doubt crowds the *imago* with a distorted and perverse content; he falsifies the truth and dignifies the lie; he misjudges the right and consecrates the wrong; he revolts against the one true God and worships false gods. But he is not wholly lacking, on that account, of a transcendent *imago*-content that confronts him throughout this perversion and judges him. Even in his rebellion, man is confronted moment-by-moment in his experience by knowledge of the one true God—disclosed in nature and history around him and in conscience within. He is unable wholly to destroy this knowledge in his very corruption of it. Therefore conscience, like a sheriff, marshals him constantly before the judgment throne of God. You will discern here the familiar outlines of the Bible doctrine of general revelation, pieced together from Psalm 19 and Romans 1 and 2.

From the outset this exposition sets human experience in the context of revelation and faith. But it does not devalue the intellect, as does contemporary theology. Nor does it exaggerate the role of reason, as does Thomistic philosophy. Before the Fall, man's reason was subject to God and his will subject to reason; therefore, his voluntary actions were conformed to truth. After the Fall, man's reason was in the service of a will in revolt against God. Yet man is not on that account without some knowledge of God and the truth and the right, however much he may distort them.

Redemption aims not simply at man's restoration to obedience, but to truth as well. It seeks his return both to the service and to the knowledge of God. The immediate end of redemption is renewal of man's knowledge of God for the ultimate end of man's total conformity to the image of Jesus Christ. Redemptive revelation and regeneration, therefore, encompass the predicament of the whole man, who was fashioned by creation for the knowledge and service of God. Redemptive revelation and regeneration seek reinstatement of intellect, no less than of volition and emotion, to the fellowship of divine conversation. If it were not so, theologians and seminarians could proclaim the great fact of special divine revelation, and yet would be free to stuff this form with a thought-content and a word-content of their own. But God wishes man both to walk in his ways and to think his thoughts after him; hence the language of revelation, like the language of prayer, takes the form of concepts and words.

Carl F. H. Henry, "Revelation and the Bible (Part II)," *Christianity Today* 2, no. 19 (June 23, 1958): 15–17.

Chapter 10

YEA, HATH GOD SAID ...?

Westminster Press has just issued a volume on *The Inspiration of Scripture* by Dewey M. Beegle. This publication holds special interest through its issuance by a denominational publishing house at a time when ecumenical discussion is centering on Scripture and tradition; through the fact that its author is associate professor of Hebrew and Old Testament at Biblical Seminary in New York, whose founders emphasized that the Bible should stand at the center of the theological curriculum; and through the fact that many evangelical institutions and movements are presently engaged in spirited conversations on the subject of Scripture.

The author "frankly acknowledges his genuine belief in the inspiration and authority of Scripture" and concedes that "few areas of Christian life and thought ... do not lead back eventually to the issue of inspiration." He urges "by the inductive method ... a reverent approach to Scripture that resolves at all costs to let God's Word speak for itself." Christian theology can in fact become endangered through "superbelief" (such as a docetic view of the Incarnation or a dictation view of inspiration). "Is one justified ... in claiming more than Scripture does? Can there be in actuality a higher view (of inspiration) than the biblical view?"

Evangelical scholars will not hesitate to reappraise their regard for the Bible in the light of Professor Beegle's claims and comments. Most evangelical Christians hold the plenary-verbal view of the Bible's inspiration; they affirm, in other words, that the whole Bible is inspired by a divine superintendence extending to the very words. They stress the Old Testament's "thus saith the Lord," a phrase found some 1,200 times, and New Testament passages on the nature of inspiration such as 2 Timothy 3:16 and 2 Peter 1:19–21. They hold that the original writings teach nothing contrary to fact.

Evangelical theologians acknowledge that inerrancy is not formally claimed by the biblical writers. But they assert that it is a proper inference from the Bible's teaching about its own inspiration, and from the character of the self-revealing God.

It must be granted, as Professor Beegle insists, that the scriptural writers do not expound the doctrine of inspiration (or any doctrine) with "the detail and completeness of systematic theologians"—including, we might add, of Beegle's own treatise. "Scripture does not tell us the mode or means by which God revealed his message to his inspired servants." It may be noted that evangelicals do not adduce verbal inspiration as a full answer to the question of *method,* but rather as a verdict on the inspired end-product or sacred writings.

Dr. Beegle declares the biblical teaching and data to be "so complex and many-faceted that it is virtually impossible to formulate the doctrine of inspiration in any concise, general statement." We are therefore hardly prepared for his own attempt to account for the Bible in the main by an "extraordinary help of the Holy Spirit" which here sinks to mere intuition and there to mere illumination. No precise definition is given of the nature and content of inspiration, but disturbingly general statements appear: "While there is some justification" for a distinction between inspired men and the inspiration of a compiler of a book, "the idea has been carried too far in some instances." Or, "inspiration had to do with the understanding of the historical record, not the inerrancy of every word incorporated from the sources."

We are told that "only a general statement of the range or extent of revelation and inspiration can be given." Our dissatisfaction is doubled by Professor Beegle's downgrading of past discussions of inspiration from the second through the nineteenth centuries as "essentially general affirmations of the divine and human aspects of Scripture" in which these two facets are nowhere "explicitly reconciled." If, as Beegle thinks, "the data of Scripture do not warrant the 'fixed' meanings" which evangelical theologians assign to the terms "revelation" and "inspiration," their intelligibility demands a clear statement of what fluid meanings define these supernatural activities.

Beegle is far more explicit in stating the position he rejects: "The sovereignty of God, the honor of Jesus Christ, and the trustworthiness of biblical doctrine are not at stake in accepting a view of inspiration that rejects the qualification of inerrancy." "We can speak of the Bible as being inspired from cover to cover, human mistakes and all." Yet "there is no need to posit *unique* inspiration for every word of the Bible. There are degrees of something in Scripture, and it is more than just degrees of revelation."

The author at times overstates conservative counter-claims in seeking to discredit them. Champions of the high view are made to say that "without a perfect original text one could just as well turn to Buddhist or Hindu literature." They are sometimes pictured as requiring repudiation of the entire content of the Bible once its inerrancy is surrendered, and as holding that the whole edifice of belief in revealed religion thereby collapses. The author should stipulate those "groups within Protestantism" which "during the last seventy-five years" have made inspiration "the pivotal doctrine of the Gospel" and hold as "popular opinion ... that Christian faith is impossible without belief in the inerrancy of Scripture." Again Beegle identifies as "a major contention" the view that whoever abandons inerrancy "will eventually ... become an extreme liberal." Yet Beegle himself quotes Charles Hodge and B. B. Warfield as emphasizing that the rejection of scriptural inerrancy does not destroy the case for theism and that the burden upon unbelief remains fully as great. Surely evangelical theologians do not make an inerrant record the *primary* purpose of inspiration. Taken simply as trustworthy records the Scriptures confront the reader with adequate evidence for biblical theism and for faith in Jesus Christ. While the author finally concedes that evangelical leaders "now acknowledge" that belief in scriptural inerrancy is not necessary for salvation, he attacks an alfalfa dummy in making evangelicals contend that inerrancy is the ground of the whole Christian faith.

Beegle's announced objective is to demolish the premise of inerrancy. A. G. Hebert's view is endorsed that inerrancy is "a new doctrine" and that "the modern fundamentalist is asserting something that no previous age has understood in anything like the modern sense." He links the doctrine of inerrancy to a "deterministic definition of divine sovereignty" and insists that it "leads eventually into the mechanical or dictation theory of inspiration": "Unless God dictated his revelation word for word, there is no assurance that the Old Testament writers caught all the nuances or overtones of God's self-disclosure." Thus to advocates of inerrancy he imputes what they disown and repudiate. Temporary retention of the belief, he tells us, may be psychologically valuable in a transition time while one is filling it with new meaning. Since evangelicals ordinarily refuse to detach psychological value from objective truth, and consider reprehensible the retention of terms or doctrines through the device of redefinition, it is remarkable to find an evangelical scholar thus justifying the doctrine.

But Professor Beegle's hostility extends also to the plenary-verbal inspiration of the Scriptures. He deplores not only inerrancy, but identification of the position of Scripture and of the Apostolic Church as "verbal plenary": "Only when Scripture and history of doctrine are read with the presupposition of inerrancy is it possible to extend the twentieth-century formulation of verbal plenary, inerrant inspiration back through church history and even into Scripture itself."

In rejecting verbal inspiration—that is, an inspiration that extends to the words themselves—Beegle views Matthew 5:17, 18 as an attack by Jesus upon the Pharisaic tendency to stress the letter rather than the spirit of the law. But Beegle does not even consider that spirit and letter are not necessarily antagonistic, or that Jesus may seek spiritual fulfillment of the letter. Hence espousal of verbal inspiration is subtly but unconvincingly equated with Phariseeism in contemporary form. The Apostle Paul's "uncertainty" over whom he baptized (1 Cor. 1:14–16) and his contrast of spirit and letter (1 Cor. 2:1–16) are held to preclude his verbal inspiration. But no mention is made of 1 Thessalonians 2:13, "For this cause also thank we God without ceasing, because, when ye received the word of God which ye heard of us, ye received it not as the word of men, but as it is in truth, the word of God ..."

For Beegle Scripture's function is to record and transmit that portion of redemptive history which suffices for belief in Jesus Christ and thus for eternal life. "By proper methods of interpretation human reason can distill the relevant aspects of Scripture."

Obviously the author narrows the Bible's profitability from apostolic indications of its value (cf. 2 Tim. 3:16). The statement that "humble submission to the Christ back of Scripture is far more crucial than one's doctrine of revelation and inspiration" is disappointingly oblique in a book presumably expounding not salvation but inspiration. And the rejection in principle of *scriptural revelation* is evident from Beegle's emphasis that "technically speaking ... the Bible is a record or witness to revelation," in contrast to the Church's traditional position that the Scriptures "*are* special revelation."

The Phenomena of Scripture

The author specially aims to construct his view not primarily from the teaching of the sacred writers about their inspiration, but from the textual phenomena (which Dr. Beegle calls "the facts" in contrast with "the doctrinal statements").

The author faces us with a series of dubious disjunctions. When he states that "aside from the ultimate authority of the triune God, Scripture is our highest authority," he apparently deprives the Bible at any point of full divine authority. Against an appeal to divine sovereignty in expounding inerrant inspiration, Beegle argues that a sovereign God would achieve his purposes through variety rather than through one method.

In sweeping departure from 2 Timothy 3:16, Beegle passes this judgment on the Old Testament canon: "The books of the Old Testament range from works of unquestioned authority and revelational content to those of questionable authority and rather insignificant value. Some portions of the apocryphal books appear to have greater worth than some sections of the canonical books ..." As Beegle sees it, mere intuition (religious genius or spiritual insight) may account for the historical investigations represented in the writing of Luke's Gospel and the Acts. Nothing more than illumination is needed to account for a number of other scriptural passages.

From this verdict the distance is not far to an attribution of inspiration to some non-canonical writings alongside the denial of inspiration to elements of the canonical. Does the setting of canonical limits, Beegle asks, "mean that every word within these limits is uniquely inspired of God, while every word outside the canon is not inspired?"

Yet in discussing the New Testament canon, Beegle tells us that the book of Jude (despite its alleged citation of apocryphal literature as authoritative) "has an authoritative ring which sets it apart from ... apocryphal books and from the writings of the early church fathers." But if both canonical and non-canonical literature are inspired, and if Scripture is errant, does not the designation of canonical rest simply upon arbitrary authority or subjective preference?

Original and Copies

We are told that "the Bible makes no essential distinction" between autographs, copies, and translations, and that all three "derive ultimately from God and that all are authoritative." If this assertion implies as it does a biblical denial of the unique inspiration of the original writers, or an equivalent inspiration of copyists and translators, it is wide of the facts. Inerrancy of autographs would assertedly require identical inspiration for compilers of early sources and for scribes. Since Jesus and the apostles appealed to the extant Old Testament manuscripts as inspired, they assertedly assigned no greater authority and accuracy to the autographs than to the fallible copies, so that inerrant originals are dispensable.

This theory discounts the biblical emphasis on the Spirit's unique superintendence of the original writers. Beegle ignores the fact that the inspiredness of the translations is not inherent but derivative from the original autographs. The Holy Spirit's use of errant copies to bless the Church is made to dispense with the need of inerrant originals. But one might as well as dispense with the sinlessness of the God-man because the Spirit blesses the ministry of devout but errant saints. The argument that if God could have given inerrant originals he could also have provided inerrant copies is irrelevant; if God could have become incarnate in Christ he could also have produced sinless believers. The life and the activity of the Church are not set in the dimension of perpetual miracle, but presuppose the once-for-all prophetic-apostolic disclosure. The translations are indeed un*corrupted* by error, and are adequate for the Church's mission in the world, but their value derives from their fidelity to the best manuscripts, and hence ultimately to their fidelity to the autographs. The apostles speak of the divine inspiration of the *writers* of Scripture, not of the transmitters of it. The assertion that New Testament writers "were not concerned about the autographs as such, nor were they exercised over the difficulties in transmitting the original text" is a misguided verdict of deductive speculation, and is contradicted by an inductive study of the Bible (cf. Rev. 22:18, 19).

Beegle emphasizes that "God did not purpose to maintain in transmission the accuracy of the autographs" but trusted the fallibility of devout human channels to maintain "the level of truth necessary for achieving his purposes." The admitted "suffi-ciency" of the present translations is made to imply the superflu-ousness of superior autographs; presumably only the corruption of all translations would constitute an argument to the need of inerrant originals! So the Westminster Confession's statement that divine providence has kept the Scriptures "pure in all ages" is turned into evidence against an original inerrancy while the Confession's related emphasis that the autographs were "immediately inspired by God" is ignored.

The testimony of Jesus and the apostles is bent to support the errancy of the autographs. Beegle disregards Paul's assertion that the glory of the Jews was their entrustment with "the oracles of God" (Rom. 3:2) and instead asserts that inerrancy of autographs is a modern apologetic artifice arising from a discovery of errors in the copies. Inspiration is said, quite properly, to be "involved in" a process that includes a chosen speaker or writer and his message, whether oral or written, so that the end result, or sacred writings, are to be viewed as inspired. But Beegle shies away from the inspiredness of the writings, in order to throw the primary force of inspiration upon the person. Once this step is taken, the divine intention to produce a corpus of sacred literature is inevitably obscured.

Beegle's position is that Scripture does not teach the doctrine of inerrancy, and that the biblical phenomena require errancy of the original manuscripts and a doctrine of inspiration that conjoins the revelation of a perfect God with an imperfect Scripture. Those who argue for inerrancy, he claims, abandon induction for deduction. But Beegle himself concedes that "perfect objectivity is never achieved" in interpreting the evidence; deduction therefore is also an element in constructing his view. Besides, not a single text lines up the teaching of Jesus or the apostles on the side of the errancy of Scripture which Beegle proclaims. Beegle denies that Jesus believed and taught the inerrancy of Scripture. Yet nowhere in Jesus' teaching does one find a hint of the errancy of the sacred writings; he deplores those who misinterpret or who neglect or who depart from the Scriptures, but his appeal to the Old Testament is always to adduce and enforce its authority rather than to question its reliability. Nowhere does

Jesus teach or imply the divine revelation or inspiration of error. When Jesus speaks of error, he criticizes the current traditions in the light of scriptural revelation; he does not promote doubt over the full accuracy and trustworthiness of the narratives, but rather invokes them to rebuke those who hold speculative views: "Ye do err, not knowing the Scripture." The emphasis on error leads Beegle to the incongruous insistence that Jesus' rebuke of the Sadducees for not knowing the Scriptures (Mark 12:24) and his emphasis on the inviolability of Scripture (John 10:35) presupposed errant Scripture because our Lord's appeal was to extant manuscripts.

The emphasis on the errancy of the apographs, or transmitted texts, places Beegle in a neat dilemma. On the one hand he stresses that the present texts are *Scripture*; on the other, he repeatedly emphasizes the fallibility of these texts (thinking thereby to discredit the premise of inerrant autographs). He concedes that the Dead Sea Scrolls attest that the text of the standard Hebrew Old Testament available today is "essentially" the same as Paul's. Textual variants ought then to be as distressing to Beegle as to advocates of a higher view of Scripture, since he assimilates the quality of the autographs to that of the present texts.

The Nature of Inspiration

Beegle initially describes the original writers as "uniquely inspired" in distinction from the scribes who share the "degree of inspiration common to all devoted men of God" (whatever that may be!). But this difference of subjective inspiration assertedly makes no difference in the written records as between autographs and copies.

We are told, for example, that Luke did not consider his Gospel inspired. Beegle does not mention the significant fact that Paul (who wrote 2 Tim. 3:16) in 1 Timothy 5:18 quotes a passage from Luke's Gospel and designates it "Scripture." And when Paul depicts Scripture as inspired of God, is not his primary reference to the original writings? And is it not to the written product that he attributes inspiredness? If Paul is mistaken at these points, his unique inspiration would seem inferior to the "common inspiration" of twentieth-century theologians who supposedly can put us right about the matter. Mr. Beegle nowhere tells us what inspiration uniquely accomplished in and through the original writers. He simply rejects "the idea that inspiration is the constant factor throughout Scripture." And he repudiates the close connection between inspiration and canonicity. We are told that the inspiration of Luke was "not likely" of a *different kind* from that of God's servants down through church history nor from that of any man today, and the same is said of Mark. In fact, Professor Beegle finally dissolves "unique inspiration" for some Bible books. "If Isaac Watts, Charles Wesley, Augustus Toplady, and Reginald Heber had lived in the time of David and Solomon and been *no more inspired than they were in their own day*, some of their hymns of praise to God would have found their way into the Hebrew canon."

At this level inspiration—unique or otherwise—seems hardly any longer to retain any element that is identifiably scriptural. Beegle contends, however, that as the *record* of sacred history consummated in Christ the canonical Scriptures are distinctive and in this general sense "equally inspired" and that "the canon *as a whole* will always rank as uniquely inspired literature." But the introduction of this claim after the earlier deflation of both canonicity and inspiration leaves one with a feeling of rhetorical profuseness.

When he contends, moreover, for the inspiration not of translations as such, but of "all reasonably accurate translations," one wonders why inspiration should be linked with the precise repetition of mistakes in supposedly errant originals. Yet Beegle goes further, and invokes as a confirmation of inspiration a translation's pragmatic serviceability—however faulty it may be—in bringing readers under the Spirit's conviction.

The value of all creedal statements on inspiration formulated in the sixteenth and seventeenth centuries is questioned on the ground that they were "precritical in nature and … neither elaborated nor reconciled the divine and human elements of Scripture in any systematic way." One wonders what the implications of this judgment would be were the doctrine under scrutiny that of divine incarnation rather than divine inspiration.

Twentieth-century champions of inerrancy have included Charles Hodge, B. B. Warfield, Edward J. Young, and others. Mr. Beegle in passing quotes a number of contemporary evangelical scholars—Bernard Ramm, Edward Carnell, James Packer, Kenneth Kantzer, Philip Hughes, and Carl Henry—where their statements are somewhat serviceable to his view. But none of these scholars would endorse the main positions of the book, and their differences are unmentioned.

While Beegle deplores the "all or nothing" view of most evangelicals, whose position he overstates, he himself acts on the principle he condemns. He affirms "inspiration—translations—copies and originals in the same sense" over against "translation—no inspiration"—thus distorting the evangelical distinction between the mediate inspiration of copies and translations and the immediate inspiration of the autographs. If the present errant manuscripts are trustworthy and authoritative, we are told, inerrant originals are superfluous. This position reaches ludicrousness with the implication that the apostles made error authoritative, and we should follow their example: "If Jesus and Paul and Peter considered the errant manuscripts of their time as trustworthy and authoritative, should we not …?"

The Quality of Bible Doctrine

The importance evangelicals attach to inerrancy, Beegle notes, has to do with doctrine. He rejects the emphasis that the biblical writers can hardly be considered trustworthy teachers of doctrine if they err in their doctrine of inspiration. He argues that they are not untrustworthy because they are trustworthy only in much rather than in all. But he does not demonstrate (nor can he) that if mistaken about their own inspiration their doctrinal trustworthiness is unimpaired, nor how the strands of truth and supposed error are to be segregated.

Beegle no more defends the infallibility of Bible doctrine than the full trustworthiness of Bible history. Take the difficulties in the synoptic record of the Olivet discourse. These are "likely" explained on the premise that the disciples "confounded some of Jesus' statements about the destruction of Jerusalem with some of his remarks about his second coming," unless "the difficulty lay in the original statement of Jesus." In any event "erroneous elements of doctrine" existed in the original Gospels. The implications of the view that Jesus' teaching was ambiguous, or of the view that his disciples inaccurately understood him, cover a territory that only the author's personal surmise holds within quite narrow boundaries. He limits it to the fuzziness of "details of doctrine … as one nears the fringes of truth." But Beegle finds a "diversity of doctrinal data" in respect to the Atonement no less than eschatology. Fuzziness thus encroaches on biblical truth itself.

When Beegle tells us that "in all essential matters of faith and practice Scripture is authentic, accurate and trustworthy," he bequeaths us the problem of discriminating what is essential. He asserts that according to the New Testament "Christ and the gospel" (not the Scriptures) are the determinative standard of trustworthy and authoritative doctrine. But we know no Christ nor gospel other than the Christ and Gospel of the Bible. And

Beegle asserts their errancy, and the possibility of Jesus' ambiguity and of his disciples' misunderstanding. The valid procedure, he now tells us, is "to accept the view that accounts for the most Biblical data related to the subject." But how often need a truth be affirmed in Scripture in order to be biblically true? For Beegle the *Kerygma* is obviously not "what the Bible teaches." The doctrinal content of the revealed Gospel seems disappointingly unprecise when we are told that "the Biblical writers shared unequivocally some doctrines that cluster around Jesus, the incarnate Christ, and the way of salvation."

Although acknowledging "the validity of concern" over the admission of error in Scripture, Beegle replies obliquely that spiritual security can be found only in daily commitment to God. This reply, if adequate, would dissolve any value whatever in Beegle's insistence on the (limited) trustworthiness of Scripture.

The important role of revealed truths is understated: "The only protection God has provided (against doctrinal deviation) is the Holy Spirit's working dynamically in a committed heart, mind, and body. This is sufficient protection for salvation, but it is still not certain protection against false doctrine." But the real issue is glossed over: it is not whether the Bible can be misunderstood, but whether the Bible, properly understood, informs the mind with revealed truths.

We are told that "all of Scripture does not come under the category of supernatural revelation" and that "all Biblical doctrine is not infallible."

Logic and the Truth

The logic of the book is sometimes woefully weak. Beegle deplores the syllogism "God is perfect, God revealed himself in the autographs, therefore the autographs had to be inerrant"—or the assumption that God, if he truly reveals himself, must "reveal himself inerrantly"—without examining the alternatives. The claim is made that the Bible is both human and divine, but logic should compel him to ask how it can be both divine and erroneous. Beegle rejects the alternative "either the autographs were inerrant, or else human fallibility infected all of Scripture." If there is another alternative, it would greatly enhance Beegle's argument if he would actually segregate the infallible from the supposedly fallible elements and indicate on what objective principle this determination is made. If divine revelation is intelligible communication, Beegle can hardly mean that God conveys propositions that are partially true and partially false, and that he inspires both inerrant and errant words. When Beegle proclaims that "the Bible ... does not teach that unless a thing is *totally* true it cannot be inspired," the word he italicizes is dispensable, and the alternative he implies is that God inspires untruth. The untenable position to which Beegle is led is seen in his assertion that "Stephen, even while under the inspiration of the Holy Spirit, probably made a mistake ..." and evidently "it seemed good to the Holy Spirit to let Paul use" erroneous figures "without informing him that he was technically wrong."

In effect Beegle espouses the view that under the Holy Spirit's inspiration a chosen divine servant may blend truth and error while a twentieth-century scholar without such unique inspiration is able to distinguish the truth from falsehood. Since Beegle disowns the assumption that "God had to reveal himself inerrantly," is not the incongruous theological alternative that divine revelation deviates from the truth? The outcome of any such religious epistemology must surely be skepticism.

Yet the author does not hesitate to assail the logic of the biblical writers. Of Matthew's application of Hosea 11:1 to the return of Jesus from Egypt, he writes: Matthew shared the "Jewish mode of thinking"; "his logic in this instance bears the marks of his day"; and he used a "method of proving (that) does not conform to all the facts." Instead of concluding from this that Matthew was illogical and reached a false conclusion from assertedly improper premises, Beegle champions "essential truth" (devoid of "erroneous nonessentials") while repudiating "absolute truth." "By shifting the line of defense from 'absolute truth' to 'essential truth' it is possible to reckon with all the phenomena and teaching of Scripture and to have a sound view of authority as well." "Essential truth" is illustrated to include fallacious conclusions resting on illicit premises.

In an error-leavened Bible the author distinguishes God's Word (which always accords with the facts) from man's word (which reflects fallible opinion). But on what basis is the distinction between these strands of truth and error made? Surely not on the ground that a statement is biblical, since even the autographs are held to err. Even statements undiscredited by scientific considerations may still come into question, and if confirmed by science, these scientific verdicts are revisable and reversible. Yet Beegle tells us that "the key events of redemptive history are to be ... authenticated, insofar as is possible, by the same criteria employed in checking all other historical data." It is no real solution to insist, as Beegle does, that "one must decide which parts of the Bible are mistaken or else one is unwittingly accepting error as truth. ... Everyone who believes in the validity and indispensability of Scripture is confronted with the inescapable duty of using one's rational powers to ferret out the mistaken elements in Scripture." If this is indeed an inescapable duty, Beegle needs to be reminded that both the prophets and apostles, and Jesus of Nazareth, neglected to enjoin this responsibility upon the children of God.

Beegle is finally driven to espouse a highly unsatisfactory theory of truth no less than of revelation and inspiration. He tells us there is "certainly some truth" to Kierkegaard's notion that a heathen praying passionately to an idol is actually "in the truth." Beegle thus detaches true worship not simply from Scriptures in-errant and verbally inspired, but from true concepts of God as well.

Existential interpretation is dignified as "new Reformation theology." It seems hardly fair to credit this "new Reformation theology" with reminding the Church that revelation and inspiration "must be actualized in the lives of persons" while the evangelical tradition is depicted as stressing the role of the Book (presumably unconcerned about appropriation). Beegle never really criticizes Barth for his refusal to affirm the inspiredness of Scripture.

Beegle's break with the evangelical-biblical view is evident in his declaration that contemporary theologians are "technically accurate in defining revelation and inspiration in terms of personal communication between God and man," alongside his revolt against the intellectual or doctrinal element. In common with much recent religious philosophy he apparently rejects the unity of truth: "There are two different kinds of truth: objective and subjective." He assures us that so-called "it-truth," which deals with "the impersonal world of things and objects," is not untrue. This does not, however, grip important questions such as: is divine revelation communicated in the form of truths? and does man have valid knowledge of God as the object of religious experience? The section on "Revelation and Doctrine" is disappointingly imprecise. It repudiates in principle, however, the possibility of revealed doctrines: "It is imperative ... that revelation and doctrine be distinguished."

The assertion that "propositional truths, like doctrine, cannot he considered as revelation because they cannot save" is misleading. No evangelical scholar holds that doctrine saves. But evangelical Christianity contends that there are revealed truths or doctrines, and this Beegle denies. Evangelical scholars contend also that revealed truths have been objectively inscripturated by divine inspiration, and that they have the status of divine revelation—whether or not the contemporary man accepts or rejects them—and this Beegle also denies.

Beegle does affirm that Scripture contains objective truths (must not whatever truth it contains necessarily be objective?). If the "elemental ideas of God and Christ" set forth in the scriptural record are "classified ... as doctrine, then a minimal core of doctrine is basic to genuine faith." In a prize understatement we are told that "Paul recognized that teaching had a part to play." The essential point, says Beegle, is that "the objective truth of Scripture, whether defined as doctrine or not, is the means by which the Holy Spirit leads to subjective truth"—and it is the latter, Beegle has earlier assured us, that is revelation.

In this century, Beegle acknowledges, the inseparability of ideas and words has become increasingly clear. But inerrancy of ideas does not, he contends, require "the inerrancy of all words"; rather, it necessitates only "correct key words." Beegle realizes that the wedding of words and ideas drives him to the further admission of "incorrect ideas" in Scripture, and his next apologetic artifice is to contrast "correct key ideas" with "erroneous non-essential ideas," which are linked in turn with "correct key words" and "erroneous words" leading finally to a distinction between "the essentials and the non-essentials in Scripture." This obviously settles nothing, since Beegle will hardly concede that everything unessential in Scripture is expressed in erroneous ideas and words, and on his theory he can hardly protect essentials from error.

If skepticism is a consequence of Beegle's view of revelation, it is also a consequence of his view of language. We are told that "words are symbols that cover areas of meaning, and the area varies from individual to individual. ... Consequently no two people speaking the same language necessarily mean the same thing by the same word. ... Scripture is no exception." Such passages deny any identity of meaning in the use of words (and contradict Beegle's earlier assertion of the wedlock of words and ideas). Nonetheless the author expects evangelical readers to understand his assault on canonical inspiration or he would not have bothered to write this book. In a more cautious statement Beegle adds that "language cannot possibly convey ... all the facets of personality and character." From this he draws three conclusions: first, that despite the symbolism of metaphorical language the human mind is able to distill concepts which amount to literal truth (would not this feat be fully as miraculous as inerrant inspiration?); (2) the necessity for exalting Jesus above the Scriptures (could this superiority then be expressed in words?); (3) Scripture cannot he described as inerrant since language is incapable of absolute communication (why does Beegle then assume that Scripture's supposed errancy can be absolutely communicated?). Beegle downgrades the God who intelligibly speaks his revelation, and the adequacy of human language to articulate will and word—and the reason he does so is his lack of a theistic view of language. The Creator who fashioned human nature as wholly serviceable to the Incarnation also fashioned human speech as a wholly serviceable medium of divine revelation and inspiration.

Faith and History

The crucial issue, Professor Beegle says, is one's estimate of "fact and history in Scripture," or perhaps better, the soundness of that estimate. With an eye on Bultmannism, he insists that subjective faith is threatened once we surrender the key elements of sacred history. "Faith is rooted in fact." Evangelical Christianity stands with Paul's "bold" affirmation that faith is futile apart from Christ's resurrection (although the equally bold prophetic affirmation "thus saith the Lord" is not taken literally). Beegle repudiates the liberalism of R. H. Pfeiffer, who divorced faith from all miracle, and not simply (as Beegle does) from the miracle of scriptural inspiration. Conceding that no history is absolutely objective, and that all history involves subjective elements, Beegle notes the "new Reformation" theology's dual definition of history and its dialectical relating of time and eternity. Quoting J. Gresham Machen's statement that belief in the Virgin Birth may not be necessary to every Christian, he asserts that Machen "has shown the impossibility of prescribing a minimal core of biblical events to which assent must be given before saving faith is possible"—which does violence to Machen's intention and his conclusion. The thrust of Beegle's exposition is to excuse doctrinal doubts and to stress how little Christians may believe.

The final appeal for belief in the Virgin Birth and the Resurrection is merely pragmatic. "As a general rule, churches with ministers and leaders who have consistently denied, or at least minimized" these particular doctrines "have tended to lose the sense of mission."

The complaint can be registered no less effectively against those who have abandoned the high view of the Bible, which carries these miracles with it. Beegle quotes contemporary adversaries of the high view approvingly despite their rejection of it for divergent reasons which often cancel each other out. If the author had followed a different course, asking where the repudiation of the high view leads contemporary theologians in their conflicting expositions of the essential content of the Christian revelation, the result might have been therapeutic. In the closing words of the book Beegle shifts the argument from the theoretical question of the nature of inspiration to the pragmatic serviceability of extant translations and copies, and he attributes divine inspiration to devout but fallible ministers in every age of church history.

The conclusion of Beegle's discussion of the historical trustworthiness of the Bible is distressingly imprecise. He discards as extreme the view that faith in Christ can coexist with doubts about "the truth and relevance of much" that Scripture declares. He wants "a mediating view" between Bultmann's rejection of trustworthiness and the view that the Gospels are reliable stenographic reports. Yet he minimizes even the importance of this broken historical truth: "Submission to Christ is primarily a matter of decision, an exercise of our will, not knowledge." One who begins (rather than ends) here will not kick long against the pricks of Bultmann's demythologizing.

Beegle declares that "minor historical errors in Scripture invalidate neither our faith not true doctrine." But since biblical history is not to be taken as accurate simply on the ground that it is biblical (part of the record), no reason remains for assuming any event not independently confirmed to have actually occurred. One cannot confidently distinguish major and minor events as significant and trustworthy and as unsignificant and untrustworthy as Beegle does except by an act of will. The history of theological debate has a way of bypassing such hesitancies and inconsistencies, and of urging the same compromises with less timidity and with great loss to the Christian heritage.

Concluding Remarks

Much of the difficulty over inspiration may in fact lie in the theologian's attempt to enforce too rigid a pattern of divine superintendence upon the Spirit of God. The Scriptures assert that inspiration extended not only to chosen persons, but to their sacred writings, and that the very words derive their unique authority from this supernatural superintendence. But the Spirit is no less free and creative in the realm of special than in the realm of natural disclosure of God, and no one *method* is adequate to account for the end-product. Verbal inspiredness is to be attributed to the writings, but their production presupposes a variety of activity—divine dictation, in the writing of the law on stone, or in Jesus' teaching, greater or lesser precision as the purpose of God requires, with correspondingly less or more reflection of the personality or stylistic differences of the writers. That copyists and translators have often erred is beyond dispute; textual criticism aims to undo their deviations. But that a perfect God reveals himself in half-truths is a thesis that cripples Christian theology far more than the problems facing the view of an authoritative Bible.

Dr. Beegle states that it is not his purpose "to unsettle the faith of any Christian, but the risk must be taken in order to remove the 'needless barrier' which has kept many more from exercising faith in Christ." But if he thinks either that Christian faith is rendered more secure through the promotion of the errancy of Scripture, or that the real barrier to faith in Christ lies in the doctrine that God reveals himself inerrantly, he is sadly mistaken. The evangelists whose ministries are signally blessed by God are those who confidently champion Scripture as God's Word written, while the theologians who promote the errancy of Scripture make their converts mainly in the ranks of professing Christians and not among the outsiders. "God chose to make his authority relevant to man by means which necessitate some element of fallibility. … The facts permit no other understanding of Scripture's inspiration and authority." Were the premises right, it would be in keeping with them to notch one's critical pronouncements a shade below the level of infallibility, rather than exempting one's theory of inspiration from the supposed fallibility which prevented prophets and apostles from accurately interpreting their experiences. We are unpersuaded by the author's assurances that if we accept his view of a broken Bible "nothing basic is lost," that "those essential elements which the advocates of the doctrine of inerrancy have cherished ... are more firmly supported than ever before," and that transcending this tradition will ready us "to challenge the tremendous moral and spiritual problems that confront us on every side."

Carl F. H. Henry, "Yea, Hath God Said ...?," *Christianity Today* 7, no. 15 (April 26, 1963): 26–47.

Chapter 11

LIBERALISM IN TRANSITION

As a theological force in America, Protestant liberalism is now open to increasing fragmentation. Liberal frontiers are in a fluid state; nobody seems able to chart lines of fixed differentiation authoritatively. A crumbling of positions, along with some realignment of loyalties, is setting in. The term "liberalism" is not self-definitive; its only common feature is a methodology; but the conclusions it draws from that methodology, which involves tentativeness, are constantly being revised. The one sure fact is that liberalism has less a character of its own than a settled temper of antipathy toward central aspects of biblical supernaturalism.

Plurality and variety have in fact marked liberalism since its beginnings. Under the banner of Schleiermacher there emerged in America, as H. Shelton Smith has noted, the traditions of (1) enlightenment (rational liberalism), both deistic and pantheistic, but Unitarian in either case; (2) transcendentalism (romantic liberalism), championed by New Englanders like Theodore Parker and Emerson, whose revolt against Locke was informed by Kant, Schelling, and Hegel in the direction of epistemological intuitionism; (3) Christocentric liberalism, which held a more radical view of sin and appealed to a Christological "norm," as with Horace Bushnell, W. N. Clarke, W. Adams Brown, and Walter Rauschenbush; (4) empirical liberalism, which erected experience as the only norm and derived "truth" from process, as with James, Dewey, and Wieman.

The early 1930s proved a moment of judgment upon liberalism. Pressed from the right by the logic of evangelical stalwarts like J. G. Machen (in view of what liberalism wished to preserve) and from the left by the logic of naturalistic humanism (in view of what liberalism disowned), and pressed from behind by the pressures of post-war history, so-called post-modern liberalism sought to correct its positions. On the premise shared by Barth and by Machen, that "modernism is heresy," both European neoorthodoxy and American evangelicalism called liberalism to higher ground, the former to an authoritative scriptural revelation and the latter to vertical divine confrontation. In these circumstances, liberalism was increasingly on the defensive, became less creative than its champions boasted, and espoused a guarded apologetic.

The emerging "realistic theology" halted short not only of evangelical positions but of Barthian commitment. The new note of realism in American liberalism was struck firmly within remaining liberal postulates. Reinhold Niebuhr, Robert L. Calhoun, Paul Tillich, H. Richard Niebuhr, Walter Marshall Horton, John C. Bennett, H. Shelton Smith, and L. Harold DeWolf emerged as chastened liberals who refused to move to Barthian positions. At the time when Continental theology was most thoroughly influenced by neoorthodoxy and the impact of Barth and Brunner was at its height in Europe, a poll by *Christianity Today* disclosed that more American ministers still chose to be designated as liberal (14 per cent) rather than as neoorthodox (12 per cent). It was younger scholars studying abroad, much more than

American theologians, who accounted for neoorthodox gains in America.

Barth's supernaturalism (the Virgin Birth included) and his insistence on the absolute uniqueness of special revelation, and hence the rejection of general revelation, and a one-sided fideism (his denial of the necessity for any kind of philosophical apologetics for Christianity), were among the stumbling blocks. Instead of displacing liberalism in America, crisis-theology was welcomed simply as a form of liberal self-criticism. Every influential crisis-theologian on the American side not only began as a liberal, but also remains a liberal in methodology—not simply in the acceptance of organic evolution and biblical criticism, but in the rejection of special supernatural revelation and redemption. It is not surprising, therefore, to hear it said that Horton's prognosis in the 1930s ("liberalism has collapsed") was premature, and to learn that Niebuhr now considers many of his earlier broadsides against liberalism too sweeping.

After a generation of fermentive reflection and dialogue, the most prominent leaders in American liberal ranks are leaving the scene through either death or retirement—the two Niebuhrs, Tillich, Van Dusen, Shelton Smith, and others. The younger liberals acknowledge that no "new flag" is flying. It is a time for second thoughts, they say. Some, lacking a recognizable theology, are prone to substitute a conscience on political or sociological issues—particularly the race question. Their main excursion into dogmatic concerns, one is tempted to say, is simply a wild distortion or misrepresentation of evangelical views (the doctrine of original sin is made to mean that every man is "a bag of pus," the doctrine of substitutionary atonement that God "becomes loving only when he sees blood sprinkled around," and such calumnies).

It is clear that most liberals remain wholly out of touch with the massive works of evangelical orthodoxy—dismissed as irrelevant simply because the problems they addressed were of no immediate concern to liberals. While they grant the resurgence of "erudite evangelicalism," some liberal denominational leaders maneuver to crowd the book tables at ministerial conferences with anything and everything but solid evangelical publications, as if to concede that liberalism today can survive only in a climate that is specially protected.

Among the regrouping liberal forces is a movement which H. Shelton Smith, one of the editors of *American Christianity*, designates as Christocentric realistic liberalism. Smith identifies himself with this wing, which he calls liberalism's "reigning" type. Its emphases are on divine transcendence as well as immanence, divine revelation (general as well as Christian), God's sovereign judgment in history, the sinfulness of man, the social gospel, and an ecumenical doctrine of the Church. Its methodology remains liberal, and it readily utilizes the accepted categories and beliefs of the ruling cultural milieu as a means of communicating Christian faith. It renounces any external criterion of truth (despite its claim to take revelation seriously), since this would lead to authoritarianism. It conceives of revelation in the form not of concepts and words but of subjective awareness. Its main claim to advance lies in its Christological affirmation: to be genuinely Christian, a theology must recognize the incarnation as the hinge of history. Jesus Christ is therefore not just another man; unitarianism is rejected, and Trinitarianism affirmed.

But when one examines this Christological ingredient at closer range, its real meaning is usually seen as much less than its apparent meaning. The Trinitarianism turns out to be not ontological but economic or Sabellian. The Chalcedonian formulation is rejected as based on a substance philosophy, and the Nicene formula approved. But this "Christocentric" view has other peculiar aspects. It does not embrace the Virgin Birth or the bodily

Resurrection of Jesus Christ. Nor does it consider his teaching normative. At various points, it is said—Satan, angels, hell, eternal punishment, and so on—Jesus was simply the child of his culture. And while Jesus' "vicarious existence" is emphasized, his death is viewed as simply the culminating event of a series of acts that rendered his death inescapable. (In the words of one spokesman for the Christological realists: "If Jesus had been strangled with a silk stocking, it would have meant just as much.") Moreover, there is no doctrine of the imputation of Christ's righteousness to sinners, but simply an emphasis on divine forgiveness and moral stimulus.

Insofar as Christological realism sees that, to survive as a Christian movement, liberalism must move from an empirical to a Christological norm and thus to incarnational and Trinitarian ground, its instinct is sound. But thus far this readjustment has been hesitant and half-hearted. In Europe liberal Protestants have already passed through this zone—on the way up, or on the way down. Karl Barth convinced Continental thinkers that to take Christianity seriously, one must take divine initiative and special revelation and incarnation seriously and realize that "modernism is heresy." There are weighty objections to many aspects of Barth's theology, but not at this point. The tendency of Christological realists to console themselves with Cornelius Van Til's judgment that Barth's methodology is after all liberal, despite his conclusions, is scant comfort, for it is liberalism's conclusions that seem constantly to call for revision.

This plight of liberalism results, no doubt, from its methodological predicament. It has lost what Barth has sought to recover, a "Thus saith the Lord." The weaknesses even of Barth's exposition are well stated in the recent book, *Karl Barth's Theological Method*, by Gordon H. Clark. And right here, in the recovery of the divine authoritative note in modern theology and a new recognition of the role of Scripture as the rule of faith and practice, lies the key to the fortunes of the religious movements of our age.

Carl F. H. Henry, "Liberalism in Transition," *Christianity Today* 8, no. 6 (December 20, 1963): 10–11.

Chapter 12

CHAOS IN EUROPEAN THEOLOGY: THE DETERIORATION OF BARTH'S DEFENSES

This essay was the second in a series of six looking at modern European theology that appeared in Christianity Today *in 1964–1965. These essays were later published under the title* Frontiers in Modern Theology *(Moody, 1966).*

Among the many issues raised by contemporary theology, one question is persistent:

Why was the theology of Karl Barth unable to stem the tide of Rudolf Bultmann's theories?

No Continental theologian is disposed to conduct a postmortem examination of Barth's theology; to do so would be to suggest that its influence were something wholly past. But this is not the case. Emil Brunner regards Barth as Bultmann's greatest present contender, and many others concur that both the

Basel theologian and his theology are still "very much alive." In French-speaking Switzerland Barthian theology has always held greater sway than Bultmannian theories. And on the German scene, Heidelberg theologian Edmund Schlink thinks Barth's influence is not only far from spent but actually expanding in some quarters.

Nor are European theologians ready to minimize the differences between Barth and Bultmann, differences which have increased markedly with the years. Often, in fact, the divergences are even exaggerated—for example, by assigning more weight than Barth allows to the "objectifying" elements in his theology, or by imputing to Bultmann a denial of the reality of God in view of his stress on subjectivity. Such distortions aside, the contrariety of their positions cannot be denied. "A wide gulf," says Erlangen theologian Wilfried D. Joest, "separates the emphasis that God has *no objective reality* at all, but exists only for me, from the emphasis that concedes that there is *no objective revelation*, yet asserts an objective reality that cannot be objectified by methods of reason and must be won by faith."

Barth and Bultmann

As the Bultmann school reiterated its belief in the *reality* of God, however, and stressed the necessity of a consistently dialectical theology against Barth's exposition, this "wide gulf" seemed to disappear. Even the "Mainz radicals" speak of Barth and Bultmann as representing complementary rather than opposing viewpoints. "It is not a matter of either/or between Barth and Bultmann," says Manfred Mezger, "for each theology needs the other as a corrective." Why so? we might ask. "So Barth does not forget the *anthropological* relevance of theology," continues Mezger, "and so Bultmann does not forget the genuine root (revelation) of theology. Barth's basic principle (the absoluteness or divinity of God) has as its logical consequence that *no* advance reservations are possible for revelation." Once this is said, the Mainz school is poised to feed the lamb to the lion in the interest of a Bultmannized Barth: "We emphasize that man does not need to recognize *God first* and then recognize reality, but the recognition of reality is coincidental with the recognition of the reality of God. Barth says, 'first the dicta about God, and then the statements about man'; Bultmann says, 'every dictum about God has to be said simultaneously about man.' Barth's principal thesis 'God is God' is useless nonsense. God is not absolute in the metaphysical sense but is absolute only in the 'geschichtliche' sense of always occurring. We have not seen God and know absolutely nothing about God except what He is saying. *All* dicta of theological origin must and can only be verified anthropologically."

However much Barth may deplore existentialism, however much he may reinforce the "objectifying" factors in his theology and appeal to wider and fuller aspects of the biblical witness, his position has remained vulnerable to Bultmannian counterattack. Bultmann was one of the earliest sympathizers with the Barthian revolt against objective historical method, a revolt that Bultmann then carried to a non-Barthian climax by imparting an existential turn to the distinction between the *historisch* as mere objective past occurrence and the *geschichtlich* as revelatory present encounter. In the revision of his *Church Dogmatics*, Barth had sought to divorce dialectical from existential theology; this effort Bultmann fought vigorously. On the premise that Barth expounds the dialectical view uncertainly whereas Bultmann does so comprehensively, the Bultmannian scholars turned the main tide of student conviction away from Barth and toward Bultmann.

"The great effect of Barth's theology," remarks Bultmann, "was that it destroyed subjectivism. Barth said God is not a symbol of my own religiosity, but He confronts me. In this we agree. And we agree also in the dialectical method insofar as Barth says theological propositions are genuine only if they are not universal truths. But Barth applies the dialectical method inconsistently: many of his propositions are 'objectivizing' propositions—and this I have sought to eliminate in my own theology."

Walter Kreck, Reformed theologian at Bonn, and one of Barth's former students who still regards himself as broadly a Barth disciple, concedes that the differences between Barth and Bultmann have receded further into the background. "Both Barth and Bultmann reject objective revelation. Barth and Bultmann have dialectical theology in common, and their main difference lies in Barth's methodological rejection of existential interpretation. Bultmann fears that Barth's method leads to a false objectivity, and insists that his existential exegesis alone prevents this. Barth fears Bultmann's method leads to a false subjectivity, and insists that his emphasis alone preserves the reality of revelation." "Yet, for all their differences," Kreck concludes, "to many scholars the two positions no longer look as far apart as they once did."

An Inner Connection?

Is there an inherent relationship, a principial continuity, between Barth's theology and Bultmann's? Or is there rather a vacuum in Barth's thought that made his dogmatics vulnerable to Bultmannian counterattack? Why did Barthian theology, which held sway in Germany for half a generation, lose its hold in the face of Bultmannian existentialism? These questions press for an answer. Aside from circumstantial factors—for example, Schlink's indication of political considerations (Barth's influence in Germany was retarded by his failure to oppose Communism as strenuously as he did National Socialism)—what accounts theologically for the fact that Barthianism, which had routed post-Hegelian rationalistic modernism, could not stem the surge

toward Bultmann's revival of the old modernism in connection
with *existenz*?

Heidelberg theologians suggest two critical areas of weakness.
Schlink, for instance, doubts that an inherent principial connection exists between Barth's and Bultmann's formulations. Barth,
says Schlink, was "more systematic than historical, and he did
not deal adequately with the historical aspects of Christian faith.
After the Second World War, many problems were again raised
at this level, and it was apparent that Barth's exposition had not
really met them." Schlink's associate, Peter Brunner, singles out
"the historical facet" also as one of the weaknesses in Barth's theology which Bultmannians were able to exploit. As Brunner sees
it, Barth treated too naïvely the question of what historical reasoning can tell us about the facts in which God has revealed himself; indeed, Barth totally suppressed these facts from a purely
historical view. Bultmann, on the other hand, took his negative
approach seriously, and sought to destroy every effort to find revelation by historical investigation.

Besides Barth's indifference to the historical, exploited by
Bultmann, Brunner adduces "the decision facet" as a second
major Barthian weakness. For Barth there is no saving moment
in time (the saving moment is an eternal moment). But, observes
Peter Brunner, theology must not overlook the importance of this
time-event in which man here-and-now encounters the Word
of the Cross. Contrary to Barth, Bultmann stresses the event of
encounter with the Word here-and-now. For Barth, the salvation
of every man is settled in the eternal election of the man Jesus,
and the means of grace are significant only for the cognition of salvation, not for the transmission of salvation. Barth and Bultmann
agree this far: that without the Living Word of God here-and-now,
which is the Word of God for me, one cannot experience the reality of revelation. But when Barth detached the transmission of

salvation from the means of grace he opened the door, as Peter Brunner sees it, for Bultmann's wholly existential setting.

Does this mean that the history of twentieth-century theology will reduce Barth and Bultmann to one theological line? The Heidelberg theologians think not.

Some theologians are less reluctant than the Heidelberg theologians to identify an inner principial connection in the Barth-Bultmann formulations. They insist rather that the transition of influence from Barth to Bultmann was inevitable because of presuppositions common to both systems, presuppositions to which Bultmann allowed greater impact than did Barth. "Theologians of a later century," says Erlangen theologian Wilfried D. Joest, "will look back and see one line from Barth to Bultmann, and in this movement they will recognize the same type of theology, despite deep-rooted differences."

Actually, such assessments are not only a future expectation. Theologians both to Barth's right and to his left are already insisting that certain *a prioris* common to Barth and Bultmann explain the sudden fall of Barth's theological leadership, and, in fact, the present predicament of Continental theology. Graduate students in European seminaries increasingly view Bultmann's position as "an automatic development from Barth's"; and in the few remaining Bultmann centers they picture the dialectical Barth rather than the demythologizing Bultmann as the "fairy tale dogmatician."

The essential connection between the two theologians is the basic emphasis that God meets us personally in the Word and makes this Word his own. With this relationship in view, Otto Michel, the New Testament scholar at Tübingen, asserts that "Barth and Bultmann are two parts of one and the same movement of dialectical theology. Barth begins with the Word of God and defines this in relation to human *existenz*. Bultmann inverts this; he begins with man's *existenz* and relates this to kerygma." "Neither Barth nor Brunner," says Michel, "gave earnest weight to historical questions—the origin of certain of the biblical elements and theological content, and their relevance for dogmatic questions. The objectivity in Barth's theology is not an object of historical research. Only by way of philosophical construction does Barth avoid subjectivizing revelation."

Adolf Köberle, the Tübingen theologian, singles out the Barthian discontinuity between revelation and history as a decisive central point of contact with Bultmann's delineation. Barth's "prophetic" role, says Köberle, involved him in a broad and bold criticism of modernism in which he too hurriedly brushed aside some of the fundamental and crucial problems of contemporary theology. Regarding this broad prophetic proclamation, Köberle thinks it not impossible that Barth may exercise in dogmatics somewhat the same influence as Billy Graham in evangelism. Barth "failed fully to engage the historical background of the New Testament, and this failure gave competing scholars an opportunity to correlate the data with contrary conclusions." Köberle points to Barth's neglect of such questions as the relationship of Christianity and science and of revelation and history, and his indifference to the problem of supposed Hellenistic or late Jewish apocalyptic influence in the New Testament.

Wolfgang Trillhaas, teacher of systematic theology at Göttingen, and former student there of Barth, has broken with his mentor's dogmatics, because "Barth so oriented his theology to critical questions and to critical reason that Bultmann could snatch away the initiative."

Trillhaas recognizes the differing intentions of the two theologians, and is aware of Barth's efforts to guard his systematics against subjectivizing miscarriages of it. Says Trillhaas, "Both Barth and Bultmann had an interest in the speciality of Christian revelation. But through philosophical speculation Bultmann gave this interest a radically destructive interpretation, whereas Barth has sought increasingly to purge himself from the earlier philosophical influences." Trillhaas considers Barth's scheme still vulnerable, however, particularly in its severance of revelation from reason.

Barth and Brunner

Among the theologians at Erlangen and Hamburg, Emil Brunner's influence is greater than Barth's. Nonetheless it is Barth more than Brunner who penetrates the mainstream of dialectical controversy. Brunner's illness has hampered his creative and productive effort and removed him from theological engagement; in the aftermath of his stroke he spends much time indoors. Brunner has become more mellow over his differences with Barth, and with a twinkle he comments to visiting students: "I'm a Barthian. I always have been." But he nonetheless considers certain facets of Barth's system unnecessarily weak. Among his favorite anecdotes is that of the lady theologian who embraced him warmly and said: "Barth saved me from liberalism, and you saved me from Barth."

The strength of Brunner's theology has always rested in its recognition of general revelation. Its weakness, along with Barth's, centers in the dialectical presuppositions that relate revelation only tenuously with history and reason. In his revision of *Truth as Encounter*, which now appears under the title *Theology Beyond Barth and Bultmann* (Westminster Press, 1964), Brunner stresses that Christianity must be more than merely negative toward philosophy. While he calls for a Christian philosophy, he does not modify his dialectical approach to revelation and reason. His philosophical treatment of the idea of truth as encounter still excludes revealed propositions and a revealed world-life view.

Brunner's theology also lost ground as he strengthened its basic personalistic philosophy. This reinforcement gave his thought an individualistic touch that—so Wenzel Lohff of Hamburg thinks—prevented Brunner "from fully appropriating the dimensions of the newer Christological and ecclesiological thought." Yet because of its clarity, Brunner's work remains useful among lay theologians. Theologian Anders Nygren of Lund notes that Brunner indeed freed the Christian doctrine of God of Platonic and neo-Platonic speculation. In doing so, however, he attached it instead, says Nygren, to "an I-thou philosophy and a kind of philosophical actualism" which represents still another compromise "between a philosophical thinking and the revelation" (in *The Theology of Emil Brunner*, Charles W. Kegley, ed., New York: The Macmillan Company, 1962, p. 183). In any event, Bultmannian theologians exploited Brunner's emphasis on the divine-human encounter for their own contrary objectives, and Brunner's affliction left him a less formidable foe than Barth.

In Europe's present theological turmoil, Brunner anticipates "a little return" to his own theology which "held the line between Barth and Bultmann" for a time. "The best option is my own," he insists. But Brunner seems to underestimate the difficulty of regaining a strategic position on the fast-changing frontier of European thought, particularly when a theology that has served for a season and has lost its hold no longer commands the center of debate.

Pro-Barthian theologians are sobered by the fact that the already bypassed options will hardly enjoy more than a limited revival. Neither Barth nor Bultmann is likely to dominate the European theological situation again. Some scholars are now asking if the deterioration of Barthian defenses under Bultmannian assault, and the subsequent collapse of Bultmannian positions, perhaps portends a radical reconstruction of Continental theology.

Barth registered his most comprehensive Christological emphasis immediately after World War II. But in deducing theological positions from Christological analogies, he tended to overlook empirical reality. This weakness also characterized his approach to ethical problems and to critical historical investigation. While many scholars felt it necessary, therefore, to go beyond Barth's compromised historical interest, they were forced nevertheless to keep in touch with Barth because of his active participation in the theological controversy. At the age of 78, however, the ailments of declining years turn Barth's thoughts more often to "the tent that is beginning to be dissolved," as he puts it. While he continues his monthly student colloquiums in the upstairs room of Restaurant Bruderholz near his home, Barth's creative work has begun to lag, and he feels unsure about completing his *Church Dogmatics.*

Busily but cautiously Barth has been modifying his theology in the direction of objectivity in order to escape Bultmannian expropriation. "Barth has become almost a Protestant scholastic again," chuckles Gerhard Friedrich, the Erlangen New Testament scholar; "more and more he leans on the historical rather than the existential." But the feeling is widespread that the revisions in Barth's theology are "too little and too late." The moving frontier of theological debate is shifting beyond the Barth-Bultmann discussion in a manner that brings some of their common *a priori* under fire. This means that the revisions in Barth's theology have lagged too long to have any direct impact upon mainline Continental theology.

The New Frontiers

The formative theology of the foreseeable future is not likely to be Barth's, Brunner's, or Bultmann's, but rather an alternative to all three.

The *Heilsgeschichte* school is calling for a fuller correlation of revelation and history. The traditional conservative scholars have long attacked dialectical theology in even wider dimensions. And a revolt against dialectical theology has been under way among several followers of Wolfhart Pannenberg of Mainz, a former student of Barth. In his bold insistence on objective historical revelation, Pannenberg represents the farthest contemporary break from Barth and Bultmann and the dialectical theology.

Says Pannenberg: "Barth and Bultmann both insist on the kerygmatical character of the Christian faith and tradition, and both assign the Christian faith (kerygma) independence over against the truth of science and philosophy. Both Barth and Bultmann refuse to bring Christian tradition in relation to the realm of objective knowledge." In spite of his "apparent objectivism," protests Pannenberg, "the later Barth remains a disciple of Herrmann, as is Bultmann." And, he adds, "Bultmann is the most faithful exponent of the dialectical theology—more so than Barth."

As Pannenberg sees it, the dialectical theology undermines both historical revelation and the universal validity of Christian truth. He insists that "if one really takes history in earnest, he will find that God has revealed himself *in history*." He maintains the necessity of knowing something about the historical facts on which Christian faith depends. Moreover, he strikes at the dialectical theology's disjunction of revelation and reason, and at its consequent refusal to relate Christianity to the realm of objective knowledge.

Carl F. H. Henry, "Chaos in European Theology: The Deterioration of Barth's Defenses," *Christianity Today* 9, no. 1 (October 9, 1964): 15–19.

Chapter 13

A REPLY TO THE GOD-IS-DEAD MAVERICKS

Religious professionals took the lead in crucifying Jesus of Nazareth; now they are conspiring to kill the Living God also.

Standing by, consenting, and in fact strongly advocating the death of God, are numerous theologians. In Christian schools they seek to rally a task force of confirmed God-slayers. The ranks include Altizer at Emory University (Methodist), Hamilton at Colgate Rochester Divinity School (Baptist), and in some respects Van Buren at Temple University (interdenominational).

A full public hearing of their views is encouraged by the ecumenical Sanhedrin. Their faith-and-order dialogue easily and swiftly seems to embrace almost every theological novelty. Meanwhile, it largely ignores traditional evangelical views or disdains them as heresy—the sole heresy at that—even though biblical supernaturalism is not only the historic faith of Christianity but also the sincere faith of most churchgoers.

Conflict over the supernaturalism of the Bible is age-old. In the ancient world, both Judaism and Christianity contended constantly against polytheistic myths. In the Middle Ages, a mist of

147

scholastic speculation and popular superstition often beclouded the Living God. Aided by this climate, modern philosophers swiftly recast the God of the Bible to suit their many rationalistic preferences. One anti-biblical theory quickly encouraged another, until Marx dramatically countered Hegel's *God is everything* with the atheistic credo: *God is nothing,* and dialectical materialism everything.

Although anti-supernaturalism is not new, Christian leaders like Billy Graham, Charles Malik, and D. Elton Trueblood remind us that the tide of atheism is rising to unprecedented heights with alarming speed.

"Never in my life," writes Trueblood, professor of philosophy at Earlham College, "have I known a time when the attacks on the Gospel were as vicious as they are now. I see about me a far more militant atheism than I have ever known, and I see it pressed with evangelistic fervor."

Evangelist Billy Graham thinks the daring wickedness and unbelief of the modern world, when seen alongside divine judgment on earlier civilizations, may perhaps signal "God's last great call" to a generation at the brink of destruction.

And the former chairman of the United Nations General Assembly, Charles Malik, notes that while organized society and governments in the Western world have taken no formal, official stand against religion and against Christ, "we see very virulent movements of secularism and atheism."

This atheistic propaganda is spectacular not only for its scope and savagery but also for its entrenchment in Protestant institutions. A century ago when Ludwig Feuerbach lapsed to the view that a supernatural God is a product of human imagination and desire, his teaching career at Erlangen University, a center of Lutheran theology, ended abruptly. Feuerbach's revolt against the inherited religion was extended by Lenin's insistence that the capitalists advanced faith in God in order to comfort the (supposed) victims of their (supposed) exploitation—a theory that required the crudest of caricatures of the Founder of Christianity, the carpenter of Nazareth. But the revolt against Christianity carried Communists like Stalin, once a Greek Orthodox seminarian, outside the church in their defection to atheistic naturalism. Today, however, scholars disseminate their God-is-dead propaganda from Protestant institutions whose support comes from sacrificial, devout believers interested in promoting Christ's Gospel. As Trueblood comments, "Some of the most damaging attacks on the validity of the Gospel are coming from those who claim some kind of marginal connection with Christianity."

At the Montreal Faith and Order Conference of the World Council of Churches, a Russian Orthodox churchman told New Testament scholars of the Bultmann school (which contends that the miracles of the Bible are myths) that "in Russia we do not need theologians to tell us" that the gospel miracles are myths: this is part of the Communist creed.

Few people would deny another's right to be an atheist (although the Roman Catholic Church only recently faced the issue of one's right to be a Protestant). But for the sake of God and integrity let such propaganda be peddled not in Christian schools but in institutions dedicated to unbelief.

The current point of crisis in theism—namely, belief in a supernatural mind and will—is a by-product of the nineteenth-century modernist defection from the historic Christian faith. Radical German higher critics presumed to derive biblical religion from an evolutionary process that dispensed with supernatural being and revelation. Brilliant scholars like Cyrus H. Gordon and William F. Albright have long since exposed the indefensible rationalistic bias of these critics. Albright considers virtually all their arguments against early Israelite monotheism "as invalid and some of them as quite absurd" (*History, Archaeology, and Christian Humanism,* McGraw-Hill, 1964, p. 99). One God appears throughout all the history of Israel as an indictment against the multitude of deities cherished in the pagan world. The Canaanites named seventy, and the Babylonians alone listed thousands of divine names. But the Old Testament names one God alone who is in supreme control of reality, one God over all nature, over all men and nations.

What radical German critics could not fully achieve in their evolutionary assault on the religion of the Bible, German philosophers have more nearly accomplished. Their prejudices have often been borrowed and carried to still further extremes by enterprising, crusading Americans mounting an attack on the reality and claim of the Living God.

Almost everywhere in non-evangelical Protestant theology today, there links the destructive notion—so unstable a basis for faith, so highly serviceable to unbelief—that man can have no cognitive knowledge of transcendent Being, no rational knowledge of the supernatural world. For almost a century modern theology has built its "case for Christianity" on this highly vulnerable foundation. Time and again the superstructure has bent in the winds, and periodically it has even tumbled. But the architects of religious liberalism have simply erected new skyscrapers atop the crumbling ruins. It remained for the death-of-God theologians to find the courage to be consistent and, instead of trying to float religious principles in midair, to level them to the ground.

Behind this malformation of contemporary theology stands Immanuel Kant, who two centuries ago tried in a highly vulnerable way to salvage remnants of a supernaturalistic view from the supposedly scientific attacks of David Hume. A thoroughgoing empiricist, Hume virtually reduced reality to sense impressions and man to animality.

In his reply, *The Critique of Pure Reason,* Kant granted to Hume what neither Augustine nor Luther nor Calvin would have conceded, nor before them Moses, Isaiah, and Paul. In a costly surrender, Kant contended that all man's knowledge comes from sense experience alone.

Ever since Kant's influence affected modern theology, evangelical theologians have protested this needless relinquishment of cognitive knowledge of the spiritual world. They have emphasized that the God of the Bible is a rational God; that the divine Logos is central to the Godhead and is the agent in creation and redemption; that man was made in the divine image for intelligible communion with God; that God communicates his purposes and truths about himself in the biblical revelation; that the Holy Spirit uses truth as a means of persuasion and conviction; and that Christian experience includes not simply a surrender of the will but a rational assent to the truth of God. In brief, although fundamentalist theology was lampooned for half a century as anti-intellectual, nothing is clearer than the fact that in American Protestantism, only the evangelical movement energetically espoused the role of reason in religion.

The non-evangelical movements, meanwhile, increasingly minimized the place of reason in religious experience. Three times in the twentieth century the formative theology of Europe has collapsed, and in America the God-is-dead aberration now has emerged as its most widely publicized successor. There is an inner logical connection between these developments; namely, the inadequate reply of contemporary theology to Kantian criticism—or, seen from the other side, its failure to insist on rationality as a divine perfection, and on the intelligible character of divine revelation and of Christian experience.

The road from Ritschl's modernism to the atheism of Altizer and Van Buren is not so circuitous as liberal Protestant seminaries imagine. One can get there swiftly by not allowing fancy rhetoric to detour him from attention to logical implications. A course in neo-orthodoxy or in existentialism may provide a long vacation on the way, but only an act of will—and surely not any logical necessity—requires such a delay.

A theological road map of the main route shows something like this: (1) Kant's philosophy excluded rational knowledge of God, grounded the case for theism in man's moral nature, and surrendered universally valid religious truth. (2) Ritschlian theology surrendered God's rational revelation, held that in contrast to scientific truth the truth of religion falls into the sphere of value judgments, and located the essence of Christian experience in man's trust or surrender of will. (3) Although Barthian theology reaffirmed God's special self-disclosure and the distinctiveness of Christianity as the only redemptive revelation, it espoused its own inadequate theory of religious knowledge: divine revelation is assertedly not communicated in objective historical events, concepts, and words, but consummated dialectically in individual response. (4) Existential theology extended this emphasis on personal encounter (as against rational, propositional revelation) by dismissing all historical props and logical supports for faith. Said Bultmann: The Bible gives us, not new truth about God, but new truth about ourselves. Spurning the miracles as myths, Bultmann contended that faith is existential and rests in the apostolically preached Christ rather than in the Jesus of history.

The obscurity of God has, in fact, been a necessary consequence of every recent theology that asserts the reality of God and also his non-objectivity and yet concedes that religious experience nowhere includes universally valid religious knowledge. While existentialist theologians correlate the "silence" of God with existential awareness of Divine presence, the most influential existentialist philosophers turn this emphasis on God's "absence" in quite another direction. Heidegger both denies God's "existence" and revives Nietzsche's emphasis on the "death of God." Sartre views the silence of "the Transcendent" as among life's profoundest problems, while Jaspers reduces the search for God to essentially "a search after the self"—a quest for divine reality in the primal depths of our own being.

It is therefore quite understandable that (5) Paul Tillich, who likewise viewed faith as existential rather than as rational, considered all qualities ascribed to the Unconditioned as symbolic, and not as literally true. Thus Tillich inverted the central emphasis of both neo-orthodox and existential theology on God's *self*-disclosure; personality lost its status as an inherent perfection of divinity and instead became a way of viewing the Unconditioned in relation to us. As against a supernatural deity independent of the cosmos, Tillich deliberately emphasized the Unconditioned ground of all being, a god of the depths; transcendence survived mainly as a notion of the limit or boundary.

Significantly, the God-is-dead school found encouragement in Tillich's theology of the impersonal Unconditioned, so deliberately contrasted with the transcendent personal God of the Bible. A more profound symbolism than any Tillich himself postulated is the fact that his death came shortly after a conference in which Altizer singled him out as spiritual father of the secular theologians. A passage from a recent book by J. Rodman Williams serves to illuminate this ready transition of existential theories to the secular point of view: "Existentialism, philosophical and theological, atheistic and non-atheistic, non-Christian and Christian, is quite closely related to the obscurity of God. It matters not whether this be the 'silence of God' (Sartre), the 'absence of God' (Heidegger), the 'concealment of God' (Jaspers), the 'non-being of God' (Tillich), or the 'hiddenness of God' (Bultmann). ... The obscurity of God might indeed be called 'the Eclipse of God' " (*Contemporary Existentialism and Christian Faith,* Prentice-Hall, 1965, pp. 63f.).

The penalty now being extracted from Protestant ecumenism for its increasing suppression of evangelical theology is the dooming of its own religious alternatives to irrationalism, and the inevitable decline of those alternatives to the silent contemplation of the death of God.

In a series of swift strokes, we may summarize this tragic twentieth-century decline from historic Christian theism to current secular atheism:

Historic Christianity expounds *objective rational theism;* that is, it affirms God's intelligible revelation and man's created capacity to know the supernatural in valid propositions.

Post-Kantian liberalism teaches *objective non-rational theism;* here faith is no longer thought to include intellectual assent to divinely revealed truths but is viewed as personal trust and obedience.

Neo-orthodoxy (dialectical theology) proclaims *non-objective non-rational theism;* here the radical transcendence of God is said to preclude objective rational revelation, and individual response replaces propositional disclosure.

Existentialism depicts *non-objective, non-rational, non-miraculous theism;* here miracles are downgraded to myth, and the supernatural survives merely in the attenuated form of elements of experience that transcend scientific inquiry.

Tillich's "Unconditioned" signifies *non-objective, non-rational, non-miraculous, non-supernatural, non-personal theism;* here the supernatural yields to the ground of being, while personality and all other attributes are regarded as symbolic rather than as literal representations.

Death-of-God speculation then yields *non-theism*.

————————

Before examining the argument presented by the God-is-dead contenders, one might well ask what gives their views a semblance of credibility. Even in biblical times the temptation apparently arose to serve as God's pallbearer; but the Psalmist's statement, "The fool hath said in his heart, 'There is no God,' " suggests not only that unbelief is high folly but also that the fool had enough discretion to keep his unfounded doubts to himself. As a *theology*, the death-of-God view is doubtless unworthy of serious consideration; for if God is really dead, theology (the science of God) has lost its object and becomes sheer nonsense. But what is it that now lends the semblance of credibility to this increasing doubt about the reality of the supernatural?

Who of us cannot give an answer? And surely the reply need not begin with science, for the real place to begin is with the problem of preoccupation with the things of this world.

We plunge into this preoccupation from our very childhood, even from the cradle. Every waking moment we seem driven to physical adjustment, but what necessity is ever laid upon us for spiritual decision?

My mother was Roman Catholic and my father Lutheran; in a sense, I was nurtured at the juncture of the Protestant Reformation. Yet we had no prayers at home, nor Bible reading, nor grace at table. There was church at Christmas and Easter, and we children were sent to an Episcopal Sunday school. There, just before my confirmation, the parish priest learned to his dismay that I had never been baptized; within a few days, accordingly, I was both baptized and confirmed. I still vaguely remember the priest's words to the godparents: "Seeing then, dearly beloved, that this child is now regenerate, and an inheritor of the promises of God ..." But I was no more regenerate than a Sears Roebuck catalogue. And I was a stranger to God's promises.

As a pagan newspaperman on Long Island in my twenties—editor of a suburban weekly, and stringer for New York dailies like the *Times* and the *Herald-Tribune*—I had "enough experience" (or "little enough") of "Christianity" to consider God a candidate for the obituary page.

If what the God-is-dead faddists mean is merely that the Deity is widely ignored as irrelevant and even obscured in much of the churchianity of our times, then I am quite ready to join their picket line against this high outrage. But I do not believe that this is all they mean, nor that it is the most important factor for assessing their views. Yet we dare not allow the fact of this cultural irrelevance of the Living God to be lost on us.

What of the multitude of members who consider church attendance, even if only sporadic, as little more than a respectable cultural custom, and who shun active identification and evangelistic engagement?

What impression of spiritual priorities do representatives of our so-called Christian nations make upon the pagan world?

Do not most statesmen conduct their political dialogue in the United Nations with no consideration of the will of God in national affairs?

Do we not promote staggering scientific successes as if human destiny depended more upon space exploration than upon human regeneration?

Is not the pearl of great price, for which Jesus said a wise merchant would exchange all that he had, still the most neglected commodity in our free-enterprise market?

Are not many intellectuals on our campuses now weighting thought against belief in the supernatural?

How neglected must God be, to be culturally and academically dead?

And what about those of us who are recognized as symbols of Christian commitment? How does our personal identity reflect our profession of the reality of God? What difference does it make in me as a person that the range of human experience includes the possibility of a relationship with the Living God? How does this reality bear on the routines of life—on fidelity to conscience, on fidelity in work, on fidelity in love? What do we do and say and think that demonstrates the presence of God in our lives? What discernible difference does it make today that we know God lives, and that Jesus Christ, the Son of the Living God, is risen from the dead?

Let me answer for the many thousands who would jump to their feet at this point.

When I was first challenged to believe, to confess Christ personally as my Saviour, to yield my life to the Living God, I realized from the moment of conversion that the New Testament does not exaggerate the contrast between faith and unbelief by its analogies of life and death, of light and darkness, of hope and doom. To know God personally, to share the forgiveness of sins, to experience the energy of the Holy Spirit in one's life, to enter into Christ's victory over sin and death—can anything be compared to this spiritual breakthrough except the discovery of a whole new world overflowing with life and power and purity and joy? Those who know that the Living God spectacularly transforms human lives dare to pray that in our fast-fading century some dark-skinned African may rise as a modern Augustine, or that Mao Tse-Tung may yet become the Billy Graham of Asia.

True as it is in our day, as in Paul's, that "not many wise, not many mighty, not many noble" give their earthbound hearts to Christ, yet the cloud of witnesses is diverse and innumerable.

Billy Graham recalls a day when, putting the promises of God to the test, he found a spiritual reality about which he could not remain silent. "To many who are perishing in their sins, it is foolishness; but to us who are saved the Gospel is the power of God," says Graham. "After nineteen hundred years, the Gospel has lost none of its ancient power."

Charles Malik, too, recalls his spiritual revolt and rescue in essentially New Testament terms: "I meant to kill him [Christ] but I did not succeed. He triumphed over my evil desire. He lives now and sits gloriously on the right hand of God. I am cleansed from my sins because he actually and completely died exactly as I meant him to, but through the power of God, he actually and completely rose from the dead on the third day. ... I beg his forgiveness, and what overpowers me is that he forgives me."

Nor will the secular theologians succeed in their attempt to kill God, their bold plan to make religion effective by deleting its supernatural elements. These professional pallbearers, hired by the Devil, who advocate God's death ostensibly to make Christianity relevant to the modern man, are motivated by concerns quite apart from the weak power of supernatural realities over modern life. They actually insist on God's necessary irrelevance and unreality. They attack the existence of a transcendent spiritual realm, repudiate supernaturally revealed truths and precepts, and administer last rites to the God of the Bible.

What grounds do they claim for their case? Science, they say. So, whereas Christianity was really the mother of Western science, these academicians, not content to tolerate her even as a disaffected mother-in-law, now aim to banish the religion of the Bible as a veritable outlaw.

Empirical science, we are told, precludes any knowledge of supernatural entities; therefore the Christian religion can survive in our time only by eliminating all supernatural and transempirical elements. In keeping with this conviction, secular theologians discard the metaphysical aspects of revealed religion and reduce the relevant subject matter of theology to what is historical, human, and ethical. According to Van Buren (who assures us that, after all, only this ingredient is essential), what remains of Christianity is the man Jesus—his life and death and availability for others, his values, and the contagion of his perspective. In a word, 1966-styled Christianity is Jesus' example of *agape* (love).

The secular theologians rest their case on a series of highly vulnerable assumptions. They blunder, in fact, in six respects.

The first blunder is their veneration of empirico-scientific categories as the filter for screening the whole of reality. Whoever considers this methodology as all-inclusive is automatically trapped in nature.

The second blunder is their naive notion that *agape* (or the moral value distinctively associated with Jesus) is really discerned and validated by this empirico-scientific approach. No less ardently than the American God-slayers, the Communists appeal to science to support their dogmas; and they scorn any appeal to *agape* as needlessly impeding the realization of a state-stipulated ethic by swift and violent revolutionary means.

The third blunder of the secular theologians is their notion that contemporary science tells how the universe is objectively structured. While nineteenth-century science entertained that presumption, twentieth-century science is more modest and presumes to tell us only what works. Most scientists, happily, are more ready to revise their notions about nature than many theologians their strange dogmas about what scientific theory demands. When Bultmann, for example, proposes an up-to-date revision of biblical cosmology in the name of science, he quite forgets that contemporary science no longer stipulates the objective constitution of reality. Thus he perpetuates a discarded nineteenth-century scientific mood.

The fourth blunder of the secularists is their selective appeal only to those scientists who share their naturalistic bias. Yet hundreds of highly qualified scientists earnestly believe in the reality of the supernatural and in the relevance of revealed religion. The American Scientific Affiliation is composed of professional scientists who espouse biblical theism. In a recent essay, Dr. Vannevar Bush of Massachusetts Institute of Technology declares it a misconception "that scientists can establish a complete set of facts about the universe, all neatly proved, and that on this basis men can securely establish their personal philosophy, their personal religion. ... Science never proves anything, in an absolute sense. ... On the most vital questions, it does not even produce evidence" ("Science Pauses," in *Fortune* Magazine, May, 1965). Dr. Bush goes on to warn against leaning on science "where it does not apply."

The secularists' fifth blunder is to believe that they can reject the Living God and yet retain the Jesus of the Gospels. For Jesus acknowledged Simon Peter's confession of him as "the Son of the living God" (Matt. 16:16) and attributed this recognition to God's special disclosure. If he was mistaken about God, why should Jesus be trusted about the good? Even Nietzsche sensed that the death-of-God requires the renunciation of Jesus Christ and called for a "transvaluation" of Christian values—that is, for an overthrow of the morality of *agape* and a return to the old pagan views.

The sixth blunder is a confusion of corpses. It is not God but man the sinner who is dead—"dead in trespasses and sins," as the Bible says, and in need of supernatural rescue.

There would be less misunderstanding if "secularized Christianity" were openly paraded not as an authentic revision but as an alternative religion. For more than a century, the makers of modern theology have offered every new fashion with the sales pitch that only this scantier version was guaranteed to appeal to the modern consumer. These trim reductions have attracted no permanent patrons, however; they have merely excited the modern appetite for more abbreviated styles. The death-of-God proposal now represents the bare exhaustion of possibilities; modern man ends up with a lifeless mannequin.

When introducing each successive style as the intellectual requirement of the modern mind, the promoters of these supposed religious fashions of tomorrow have simply indulged in special pleading. Either modern man is of all men most fickle, and wholly unable to make up his mind, or he has not really demanded—as recent generations were assured in sequence—the Kantian philosophy, the Ritschlian theology, the dialectical theology, the existentialist theology, and now (as Altizer thinks) the death of God.

Evangelist Billy Graham has said that "modern atheism is as dated as last week's weather," while Bishop Gerald Kennedy reminds us that "apostolic evangelism is as fresh as tomorrow." The choice before the modern world remains the Gospel of Christ or the fables of men. Man is made for God, and without God he is not wholly man; the godless myths hold promise only for the making of monsters. To accept the death-of-God view is to head into a dead end for hope, for purity, and for spiritual renewal in our time.

Carl F. H. Henry, "A Reply to the God-Is-Dead Mavericks," *Christianity Today* 10, no. 17 (May 27, 1966): 33–37.

Chapter 14

WHERE IS MODERN THEOLOGY GOING?

Ours is a generation of gyrating theology that seems to have spun off any sure Word of God. Neo-Protestant religious currents are losing force and nearing an end of their special impact, while classic modernism, though politically a volcano, is theologically now but a bag of wind.

What significant developments define the theology of the recent past, and what can we say about them from the evangelical Protestant point of view?

1. Reigning neo-Protestant religious theory has collapsed for the third time in the twentieth century.

First, classic modernism broke down; then, neo-orthodoxy; and most recently, existentialism.

Classic modernism was the theology of radical *divine immanence.* Predicated on Hegelian pantheism, it assimilated God to man and nature, and banished miracle and special revelation. Its most influential theologian was Schleiermacher, who eagerly shifted the case for theism from supernatural revelation to religious experience—supposedly as an absolute requirement of the modern mind. But modern thought proved more transitory than the early modernists dreamed.

Neo-orthodoxy was the theology of radical *divine transcendence.* In the context of dialectical theology it reasserted divine initiative, special revelation, and miraculous redemption. Its courageous spokesman was Karl Barth, who later intoned funeral rites for the modernist message in Europe.

Existentialism was the theology of *subjectivity,* heir to the dialectical denial of objective revelation and redemption. Rudolf Bultmann was its champion, insisting that the modern mind demands, not a modernist, not a neo-orthodox, but an existentialist reading of reality. Demythologize the supernatural! Existentialize God's activity! Dehistoricize the kerygma! But Bultmannian scholars soon fell into internal disagreement and were hard pressed by external critics. Like modernism and neo-orthodoxy, existential theology has lost control at the formative frontiers of theology in our day.

2. The survival span of recent modern alternatives to evangelical Christianity is shrinking.

Anyone who scans the decades of the twentieth century with an eye on the dominant theological traditions will soon note the shortening of intervals between newly emerging neo-Protestant religious theories. It is probably accurate to say that classic modernism reigned over the influential formative centers of theological thought from 1900 to 1930, dialectical theology from 1930 to 1950, and existential theology from 1950 to 1960.

Some theologians speak of a "compression of time periods for the development of theological traditions"—from a thousand years, as in medieval times, to as little as a decade in our own day. Such continuing theological reconstruction, some observers would say, is a necessary result of the knowledge-explosion in our time; others even depict all theological formulations as fallible human theories or tentative religious models subject to constant revision.

But surely such endorsement of theological revisionism is not shared by biblically oriented Christians, who insist on a core of revealed truth by which all human traditions must be judged. One may recall the well-worded sign on a country-church bulletin board: "Our God isn't dead—sorry about yours."

European theology is now an open field; none of the many contenders has control. The revolt of Bultmann's disciples, which began in 1954 with Käsemann's rebellious critique, marked the beginning of a decade of unending theological dissent and division. The growing disagreement among post-Bultmannians over the significance of the historical Jesus was only one aspect of the religious ferment. Among those involved in the widening search for a satisfying alternative were the traditional conservatives, who insisted that divine revelation is both intelligible and historical; salvation-history scholars, who asserted that revelation is historical but that we are left to extrapolate its meaning; revitalized Barthians, who supplemented the early Barth with quasi-objective elements in the mood of the revised *Church Dogmatics;* independent thinkers like Thielicke and Stauffer; and at the frontiers, newer figures such as Pannenberg and Moltmann. But in all this turbulence, it is noteworthy that more radical thinkers like Braun and Mezger, who reduced the reality of God to interhuman relationships and inverted "God is love" into "love is God," offered but one of many alternatives in the pluralistic theological milieu. By contrast, radical secular theology in the United States won wide attention and created a special situation.

3. The death-of-God theology gained prominence in American religious discussion and was openly welcomed within the ecumenical dialogue.

The death-of-God writers gained their importance, not through Gabriel Vahanian's assertion of a modern cultural alienation from the Christian heritage whereby God has died existentially, but especially by their affirmation of the literal death of the Deity. The new radicals misappropriated and distorted the *Letters from Prison,* which Bonhoeffer never intended as a prolegomenon to religious positivism. In their common projection of a secular theology that gave centrality to Jesus in order to displace a supernatural personal God, Altizer insisted on God's ontic death, Van Buren shared his rejection of the realm of divine transcendence, and Hamilton forfeited its significance.

4. Scholars are increasingly aware of the depth of the current religious crisis. Neo-Protestantism today is readily described as a situation of theological chaos.

Some relativists speak approvingly of the "pluralistic character" of the present religious scene, as if open-end diversity were preferable to theological consensus. But many interpreters realize that theology is now in a state of confusion, even anarchy; some characterize our era as a theological shambles. Frederick Herzog describes the situation as one of baffling consternation (*Understanding God,* 1966). He characterizes it by an ancient Greek term revived in the last century to describe the vagaries of primitive religions in the Pacific islands: *aporia* (*a + poros* = "without passage," a state of distressing doubt about what course to take—where to begin, what to say, where to end).

5. There is growing realization that the force of the biblical view of God was broken through compressed and fragmented presentations that obscured important aspects of the scriptural revelation.

The present generation was proffered a Twiggy-theology, styled to make one forget that its essential form was little more than a skeleton; a mini-theology that offered high style for the new season but had to run for cover when winter came.

Man's *primal ontological awareness* of religious reality is stressed by some theologians, and in a variety of ways: as precognitive awareness that insistently raises the question of God (Herzog); as precognitive awareness that *is* awareness of God (Tillich); and as precognitive awareness of the mystery of the universe, alongside which God the Mystery assertedly reveals himself only in personal encounter (Hordern).

But others deny any point of contact whatever in man for God's revelation in order to concentrate the case for the reality of God in dialectical confrontation (Barth, Gollwitzer). Still others retain general revelation while repudiating natural theology (Brunner).

Some revive a species of natural theology (Hartshorne, Cobb).

Then there are those who rely on the new quest for the historical Jesus (Robinson, Michalson).

Linguistic theologians contend that religious language has functional utility but is not conceptually true. (This semantic obfuscation is in part a reaction against the endless and exasperating neo-Protestant redefinition of who and what God is. If the Christian concept of God must be as radically changed as it is in Whiteheadian, Tillichian, and Bultmannian reconstructions, in order to make it meaningful to modern man, would it not be more honest simply to assign to language about God a psychological significance only?)

The theology of the recent past has characteristically attempted take-off on too short runways to get airborne. The vain attempt to support the case for theism by a fragmented theology is especially evident in Barth's concentration on divine-human encounter as the locus of revelation, and in Tillich's concentration on God as the immanent Ultimate. To overcome the immanentist loss of God in man and nature, with its notion that the all-inclusive Absolute is *more* than we are, Barth insisted that God confronts men individually as the sovereign *Other*. But his assertion of personal confrontation involved also a denial of the universal dimension of divine revelation in man, nature, and history. Tillich, on the other hand, emphasized the universal dimension of revelation by anchoring the case for theism in every-man's back yard; he denied a supernatural personal God, presumably to protect the universal access to divine revelation through the Ground of all being.

So each formula goes to its own radical extreme to compensate for the compromises of another, while none incorporates in itself the comprehensiveness of the biblical revelation of God. In view of this reduction of the content of theology to isolated and distorted fragments of the scriptural view, the successive alternatives in recent neo-Protestant thought gain the unhappy character of reactions to reactions to reactions. In this connection it is noteworthy to recall how death-of-God theologians like Altizer and Van Buren depend on the theology of individual confrontation for their comprehension of the Christian religion (Van Buren completed his Ph.D. under Barth, and Altizer misunderstands historic Christianity in the neo-orthodox sense of radically transcendent individual confrontation).

6. A vast number of highly tentative religious writings reject traditional formulations, reflect the modern spirit, refuse to concede that they are anti-Christian, restate the biblical view in novel forms, and insist that the new statements express what the biblical writers really intended to say.

These speculative reconstructions stretch all the way from panentheistic Christification (Teilhard de Chardin) to God-is-dead speculation (Altizer).

Three patterns of speculative religious thought are now emerging as alternatives to historic Christian theism. All of them represent a critical withdrawal from biblical controls. All reject the reality of the supernatural or of a personal God distinct from the universal. All disown miraculous divine revelation and redemption. These three patterns are:

a) *Theories of sociological salvation.* Here politico-economic structures are emphasized as the key to human felicity. Alongside the familiar Marxist version (dialectical materialism), so-called Christian versions have been projected in the context of a secular theology by Gogarten in Germany, Van Leeuwen in Holland, Ronald Gregor Smith in England, and Harvey Cox and Paul van Buren in the United States.

b) *Theories of cosmological salvation.* These espouse a religious ontology wherein mankind gains redemption by cooperating with divine cosmic forces. Anticipations of such views were projected by Bergson in France and Berdyaev in Russia. Current examples are Teilhard de Chardin's panentheism, Whitehead's pan-psychism, and Tillich's being-itself in which all men participate.

c) *Attempted syntheses of the sacred and secular.* These diverse elements are compounded in a variety of ways by A. M. Ramsey, John A. T. Robinson, and sometimes Harvey Cox.

All three patterns agree in several basic respects in their revolt against biblical theology:

- Reality, as they see it, is one-layered; rejected is a divine supernatural-moral realm antecedent to and independent of the world of nature.

- Only within the immanent natural process do they accommodate the dimension of transcendence.

- Cognitive knowledge of the super-sensory is excluded.

- Many theological antitheses are rejected, including the traditional contrasts of Creator-creation, eternity-time, infinite-finite, supernatural-rational, good-evil, church-world, belief-unbelief, salvation-judgment.

Yet for all their common disagreements with biblical theology, the new trends nonetheless also differ significantly from one another:

- The latest attempts to synthesize the ebb and flow of the sacred and the secular proceed in contrary directions. Harvey Cox works Teilhard de Chardin in a secular direction and Bishop Robinson works secular theology in Teilhard's panentheistic direction;

meanwhile A. M. Ramsey's correlation (*The Sacred and the Secular*) is more mediating.

- Cox locates the "transcendent" (God's special activity) at revolutionary frontiers of social change and regards centrality for I-Thou personal relations as a threat to the fundamental importance of justice, which is no respecter of persons. But Robinson considers the personal as the decisive category for interpreting reality. Here, again, antithetical views have predictably emerged from an earlier dilution of justice to love.

Noteworthy is the fact that current expositions increasingly shroud the personal dimension in ambiguity. Neoorthodoxy had elevated the I-Thou encounter to decisive centrality, correlating this emphasis with the supernatural revelation of a personal God wholly other than man and nature. Existentialism diluted and restated this relationship in terms of transcendent personal encounter. But recent mediating writers weaken it still further by discarding the reality of a personal God and the emphasis on revelational confrontation. Teilhard, Whitehead, and Robinson, rejecting transcendent personal individual revelation, speak of divine-human relations in mystical and experiential terms only, and see the whole of reality as one field in which the All and the personal constitute a single cosmic movement toward interpersonalization in love.

The theological consequences of this surrender of biblical terrain are grave. In at least four respects the new views signal a strategic loss of Christian perspective:

a) The loss of God as *other* (and revival of a view of God as merely *more* than we are)—hence the forfeiture of an independent Creator of the universe who is antecedent to it and sovereign over it.

b) The loss of God's special once-for-all manifestation in revelation and incarnation. The new Christology discards the doctrine of the two distinct natures in Jesus of Nazareth.

c) The loss of an absolute distinction between good and evil. If, as secular theologians assert, "God is where the action is," must we not look for a revelation of God in Hitler as well as in Jesus? And does any reason then remain for preferring peace to social revolution? What authentically evangelical interpretation can possibly be placed on Bishop Robinson's emphases that "God is in everything and everything in God—literally everything ... evil as well as good" (*Exploration into God,* 1967, p. 92), and that "no aspect of history, however resistant to personal categories, is not ultimately to be seen in terms of spirit, freedom and love" (p. 102)? Does this not undermine a lively sense of moral conscience in the presence of evil—and quite understandably breed a "new morality"? In the name of a Christian view of God are we to expect the six million Jews who died in Hitler's Germany to discern God's spirit and love in Nazi bestiality? Could such speculation ever have evoked the indignation that shaped the Barmen Confession over against Nazi tyranny?

d) The loss of a final judgment and separation of the righteous from the wicked.

In short, the emergence of the frontier tendencies signals the collapse of the neo-orthodox attack on modernism and the reappearance of a pre-Barthian theological mood. The influence of Schleiermacher is once again registering its force. Defection to pre-Barthian modernism is attested by several features of the current trend:

- Its vague concept of divine personality, not as wholly *other* personal Creator and Redeemer of man and the world, but as a loosely defined quality structuring the whole of reality.

- Its evasion of a metaphysical objectification of the God-idea and confinement of the content of religious affirmations to statements about God-in-relation to us. Here one finds a revival of emphases in Kant and Schleiermacher. God becomes a postulate demanded by man's moral nature, but the reality of God is asserted without the existence of God as an objectively metaphysical being. The mood is anticipated in Kant's *Opus Postumum:* "The concept of God is a concept of a subject outside me *who imposes obligations* on me. ... This Imperious Being is not outside man in the sense of a substance different from man. ... The All, the universe of things, contains God and the world ..."

- Its shift of emphasis away from divine initiative to human exploration in the theological arena. This trend so adjusts Christianity to one segment of the contemporary mind by removing the reality of revelation and by conforming theology to speculation that it makes revealed religion superfluous. It

rejects the religion of the Bible as a form of mental
bondage to the culture of the past, while enslav-
ing itself to modern prejudices as a true mirror of
the Divine.

The new theories, in short, sacrifice what biblical theism preserves: an authentic view of a supernatural, personal God and of
his relations to man and the world—the living, sovereign Creator
and Preserver of men and things and moral Judge of the universe,
who became incarnate in Jesus Christ in order to offer redemption to a fallen race.

*7. The case for theism is now "up for grabs"; issues are pressing
to the fore that reach back through the long history of philosophy
and theology and demand a comprehensive depth-investigation of
theological concerns.*

Disciplined students are becoming impatient with short-shrift,
emaciated approaches promoted out of all proportion by denominational publishing houses, and advanced in ecumenical discussions that are shaped to preserve a certain "theological mix" in
dialogue but that routinely underrepresent the existing support
for historic Christian theism. The proliferation of subjectivistic
theories about God has lost its excitement and is becoming wearying; scheme after scheme now has only a half-day popularity
or a one-campus visibility.

In any generation, the truly influential theologians are not the
clever itinerants who pick and choose which issue to attack and
which to avoid but those who spell out their views comprehensively and systematically in a classroom context, and in relation
to the history of ideas (e.g., Barth, Brunner, Bultmann, Whitehead,
Tillich, Teilhard; among evangelicals, Machen, Berkouwer, Clark,
Dooyeweerd, Van Til, Carnell).

The death-of-God theology is increasingly seen, not as merely a radical deviation, nor as simply a malignant surface growth, but as a conjectural development rooted in the basic concessions of recent theological speculations and rising from them as a matter of logical inescapability. The unifying negation in the entire tradition connecting Ritschl-Barth-Bultmann-Altizer and the linguistic theologians was supplied by Kant: Man can have no cognitive knowledge of the supernatural. The predictable result is metaphysical agnosticism. Whoever overturns that premise (and neither Isaiah nor Paul would have changed his mind about the truth of God had he read Kant's *Critique of Pure Reason*) strikes a knockout blow against the basic bias in contemporary theology.

There is now a growing demand for a comprehensive investigation of theological concerns in which the prejudices of our present age are compared and contrasted with those of earlier ages, and assessed anew in the context of the biblical exposition of God.

8. The sacred religious motifs to which Judeo-Christian revelation gave a decisive meaning are now used in so many senses by theologians and clergymen that institutional Christianity has become almost a modern Tower of Babel.

The term "God" is so diversely employed that *The Encyclopedia of Philosophy* (1967) declares it "very difficult—perhaps impossible—to give a definition ... that will cover all usages" (III, 244).

Gerhard Ebeling says we are dying of "language poisoning"; I prefer to say, of Word-distortion.

Consider the lessons so clearly taught by the drift of twentieth-century religious thought:

- The disjunction of the self-revealing God from the word of prophets and apostles as the Word of God leads to the loss of the self-revealing God. Barth's

bold effort to revive a theology of the Word of God
faltered when he refused to identify the scriptural
word with God's Word.

- The dialectical dogma that divine revelation is never
  objectively given (in human concepts and words
  and in historical events) leads to the subversion of
  divine revelation into human self-understanding.
  Bultmann not only subverted dialectical divine disclosure into existential half understanding but lost
  the incarnate Word as well.

The next move was inevitable—either the *wordless God* (the
"silent" God, the "hidden" God) or the *"Word" without God* (secular Christianity).

Already the "death-of-God" theology as an option has
exhausted itself and is ready for burial except by the faddists.
Its proponents are divided internally: Vahanian's emphasis that
God is existentially dead for modern man was misappropriated
by some who argue for God's ontic death; Altizer's position is an
embarrassment to other death-of-God theologians because it
lacks significant epistemological underpinning. According to Van
Buren, the empirical scientific method "excludes" miracle and
the supernatural; yet he inconsistently condemns the unique
values associated with Jesus to the same guillotine. The truth
is that the scientific method is an impotent arbiter of these concerns. Scientists who must live daily with the scientific method
are as "modern" as Altizer, Hamilton, and Van Buren; yet many
recognize the limits of their method and confess that it cannot
settle the issue of the reality of the supernatural.

But that is not yet the terminal stage of a sick theology.
Contemporary theology cannot stop with God-is-dead bulle-
tins, for that headline has already exhausted all possible reader

interest. What more can one say about God, once he has said that God is dead? People don't care to linger long around a corpse. Book sales are falling off, and publishers are looking for new trends on which to capitalize.

9. "The resurrection of theism" after the death of God can be a live option if the evangelical vanguard becomes theologically engaged at the frontiers of modern doubt.

The time is ripe to recanvass evangelical rational theism with its emphasis on the revelation and manifestation of the Logos as the critical center of theological inquiry. A new prospect for systematic theology is at hand, and a growing demand exists for a comprehensive worldview that does full justice to the real world of truth and life and experience in which man must make his decisions.

In the Western world today only three major options survive. Sooner or later one of these will carry off the spiritual fortunes of the twentieth-century world. Each of these views, significantly, holds that man can know the ultimately real world. But each differs from the others in important ways about ultimate reality.

One view is Communism, which dismisses the supernatural as a myth.

The other views, to which neo-Protestant agnosticism has forfeited the great modern debate over the faith of the Bible, are Roman Catholicism and evangelical Christianity. The really live option, in my opinion, is evangelical rational theism, a theology centered in the incarnation and inscripturation of the Word (a theology not of the distorted Word but of the disclosed Word). This, I feel, offers the one real possibility of filling the theological vacuum today.

Evangelical Christianity emphasizes:

- The universal as well as once-for-all dimension of divine disclosure.

- Authentic ontological knowledge of God.

- The intelligible and verbal character of God's revelation.

- The universal validity of religious truth.

10. The problem of God is the critical problem of the next decade (1968–1978) and is the fundamental issue for all mankind.

For Americans, the problem of God is more decisive for human life, liberty, and happiness than the issues of the American Revolution two centuries ago. For Protestants, the problem of God is more decisive than the issues of the Protestant Reformation four and a half centuries ago. For Christians, the problem of God is as decisive as the confrontation by Christ's disciples of the polytheistic Greco-Roman culture of their day, and of their own preparatory Hebrew heritage. For modern man come of age, the problem of God is no less decisive than was that ancient conflict between man's trust in the gods of pagan superstition and trust in the revelation of the sovereign Creator-Redeemer God. The problem of God now stands before us as the critical problem of the next decade, and it is the fundamental issue for all mankind.

Carl F. H. Henry, "Where Is Modern Theology Going?," *Christianity Today* 12, no. 11 (March 1, 1968): 3–7.

Chapter 15

JUSTIFICATION BY IGNORANCE: A NEO-PROTESTANT MOTIF?

*Henry gave this address at the Evangelical Theological
Society annual meeting on December 29, 1969.*

Of all the New Testament doctrines mythologized by neo-Protestant theologians, none has fared worse than justification by faith.

One ploy of recent modern theology has been a constant appeal to the majestic Reformation principle of *sole fidei* in an attempt to divorce Christian belief both from the certainty of objectively revealed truths (in the inspired prophetic-apostolic Scriptures) and from any firm grounding in external historical events (particularly the substitutionary atonement and bodily resurrection of Jesus Christ).

To be sure, the Bible's rejection of salvation by human effort rules out man's ability to relate himself acceptably to the Living God by the genius of the human mind no less than by the energies of the will and emotions. God's thoughts and God's ways are higher than man's—higher still than sinful man's, who cannot achieve divine acceptance whether by intellectual ingenuity or by moral striving.

But the lifeline of the Protestant Reformation was its redis-covery of the Scripture truth that God offers to penitent believers, hopelessly guilty in their strivings to achieve salvation by works, the benefits of Jesus Christ's mediation on the Cross. God acquits sinners, solely on the ground of a righteousness that he himself provides, a righteousness made known by intelligible divine rev-elation and embodied in the life, death, and resurrection of Jesus of Nazareth, a righteousness available to sinful men by faith alone.

But modern theologians have extended the Protestant prin-ciple of soteriological justification into a perverse speculative theory of epistemological justification by skepticism. Many neo-Protestant writers contend that the religious-ethical prin-ciple of justification solely by faith must be expanded to include a religious-intellectual corollary. In deference to divine revelation, man not only must renounce speculative rationalism, but suppos-edly must also repudiate all cognitive knowledge about God in order to give faith the right of way. Some recent statements con-sequently expound justification by faith in a manner that would destroy both the indispensable historical content and the indis-pensable knowledge content of revealed religion. "Justification by faith" becomes an abstract speculative principle through which its neo-Protestant advocates undermine much, if not all, that the New Testament and the Protestant Reformers considered essential to their exposition of the doctrine.

According to the contemporary view, intellectual faith-justification requires the rejection of any claim to divinely revealed truths, to the historical factuality of saving events, and to the scientific credibility of biblical miracles. Faith that justi-fies, it is said, has nothing to do with revealed information and external events: it is essentially trust in God devoid of cognitive knowledge.

That faith should liberate man's conscience, rather than burden it, was indeed one of Luther's emphases. But to turn this freedom into a theological necessity for emptying Christian belief of revelational truths and of the historical actuality of redemptive events is to misappropriate and pervert a Reformation principle.

Yet almost every influential neo-Protestant theologian in the recent past—including Karl Barth, Emil Brunner, F. Gogarten, Rudolf Bultmann, Paul Tillich, and the Niebuhrs—has wrongly used "justification by faith alone" to discount or dismiss the cognitive content and historical foundations of Christian faith. Some have done worse than others: they have turned justification by faith into an apology for non-Christian theology while at the same time evaporating the great distinctives of biblical religion. Some statements virtually reduce faith to courageous ignorance.

The early Barth contended that God confronts man and precipitates spiritual crisis by exposing the ambiguity of man's religious life. Barth insisted, however, that divine revelation does not convey truths and that faith is a "not-knowing" (*The Epistle to the Romans,* London: Oxford University, 1933, p. 88). His later attempts to rescue an intellectual or cognitive significance for faith came too late and were, in any case, too halting. Barth's early emphasis on a cognitively contentless revelation was nonetheless coordinated with God's exclusive revelation in Jesus Christ; later theologians, traveling the same route of "not-knowing" faith, freed divine disclosure from a necessary connection with Jesus Christ.

Every one of the dialectical and/or existential theologians insists that any and all religious truth-claims are ambiguous; existentialism's repudiation of every attempt to speak objectively of God was, therefore, destined for special welcome. Revelation is regarded, not as an objective divine communication of truths about God and his purposes, but rather as internal and paradoxical spiritual encounter. Revelation, in this view, has for its correlate not knowledge but trust; justification by faith, in consequence, is correlated with intellectual doubt.

Bultmann considers his whole demythological projection of faith and understanding wholly "parallel to St. Paul's and Luther's doctrine of justification by faith alone. ... Or rather, it carries this doctrine to its logical conclusion in the field of epistemology" (in *Kerygma and Myth,* ed. by Hans Werner Bartsch, Harper, 1961, pp. 210 f.). Insists Bultmann: "Indeed, de-mythologizing is the radical application of the doctrine of justification by faith to the sphere of knowledge and thought. ... There is no difference between security based on good works and security built on objectifying knowledge" (*Jesus Christ and Mythology,* Scribner, 1958, p. 84). Faith is correlated with the word alone, but this word of proclamation has no basis in revealed truths or historical saving events, inasmuch as the modern worldview is assumed to have ruled out the supernatural. The act of God in the Christ-event, however, that meets man in the preached word, enables man in faith to experience authentic life.

After first whittling down Paul's entire Christology to justification by faith, Bultmann then reinterprets the latter to mean that man can experience "new life" by forgoing all self-justifying effort—a category in which Bultmann includes any confidence in divinely disclosed truths. The authority and evidential value of the prophetic-apostolic writings is excluded as a support for faith, since to buttress belief objectively would contribute to self-justification by obscuring the possibility of a new mode of existence in terms of radical faith. If authentic existence is defined as *existential* self-understanding, then assurance that rests on externally valid beliefs and objective factors must belong to inauthentic existence. Bultmann welcomes negative historical criticism for the support it gives to his theological slant. The assaults of a naturalistic philosophy of science and of historical positivism upon external miracles in nature and history enjoy free course. Reformation theology cannot base faith upon any "work," and in this category Bultmann includes any fruit of historical and scientific inquiry. Faith must rest, instead, solely upon the preached word (though it is unclear why this, too, cannot be critically viewed as in some sense also a "work"). Bultmann concentrates the entire reality of revelation upon the event of preaching. Theological propositions are true only as existential statements, and only through faith is God knowable (which is Bultmannian shorthand for authentic self-understanding).

"Faith alone" here means existential decision without dependence on supernatural supports, historical happenings, cognitive content, or external evidence. Unlike Barth, who maintained the necessity of Jesus Christ's substitutionary death and external resurrection, Bultmann retains the supernatural and miraculous only as myth and not as objective reality. For Bultmann, the essence of justification by faith is trust in God's act experienced in existential response to the preached word in the absence of objective knowledge and external considerations.

But if Bultmann insists nonetheless on the reality of God apart from our faith, while denying God's knowability outside faith, H. Braun radicalizes Bultmann's existentialism to the point where the existence of God is wholly identical with the self-understanding of man in faith. Braun reduces the New Testament doctrine of justification by faith to the ethical tension of "I ought" and "I may." The apostles sound forth Jesus' call to moral transformation in terms of the paradoxical unity of God's radical demand and radical grace. By first understanding and proclaiming the faith that unites God's demand with his grace and hence justifies, Jesus provided historical impetus for justification.

But Braun holds that justification can be verified elsewhere in human experience. Anthropology, according to Braun, is the New Testament constant, and Christology the variable. Despite his dismissal of the independent reality of God, and despite the dispensability in principle of Jesus of Nazareth (the moral paradox at the heart of the doctrine of justification might, in theory, have been uncovered by another person remarkably dissimilar to the Man of Galilee), Braun nonetheless espouses justification by faith, however deviantly.

Since faith is presumably independent of conceptual knowledge and of historical events, F. Gogarten ventures a restatement of justification that makes possible both the complete and radical autonomy of the physical and historical sciences and man's total reliance upon them in shaping the future (see *The Reality of Faith*, Westminster, 1959, chap. 10). Justification by faith is, therefore, not related to man's individual moral and spiritual predicament before God; instead, it sanctions man's shaping of the world and of history by reason and science alone, rather than their forfeiture to religious incredulity. Gogarten misappropriates Luther's great doctrine to advance his own connection of faith with secularization as a Christian phenomenon; for him, the revelation of Jesus Christ is the direct and original basis of secularization. Jesus' unreserved trust in the Father fully exposes the fact that the cosmos and history, contrary to the prevalent pagan beliefs, are not controlled by divinatory powers. As son of the Father, and in view of his confidence in the Creator, man is now wholly free to become lord of the world—so Gogarten contends—through unlimited use of reason and science.

In other words, the secularization of society assertedly has a divine mandate; man can fulfill his responsibility in the world only by aggressive reliance on reason alone rather than on faith; the limitless use of reason and science are the means by which man must advance the order, unity, coherence, and future of the world. But, says Gogarten, only faith in God as Creator frees man for this total reliance on reason. Man's understanding of the world as God's creation is, therefore, the equivalent of man's justification in God's sight. In this way the doctrine of justification, forcibly detached from the whole framework of supernatural revelation and miraculous redemption, gains speculative exposition in terms of man's freedom to enlist science to fulfill his culture-mandate in the world and history.

In America it was Tillich who carried the modern distortion of justification by faith to its extreme. Repeatedly Tillich claimed the Pauline and Lutheran doctrine of justification as the foundation of his entire theological outlook. The essence of that doctrine, he insisted, is as indispensable today as in the first and sixteenth centuries. But, as he went on to say, a reinterpretation and wholly new understanding of it are necessary: "This idea is strange to the man of today and even to Protestant people in the churches" and is now "scarcely understandable even to our most intelligent scholars. ... And we should not imagine that it will be possible in some simple fashion to leap over this gulf and resume our connection with the Reformation again" (*The Protestant Era,* University of Chicago, 1948, p. 196).

Tillich proposes to revive and reinterpret justification by faith not merely as an article of the creed but also, by relating man to God as the Ground of all being, as the comprehensive frame through which ultimate reality is to gain new power in universal human life. Tillich's radically conceived view detaches justification by faith from its historical understanding—namely, from the doctrinal biblical view of God, of Christ, of redemption—and boldly turns it into a formula for repudiating supernatural theism.

In view of man's inability to protect himself, by human striving, against devastating threats to survival and existence, Tillich expounds the implications of justification by faith for cultural autonomy. Neither right beliefs nor spiritual activity nor any other achievement on man's part, he says, can stave off the ultimate condemnation of man's efforts to failure. But justification means that man is *accepted* as he is, without even striving for acceptance; it declares that grace is available, and that man's estrangement from God is overcome in reconciliation and new being.

To see in such a presentation the New Testament content of justification by faith is to misunderstand Tillich. He calls man to no particular beliefs, to no intellectual presuppositions whatever, to no specific spiritual affirmations—not even to the definition of acknowledgement of divine grace, nor to the naming of God's Name. According to Tillich, the Protestant principle assertedly implies that "there cannot be a truth in human minds which is divine truth itself. Consequently, the prophetic spirit must always criticize, attack, and condemn sacred authorities, doctrines and morals" (*The Protestant Era,* p. 226). Protestantism must proclaim the judgment that brings assurance by depriving us of all security and must proclaim our having truth in the very absence of truth (even of religious truth). *"You are accepted,* accepted by that which is greater than you, and the name of which you do not know. ... Simply accept the fact that you are accepted!"* (*The Shaking of the Foundations,* Scribner, 1948, p. 162). Hence, in his application of justification by faith to the religious aspect of man's ethical life, Tillich divorces divine acceptance of man from specific doctrinal beliefs.

He goes still further by applying the justification theory to the whole intellectual side of religion in such a way that the skeptic is no less divinely justifiable than the striver who merely believes himself to be accepted. Doubt is said to unfold within itself an infinite passion for the truth, a faith is assertedly hidden inside skepticism. If justifying faith involves no specific content, the skeptic who has hidden faith must also be regarded as somehow in the truth and in unity with Being itself. "The paradox got hold of me," said Tillich, "that he who seriously denies God, affirms him" (*The Protestant Era,* p. xv). So then justification by faith is universally assured, even to those who find belief in God an impossibility. On Tillich's premises "there is no possible atheism": God is present in every act of faith, even if this faith expressly denies the very existence of God. If correct ideas are a dispensable "work" in relation to justification by faith, then neither incorrect ideas nor ideas in suspense or doubt can disqualify one from justification by faith—just so long as one is earnestly involved. "Go with Pilate, if you cannot go with Jesus; but go in seriousness with him!" writes Tillich of Pilate's doubts concerning the truth (*The New Being,* p. 68).

This is not all. Tillich gives an even more radical, more universal, more abstract statement of justification by faith. Not only for the skeptic, in whose doubt faith is said to be nonetheless present as a presupposition, but even for one committed to a-meaning, justification is possible without intellectual reversal. Heinz Zahrnt summarizes Tillich's position as follows: "The courage which looks despair in the face already *is* faith, and the act of taking meaninglessness on oneself is a meaningful act" (*The Question of God,* London: Collins, 1969, p. 344).

In his closing chapter of *The Courage to Be,* written in 1952, Tillich suggests that the very term *faith* desperately needs modern reinterpretation, then proceeds to analyze the experience of courage, connecting, in the face of meaninglessness, the courage to be with the power of being, or the Ground of all being.

> By affirming our being, we participate in the self-affirmation of being-itself. There are no valid arguments for the "existence" of God, but there are acts of courage in which

we affirm the power of being, whether we know it or not. ...
Courage has revealing power, the courage to be is the key
to meaning itself [*The Courage to Be,* Yale University, 1952,
p. 181].

Tillich's closing words are, "The courage to be is rooted in
the God who appears when God has disappeared in the anxiety
of doubt" (p. 190). The experience, undirected, without specific
content, that appeals to no special divine revelation but takes into
itself doubt and meaninglessness in the bald confidence that one
is accepted—this Tillich calls "absolute faith." Its sole presupposition is the Ultimate, the "God above God," beyond describable
identity. Absolute faith is faith without a theology, without words
and concepts, yet is faith in the trans-personal presence of the
Divine, the depth of things, the ultimate Ground.

For Tillich, in other words, there is no unconditional truth
of faith except one, and that is, it would appear, that no one pos-
sesses any such truth. Despite this disclaimer, however, Tillich
was somehow misled into believing justification in the Tillichian
reinterpretation to be an indispensable truth, and this at the high
cost of scuttling the biblical truth of the self-revealing God and
the truth of justification by faith in the understanding of the Book
of Romans and in the experience of the Reformers. In his exposition, justification gains a universal significance that goes beyond
Protestantism, beyond Catholicism, beyond Christianity itself.
Tillich's concept loses both the God of the Bible and the supernatural redemption and rescue of sinful man. In short, by elaborating
justification as a speculative principle the way he does, Tillich
forfeits justification as a supernatural provision of divine grace.

Quite clearly, then, with Gogarten and Tillich, the justification
principle takes on essentially post-Protestant and non-Christian
features. Not only is its content emptied of New Testament

essentials, but its form is shaped by theosophy rather than by theology. A justification that requires even Christians to give up all their revealed knowledge of God, to surrender supernatural realities, to forgo the metaphysical significance of Jesus Christ, is a justification totally foreign to the first Christians. As Zahrnt observes, if the people who longed at the waning of the Middle Ages for a more authentic way of speaking about God had thought that Luther's Reformation must necessarily end this way, they would "have put their hands over their ears in horror and cried: 'Anything but that!'" (*The Question of God,* p. 359).

Nowhere did neo-Protestant theology seriously question its speculative extensions and reformulations of justification in terms of radical faith. Rather, justification was made to imply the epistemological theory that all knowledge is historically conditioned, that faith requires the rejection of objective truths, that faith is uninterested in the historical actuality of saving events, that even the severest criticism of the natural and historical sciences could in no way jeopardize the vitality and propriety of faith: moreover, Protestantism, it was held, historically sponsored and licensed these views.

In his early writings, Barth had insisted that the revelation of the Living God is confined to Jesus Christ. He later acknowledged that this view could not rest simply on the contention that divine revelation enlists only nonintellectual trust in its exposure of the ambiguity of man's righteousness. In his earlier view, faith was considered to be implicit in the question "Who am I?" and accessible to man as man; its connection with God's unique act in Christ, therefore, seemed hardly necessary. He came to see, however, that a flat rejection of objective knowledge of God and historical revelation threatened to dissolve divine disclosure into theological subjectivism. Under counter-pressure by Bultmann and existentialists, Barth, therefore, increasingly

sought to inform faith with cognitive significance, and stressed
the external objectivity of Christ's resurrection, though he continued to place the event beyond the reach of historical inquiry.

Despite Barth's maneuverings toward revelational quasi-
objectivity in history and in cognition, not only Bultmann but
also many post-Bultmannian theologians continue to combine
their insistence on God's once-for-all disclosure in Jesus Christ
with the costly thesis that faith is consistent with radical doubt.
For all the assertion of the "new quest" of the historical Jesus,
Gerhard Ebeling, for instance, contends that the Reformation
doctrine of justification by faith is mirrored in the unqualified
abandonment of historical considerations to critical methodology: "Protestantism of the nineteenth century, by deciding
in principle for the critical historical method, maintained and
confirmed ... the decision of the Reformers in the sixteenth century" (*Word and Faith,* Fortress, 1963, p. 55). Ebeling's interest
is not the vindication of authentic as against spurious historical
claims. In his essay on "The Significance of the Critical Historical
Method for Church and Theology in Protestantism," he postulates an inner connection between justification by faith, which
assertedly requires us to live without any kind of security, and
critical-historical methodology which undercuts any assurance
that faith might find in external historical facts.

The announced effort of some post-Bultmannians to maintain some measure of historical rootage for Christian faith would
in principle sacrifice, as Van Austin Harvey rightly comments,
"the meaning of justification by faith which the 'new questers' also
want to preserve" (*The Historian and the Believer,* London: SCM
Press, 1967, p. 196). Most post-Bultmannians in fact really have
no desire to reassert a historical or rational justification of faith.
Ernst Fuchs, for example, still insists no less strenuously than
Bultmann that to ground faith in objective demonstration would

involve the human intellect in a form of illusory self-justification. A free faith would be precluded, he contends, if belief in the Gospel of the risen Christ were established by eyewitnesses: "The witnesses of a particular, repeated happening are in competition with faith, and what they have seen is in competition with the gospel which is to be believed" (*Gessamelte Aufsätze,* Tubingen: J. C. B. Mohr, 1965, III, 276). So, too, Hans Conzelmann combines historical skepticism and cognitive uncertainty with existential justification in a manner that detaches faith from objective truth about God and the factuality of Christ's resurrection (*An Outline of the Theology of the New Testament,* Harper & Row, 1969).

It becomes increasingly apparent that the dialectical-existential severance of divine revelation from rational cognizability and from external historical events leads inevitably to the loss both of special and of general revelation, since it hopelessly weakens the meaning of the term *revelation.* (Whatever else may be said about Wolfhart Pannenberg's theology—and it is not beyond serious evangelical criticism—he sees clearly that the right aim of historical method is not, as recent modern theology would have it, to plunge the believer into such uncertainty about history that he can live only by a leap of faith, but rather to ascertain knowledge about the past.) To be sure, the rejection of intelligible divine disclosure and of external divine revelation in nature and history was correlated in dialectical-existential theology, in its alternative emphasis solely on personal non-propositional confrontation, with an insistence that God confronts man only in and through his Word, Jesus Christ. Yet Bultmann's view of faith as authentic human existence, or self-surrender inspired by the symbol of Jesus Christ's death and resurrection, not only leaves in doubt the indispensability of a past unique act of God in Jesus of Nazareth, but also accommodates the logical possibility of another symbol of faith serviceable to those to whom

Christ is unknown. If the faith that justifies is a matter of existential self-understanding, divorced from dependence on objectively revealed divine truths and external historical saving events, cannot man realize his own true nature independently of Jesus of Nazareth?

Bultmann concedes this possibility only in theory; he insists that God's prior initiative in Christ must in actuality be assumed because only in the proclamation (kerygma) about Christ has authentic existence been realized.

But so-called left wing post-Bultmannians take the other option. Fritz Buri and Schubert M. Ogden contend that the neo-Protestant understanding of "justification" has as its logical consequence the radical universal character of divine grace; to identify it solely with a divine act in Jesus Christ they consider to be an arrogant theological presumption (Schubert M. Ogden, *Christ Without Myth,* Harper, 1961, pp. 145 f.). If Christian faith rests on no objective truth and no historical actualities, but depends rather upon a personal act of God in an event about which very little can be known, then radical faith becomes a universal possibility. Pointing to Bultmann's deliberate distinguishing of self-understanding from belief in the cross and resurrection of Christ as objective events, the left-wing post-Bultmannians ask: If faith is a passage from inauthentic to authentic existence, without necessary dependence on an objective historical event in the past, is such faith not a possibility for man as man? Ogden takes the coordination of justification with doctrinal disengagement seriously: the teaching that salvation is by Christ alone is labeled—not "absurdly," as Carl Braaten thinks (*New Directions in Theology Today, Volume II: History and Hermeneutics,* London: Lutterworth, 1968, p. 85), but in a way quite consistent with the existentialist premise—as "the final and most dangerous triumph" of "the heretical doctrine of works-righteousness." This heresy, he says, we can now avoid only by stressing "that God saves man by grace alone in complete freedom from any saving 'work' of any kind traditionally portrayed in the doctrines of the person and work of Jesus Christ" (p. 145).

With an eye on the unstable Bultmannian and post-Bultmannian defense of once-for-all disclosure in Jesus Christ the Word, Van Austin Harvey takes the final step. Since neo-Protestant theology equates faith with trust or decision and detaches revelation from both cognitive truth and specific historical beliefs, Harvey contends that the content of faith may be as readily mediated by historically false myths as by actual historical events (*The Historian and the Believer,* pp. 280f.). This view, he argues, "tries to take with utmost seriousness both the Protestant principle of justification by faith and the historical character of human existence, of which the morality of human knowledge is but a formalized constitutive part" (p. 288).

Thus, the neo-Protestant restatement of justification by faith as an epistemological principle attaching faith to cognitive doubt finally succeeds in destroying justification by faith as a soteriological principle that attaches faith to God's saving revelation and redemption in Jesus Christ. A formless and contentless belief—rendered so by the loss of universally valid truth and of external historical grounding—must cut itself off from necessary connections with Jesus of Nazareth, from justification by faith in an authentically biblical understanding, and must attach itself instead to radical faith as a possibility available to every man as man. It is then free to draw its life-giving spirit from pseudo-scientific dogmas about the impossibility of miracle or the irrelevance of the supernatural, or from historicist dogmas that dismiss Judeo-Christian revelation as myth by hardening modern doubt into anti-Christian finality. When justification by faith is thus perverted into the speculative theory that revelational truths and revelational history are efforts at self-justification, the essential connection of Christian faith with intelligible and historical revelation is sacrificed on the altar of scientific-historical positivism.

The recent epistemological perversion of this soteriological principle must be seen as a massive delusion of self-justification. In their self-disengagement from the cognitive content of divine revelation, neo-Protestant theologians pleaded their personal humility and protested presumptive pride in the evangelicals' attachment to the truth of Scripture. But it should be crystal clear that their modern justification of doubt is a pridefully presumptive repudiation of the rational content of the Living God's intelligible disclosure and of his redemptive acts in external history. The neo-Protestant reconstruction of justification by faith is, in fact, a massive self-delusion, a subtle self-justification of the contemporary revolt against reason and against revelation in its Judeo-Christian understanding.

A theology of this kind needs more than renewal; it needs God's forgiveness. All our theology, of course, stands always in need of purification by the inspired Scriptures; some of it needs to be purged. But can a speculative theology that guarantees its own justification in advance by correlating divine acceptance with man's courageous ignorance, hope for a pardon of which it feels no need?

Ironically enough, evangelical theology must acknowledge that Roman Catholicism, whose misinterpretation of justification the Reformation protested, today has more understanding than does the influential vanguard of neo-Protestant theologians who have miscarried the doctrine to the point of mischief and misbelief. Were it not for the emerging radicals in the Church of Rome today, not a few evangelicals would seek liaison for examining biblical justification by faith, particularly with devout Catholics who show a new respect for the Bible. The neo-Protestant perversion of justification is so much worse than the medieval misconstruction that ecumenical Christianity can now profit by hearing of what the Scholastics had to say, although it is only through what the Scriptures have to say, of course, that we, like Luther, can find the way again.

Karl Barth could speak of the revelation of God as a clap of thunder in the Swiss Alps. For Paul Tillich, faith was like a flash of lightning that in a stormy night throws everything into a blinding clarity for just a moment. Barth's thunder has worn itself silent, and Tillich's momentary light has waned. The mind of modern man, whose doubt and sense of meaninglessness even theologians venture to justify, stumbles in blindness and night. May God who justifies authentically, on his own terms, and in his own way, cause the Light to shine and the Word to be heard again. And may theology experience forgiveness of sins in a gracious rediscovery and proclamation of authentic justification by faith alone.

Carl F. H. Henry, "Justification by Ignorance: A Neo-Protestant Motif?," *Christianity Today* 14, no. 7 (January 2, 1970): 10–15. This article also appeared in Journal of the *Evangelical Theological Society* 13 (Winter 1970): 3–14.

Chapter 16

THE FORTUNES
OF THEOLOGY

*Between April and August 1972, Henry devoted five of
his "Footnotes" columns to exploring the fortunes of
theology. They are combined here under a single heading.*

Theology in the west continues to be plagued by convulsive
upheaval. Deepening controversy shadows the Church of
Rome, wherein problems of authority challenge the hierarchy up
even to the papal summit. Neo-Protestant ecumenism has now
drifted from earlier programming of faith-and-order concerns to
doubt and disorder as vexing dilemmas of the day. The Protestant
world, whose liberal leadership envisioned a Christian century
and one great world church given over to socio-political priorities,
is today more divided theologically and at odds ecclesiastically
than for a century.

No fact is clearer than the loss by many of the churches of
any sure Word of God. The distressing disarray of contemporary theology is plainly related to the ecumenical community's
ambiguity in this sphere. Prestigious modern theologians have

exercised magical gifts with words, but despite semantic ingenuity and verbal prestidigitation, their momentarily spellbinding theories have lacked abiding power. Each novel alternative in turn becomes part of the predicament of modern theology, rather than holding promise of enduring import. Protestant seminaries increasingly assign conversation a priority over proclamation, and sustained searching of Scripture progressively yields to team-taught diversity.

The Bible has much to say about God's chastisement of his people for neglect of his counsel, and it contains dire warnings against distortion and defacement of the divine Word. It is not an idle question, therefore, whether ecumenical bewilderment over an authoritative Word of God may not reflect divine judgment upon professing Christendom for its disregard of the truth of revelation. Ecclesiastical dilution of the biblical disclosure not only clouds the truth-content of revealed religion; it also forfeits the Church's distinctive cure for the secular man's spiritual lifelessness and moral suicide, and compounds his growing sense of human futility.

On the other hand, it is not forbidden to ask whether some portents may be appearing of a better day for twentieth-century theology. Has the murky tide of anti-intellectualism now perchance run its course? Will religious claims soon be correlated again with an imperative reason for human hope and faith? Has evangelical theology, as currently verbalized, the necessary potency for a spiritual turnabout? Can it now hope to become formatively influential in American life as an evangelistic message addressed solely to the needs of isolated individuals, without bearing decisively upon the national outlook and offering a social vision as well?

Reflection upon the theological ferment of the recent past may illumine the intellectual eclipse that seems to be settling

over Western Christendom. If these observations do not venture any prophecies about the near future, they may at least set
in perspective some costly theological mistakes of the near past.

*1. Non-evangelical theological alternatives to historic
Christianity put forward by neo-Protestant scholars have been
successively smitten by an unsuspected malignancy; their plum-
meting into terminal illness happens even more swiftly than their
dramatic rise to influence.*

The various neo-Protestant theologies are short-lived novelties, prominent only for a brief season; like fashions in clothes,
they yield to ongoing replacement. The fashionable theories of
our day have had even less staying power than their speculative
antecedents that were grounded in nineteenth-century enthusiasm for philosophical idealism or religious feeling or moral values.
Protestant modernism, naturalistic humanism, dialectical disclosure, existential decision, and "God is dead" postulation have, one
and all, no more obvious identifying characteristic than a high
mortality rate. The life-span of contemporary theological theories is now briefer than that of reigning scientific theories whose
champions, claiming neither revelation nor authority, openly
anticipate revision of their formulas. The theology of the death
of God sagged in audience interest not very long after a major
denominational publishing house had rearranged its book publication schedule to focus on the God-is-dead thought.

The short life expectancy of the distinctively modern theories of theology is therefore one of their most evident traits. All
influential neo-Protestant theologians of the twentieth century
have lived to see a widespread acceptance and abandonment of
their formative frontier expositions.

*2. Diagnosis of these neo-Protestant views—from the theology
of a thundering other-worldly dialectical Word to that of an explosive this-worldly God of revolutionary violence, or the more timid*

process-theology deity given to collective bargaining—discloses, amid their transientness, a developmental pattern common to them all. Their undergirding rationale involves a three-step maneuver in respect to the Bible.

First, a given theologian isolates for ridicule (as intellectually intolerable, or as a vestigial remnant of the prescientific past) those aspects of the scriptural account that his system aims to replace (e.g., for Barth, divinely revealed truths claiming objective validity; for Bultmann, supernatural reality and miracle; for Ogden, God's transcendent revelation in Jesus Christ the Word; for Van Buren, the transcendently divine).

Second, Jesus Christ is appealed to as validating the non-evangelical alternative manufactured by the contemporary savant. The prestige of the prophetic-apostolic witness and of the Reformation heritage is then likewise arrogated to the newly minted theory.

Finally, having stripped the Bible of controlling contrary elements by dismissing them as mythical or marginal, the contemporary theologian asserts that what is left of Scripture teaches or supports the new view. The modern speculations are therefore freely depicted as biblical, and as expressing either the highest emphasis, or the real doctrine, or the intention, of the sacred writers.

3. The special appeal of each neo-Protestant religious theory lies in its dramatic correlation of some urgent concern or deep longing in contemporary life with segments of the scriptural revelation that have been obscured or neglected by other recent religious alternatives. Barth stressed anew an authoritative Divine Word; Bultmann, the critical importance of personal decision; Cullmann,

---

Carl F. H. Henry, "Footnotes: The Fortunes of Theology," *Christianity Today* 16, no. 14 (April 14, 1972): 35–36.

the centrality of salvation-history; Moltmann, the irreducible importance of Jesus' resurrection from the dead; Pannenberg, the revelatory significance of universal world history; and so on. Each view gains a magnetic hold on younger clergymen through the reassertion of certain facets of biblical theology. And each theory compounds the errors of its predecessors in two ways. It first superimposes upon the Bible an interpretative framework alien to it, and then subordinates other definitive elements of biblical theology to this.

These theories, then, gain a following in the Christian community by correlating theosophical or philosophical novelties with broken fragments of the biblical revelation. The Bible is not appealed to as an authoritative Book, plenarily inspired and constituting a divinely given rule of Christian truth.

4. In regard to knowledge of God as an objective reality, the formative theological views of the last hundred years are metaphysically agnostic. This trend crested into the ecumenical vision of a world church that raised social involvement above metaphysical consensus and creedal tests. Protestant modernism emphasized the experiential values of following Christ's exemplary commitment to Divine Fatherhood and human brotherhood. While Barthian theology located faith's center in divine disclosure rather than in religious experience, it depicted revelation as paradoxical: the truth of faith, it said, defies expression in universally valid propositions. Bultmann, however, insisted that the self at the center of existential revelation is not the divine self at all; it is rather, he affirmed, the human self.

Supposedly to enhance revelation, dialectical-existential theology disowned logically consistent knowledge of God and portrayed faith as a cognitively vacuous leap. The Continental theologians therefore affirmed as Christianity's special distinctive what in the minds of logical positivists reduced Christianity to nonsense—the notion that the reality of God turns not on intelligible rational evidence and objectively valid truth but rather on personal decision and inner response. More recently such post-Bultmannian theologians as Fuchs and Ebeling, and even such proponents of external historical revelation as Moltmann and Pannenberg, have likewise deprived Christianity of any final cognitive affirmations about the ontological being of God.

This loss of the rationality of divine revelation in recent modern theology prepared the way for the notion of God's demise: if God cannot be truly known for what he assertedly is, the Living God is in epistemic eclipse. Contemporary theologians show almost cultic fanaticism in forfeiting ontological knowledge of God's nature as he is in himself. Their works remind one of Clifford Irving's supposed revelations concerning the inaccessible Howard Hughes: publishing houses are available to disclose secrets of the life and deeds of the Great Unknown; biographers tell of special access vouchsafed to them alone; readers await an up-to-the-minute revision of what the existing versions declare to be the unchanging truth. Then—at last—the necessary authorization of legitimacy is found to be missing, and the real voice and word of the Invisible Shepherd, known and recognized by his sheep, is admitted to point another Way.

5. *The attempt to resuscitate process theology as the wave of the future is faltering.* Process theology is one among many ripples on an agitated theological surface. It lacks firm basis in the Hebrew-Christian Scriptures, and is more a philosophical than a theological explanation. Its current appeal is largely limited to students unfamiliar with related proposals from earlier in this century; the present versions are much like a return of an old movie.

Liabilities of process theology are numerous. Among its intellectual difficulties, two stand out. First, it obscures God's causal relation to the universe; the emphasis that the universe is as necessary to God as God is to the universe compromises the biblical doctrine of creation. Second, its insistence that God is an aspect of the whole of reality precludes any absolute distinction between good and evil. Indeed, the more intimately God is correlated with man and history—particularly in a century vexed by devastating international wars and the social violence of Nazism, Fascism, and Communism, as well as the pervasive moral decline of the world—the more difficult it becomes to maintain any adequate view of sin.

6. *The positive significance of radical contemporary views—for example, the "theology of revolution" and "black theology"—lies in their rejection of other sub-Christian alternatives rather than in any espousal of authentic and permanently valid positions.* A commitment to violent revolutionary change cannot accommodate in any event a final theology or controlling *Logos*; what destroys all must sooner or later be self-destructive.

Revolutionary theology mounts an extreme reaction against the misidentification of the status quo as essentially just or as acceptably Christian, a costly error that the Christian Church has too often made. Black theology is a reactionary insistence that theology can be done only by blacks, a notion no less exaggerated and extreme than the assumption that God is white. To write Christian theology in terms of any culture-orientation is hazardous. The neglected emphasis that theology needs to revive is that the Christian revelation has permanent implications for all oppressed people.

7. *The unenviable consequence of neo-Protestant theology's revolt against reason and rationality is that its positions cannot be regarded as true.* It should be apparent that any movement that disowns the instrumentality of reason in establishing theological positions or in validating its objectives cannot rationally defend its own perspectives. Philosophers may speak of religion

as a "special kind" of truth, and theologians may deplore the pursuit of objective truth about God as prideful presumption; but unless the man in the street is convinced that spiritual claims belong to the same order of truth as life's other persuasive commitments, he will not take Christian claims seriously. He will turn rather to cults that claim to give such knowledge or will probe the mystical, astrological, or merely magical. The religious revolt against reason is sure to issue in a harvest of aberrant and inventive alternatives to biblical faith.

8. *The stark confusion in theology and philosophy has plummeted the prestige of these fields of knowledge to sad new lows.* General public interest in serious religious and philosophical literature has been eroded. The list of 100 best books for 1971 carried by many Sunday newspapers at year-end did not even include theology or philosophy as a category.

9. *As modern theologizers increasingly promoted their perspectives not as unchanging "gospel" but as merely "jump-off" points for contemporary inquiry, divinity students more and more forsook theology for social activism as the essence of Christian response.* Thus for many clerics God's Word and work gave way to political engagement as the focus of interest. In Germany, the appeal to socialism as informing the content of the theology of hope has so pervaded the ecumenical seminaries that Marxism now elicits notably wider loyalties among divinity students than among university students generally. A remarkable percentage of German seminarians today regard the churches not as centers for proclaiming an apostolic Gospel but as strategic springboards for promoting socio-political change.

10. *The faddish cult of irrationality in the theology of the recent past is now fast running its course and a faith at once revelationally*

Carl F. H. Henry, "Footnotes: The Fortunes of Theology," *Christianity Today* 16, no. 16 (May 12, 1972): 32–33.

based and rationally compelling is reasserting its claims. The ablest Christian apologists have always contended that Christianity speaks the truth in view of intelligible divine revelation, and that what Christianity affirms about God is the case whether men choose to believe it or not. Augustine insisted that faith issues in understanding, and the Protestant Reformers stood with him against any reduction of divine revelation to camouflaged truth. J. Gresham Machen, Protestant modernism's American arch-foe, deplored the divorce of Christian faith from supernaturally revealed information about God and his purposes. C. S. Lewis correlated devotion to the Christian faith with the service of reason. Gordon H. Clark criticizes non-evangelical theories for their contrast of faith and reason.

Mediating views—such as process theology—that reaffirm the indispensability of rational coherence to a sound religious outlook, nonetheless needlessly constrict the rational activity of God and forfeit special cognitive revelation. Such speculative alternatives to philosophical and theological irrationalism promote supposedly coherent conceptualities that, as unstable half-way positions, compromise the Christian faith and make it necessary for others to formulate an acceptable counterview. Those who reject biblical theism cannot do so on the basis of coherent reasoning, for the Christian revelation of God is rationally consistent and compelling, and, moreover, rationality has its very basis in the nature of the Living God.

11. Evangelical Christianity is unlikely to gain penetrating and persuasive significance in American life today unless it speaks a theological-ethical word to the nation and not simply to isolated individuals. The weakness of the evangelical thrust in both community and campus crusades is that it now aims almost solely at rescuing parched souls from the burning without energetically enlisting minds for intellectual perspicuity and bodies for public justice. Its witness to a Christian world-life view as a socio-cultural alternative to the empirical eccentricities of the West is meager.

Many Americans are given over to the vision of a scientific society in which cities are to be saved by technocratic planning and individuals by medical progress. Counter-cultural youth have disowned the technocratic worldview in the name of human values, but, disillusioned by the Vietnamese war abroad and social injustices at home, they tend to embrace private mysticism and to lack consistent dedication to national purpose. Not long ago the danger of revolutionary rebellion was widespread; social critics were asking whether the disenchanted young might rally to a tyrant mounting a Red charger, much as restless German youth became Hitler's Nazi storm troopers. Now the question is whether the alienated young, many of whom are dropping out of the public arena into private communes, have resigned themselves to the ambiguity of their experience and given up hope for a new direction—whether they will even bother to vote.

American society is increasingly adrift on matters of destiny and morality. The American people are sinking into a socio-political and religious-moral crisis that demands the leadership of a modern Lincoln. No society can long take a rain check on final commitments. The relevance of religious truth to public politics must not be muddled into generalities. Nor ought concern over religion in public education to leap over the question of truth in the classroom in order to debate simply whether prayer and meditation are permissible—while non-theistic teachers proceed with impunity to capture the minds of young America.

Evangelical "think tanks" intended primarily to formulate an evangelistic strategy without wrestling with the larger concerns of truth and right cannot adequately cope with these concerns. No theological outlook is now likely to exert a shaping influence on the American scene unless it moves the masses toward both a new vision of truth and justice and a new way of life in a socio-cultural context. If revealed religion is to become formatively significant on the present American scene, the Christian vanguard must address man as man as well as man as sinner; it must speak to the destiny of nations and the meaning and worth of life, while it speaks to man in his private needs and as an evangelistic target.

12. *American evangelical Christianity is by no means in an enviable position.* No academically great university reflects its views, and no voice like President Timothy Dwight's at Yale almost two centuries ago calls academia to contemplate the logic of biblical theism. Many large state and private universities crowd historical Christian perspectives out of their philosophy and religion departments. Many evangelical colleges are running large deficits; few are concerned with solid literary production, and rarely are these colleges' administrative spokesmen and scholars quoted in the public arena. In denominational circles, evangelical seminaries are continually merged out of their historic commitments or tend to become theologically imprecise through ecumenical dilution. Leading evangelical magazines have not escaped substantial circulation losses; long-range gains in readership are now usually achieved through magazine mergers. Most evangelical journalistic efforts remain too pontifical and propagandistic to interest disenchanted liberals, and too theologically unexciting and journalistically unimaginative even to pace evangelical frontiersmen. In evangelism, only exceptional churches across America have recaptured the energies that crusade evangelism hoped to stimulate; many congregations still pray that a crusade will rescue their declining cause, and usually that does not happen.

Carl F. H. Henry, "Footnotes: The Fortunes of Theology," *Christianity Today* 16, no. 18 (June 9, 1972): 30–31.

We have already noted that the present American scene shows pockmarks of moral decline and spiritual unrest. Our frontier society finds contraceptive devices a gateway to sexual licentiousness and abortion the happy solution for overpopulation; the marriage concept it scorns as a deterrent to the good life. Numbers of people reject the prevalent view of work as a means to affluence and prestige, not because they have the higher motivation of work as service, but because they expect the redistribution of wealth, more and more government welfare programs, and larger opportunities of leisure. The confused political situation among those who rely on law and order meanwhile encourages the discontent to foment disorder.

The spiritual sky is ominously beclouded. Jesus-freaks and Satan-worshipers have both come to the fore, organized ecumenism is struggling to retain power, fragmented evangelical forces are parrying a more cooperative way into the future. A vast array of cults, the big-city Graham crusades, the charismatic movement, thousands of student conversions to Christ, a widening use of television by Oral Roberts, Rex Humbard, and others, the growth of Pentecostal Catholics, and the emergence of a noteworthy Christian Jewry all crowd the religious scene today.

How are we to assess the evangelical prospect amid these forces? Some thinkers envision a new age of religious syncretism that will aim to span the differences between Christ and Confucius, or even between Matthew's gospel and Mao's. Others credit the Jesus people with launching a spiritual revolution in America. Still others think that American and European Christianity has now largely had its day, and that the evangelical future will move through Asia, Africa, or Latin America.

Many lamps of evangelical promise are agleam in the present

dark hour, and some remarkable developments of new life are easy to discern.

Amid intellectual fatigue and moral chaos on the campuses, a nucleus of Christian students and teachers openly declare their personal faith in Christ. Differing local situations may determine how this phenomenon becomes organizationally absorbed—Campus Crusade, Inter-Varsity, Navigators, or some exceptionally virile denominational work. Often the new surge moves simply under the broad umbrella of the Jesus movement. At Marshall University about 300 students declared for Christ in the span of just a few months. Inter-Varsity's triennial Urbana conference has become a well-known and respected missionary-recruiting grounds for hard-pressed denominations. In June some 85,000 gathered in Dallas for Explo '72, a nationwide student Christian conference organized by Campus Crusade.

Young Jesus-followers seem uninterested in the professional ministry as a vocation; they seek evangelistic and missionary patterns outside the pulpit. At the same time converts on non-evangelical campuses, deluged by intellectual pressures on faith and confronted by issues of social justice, are burdened about stating Christian claims in a coherent and compelling way; they do not wish to separate a Christian world-life view and socio-cultural sensitivity and evangelistic engagement. Although in somewhat smaller numbers, recent alumni of Christian colleges also show these same larger concerns, and are earmarking their graduate studies in philosophy, law, and political science for larger involvement in the cultural debate. The publication *Universitas* that has been projected by evangelical campuses aligned in the Consortium of Christian Colleges may reinforce these interests. The Institute for Advanced Christian Studies, a mobile fellowship of evangelical professors, many serving on prestigious campuses, seeks to advance Christian perspectives by sponsoring invitational scholars' conferences and research grants to mature writers engaged in frontier issues. To become more than a salvific cult that from the sidelines of culture conducts periodic forays to rescue prisoners in an alien milieu, evangelical Christianity must engage energetically in the conflict of ideas and in the struggle for public justice.

During the past century evangelicals have developed their affinity through cooperative evangelistic and missionary momentum, and evangelism, indeed, still offers the most inviting doorway to transdenominational engagement. Key 73 offers Christian believers across America an unprecedented opportunity to reach their fellow countrymen from the Atlantic to the Pacific. If Key 73, already endorsed by almost 150 American denominations and evangelical agencies, becomes merely an occasion for each participating group to do its own thing while others do theirs, it will make about as much permanent impact as a Fourth of July celebration. But if, across the nation, in block after block and precinct after precinct, believers of all races and stations come to know one another as God's concerned people, a powerful river of spiritual life could pour through our sick cities and weary land. A transcultural concentration of committed Christians, an interracial vanguard of the spiritually concerned, could become a tide of healing in our great cities, where schools and mass media are now vulnerably exposed to radical and destructive pressures that threaten to inundate the nation.

One hopes that an open Bible will be the central core from which the diverse groups will hear what the Spirit says to the churches. No evangelical movement today wholly enfleshes the Kingdom of God, and each needs to be brought from merely confirming its peculiar tenets to obediently serving the Lord of Glory. The charismatic movement today weaves through almost all strands of the religious spectrum; some devotees are oriented toward tongues-speaking, others toward healing, some toward simply a deeper work of the Spirit. Who would have dreamed, when the question was wrestled whether to invite Roman Catholic observers to the 1966 World Congress on Evangelism, that only half a decade later 50,000 Pentecostal Catholics in the United States would identify with apostolic rather than medieval loyalties? Today thousands of Catholics are meeting with their neighbors in interdenominational home Bible-study groups. Many resent not having been taught the Scriptures by their priests, at the same time these Catholics find little appeal in local Protestant churches where the Bible is also largely ignored. Throughout America, while the adult Sunday school suffers severe decline, more and more weeknight neighborhood groups are meeting for Bible study. This fact reflects, in part, dissatisfaction with theological compromise in much denominational church-school literature, and with preaching devoid of, or antagonistic to, scriptural authority. In present-day Jewry, a vanguard of Christians, including young intellectuals who insist in their synagogues that Jesus is the Christ, is restoring the Book of Acts to contemporary reading, and spurring the recent interest in New Testament charisma to an even deeper probing of New Testament Christology.[4]

A crisis in theological credibility darkens the Western world; multitudes are baffled over what, if anything, they should believe about God.

Carl F. H. Henry, "Footnotes: The Fortunes of Theology," *Christianity Today* 16, no. 20 (July 7, 1972): 21.

This theological credibility gap differs from the widely denounced political credibility gap. Government officials are often charged with withholding information or manipulating the news; religious academics, however, are not often accused of malevolent secrecy or deliberate dishonesty. Few theologians are given either to anonymity or deceit.

The complaint against neo-Protestant theologians, rather, is that they simply don't "tell it like it is." Their religious reports are inconsistent and contradictory, if not incoherent. And if theologians and clergy who claim to be divinely updated experts cannot agree among themselves, surely the public cannot much be blamed for having high doubts about the Deity and about those who claim to fraternize with him.

If modern theologians kept their supposed revelational insights to themselves, that would be another matter. Then the continual revision and replacement of their views would create little problem for the public. But as it is, theology is increasingly tagged as an enterprise of creative speculation; its queen-for-a-day tenets have less endurance than many frankly tentative scientific hypotheses.

Neo-Protestant theologians hesitate to admit that they are simply playing peek-a-boo with divinity. Two generations of modern religious theory nevertheless bear out the blunt verdict that their rumors about God have no more solid basis in objective disclosure than Clifford Irving's supposed conversations with the inaccessible and invisible Howard Hughes.

What makes the confusing theological reports—that the Deity is "in here" or "out there" or "up there" or "in depth" or "dead and gone"—a scandal is the fact that the Living God is truly accessible in his revelation. These neo-Protestant claims are intended to state the truth about God. But they so clearly contradict one another that if their proponents are not promulgating a literary hoax, they are at least profoundly mistaken. No claim is no more obviously fraudulent than that contemporary religionists convey the unadulterated truth about God. Their views cancel one another out.

Realizing this, a great many frustrated divinity students have taken a raincheck on theological commitments. For them to pursue a mod-theology for permanently valuable spiritual profit is about as rewarding, they feel, as for a squirrel to dig for nuts in Astroturf.

What neo-Protestant theologians as a class are saying about God is not only insufficient but inaccurate. At best, they proffer a mixture of truth, half-truth, and untruth—and no recent modern theologian has presented a solid criterion for distinguishing one from the other. The inevitable result is public distrust, even when these theologians happen to tell the truth about God. Their lack of theological concurrence has given rise to an adage: "When in doubt, speak as a theologian."

This widespread uneasiness over the pontifications of contemporary theologians has been nurtured not only by their ambiguity and abstruseness but also by their promotion of a pluralistic dialogue that often denies historic evangelical Christianity a voice. Champions of a quasi-official ecumenical position screen and manage the news about God. Ecumenical biblicism wears thin the seventeenth chapter of John's Gospel ("that they may be one") but leaves comparatively untouched Jahweh's message through Jeremiah: "You keep saying, 'This place is the temple of the LORD, the temple of the LORD, the temple of the LORD!' This catchword of yours is a lie. ... Do not run after other gods to your own ruin. ... You run after other gods whom you have not known; then you come and stand before me in this house, which hears my name, and say, 'We are safe'; safe, you think, to indulge in all these abominations" (Jer. 7:4 ff. NEB).

Among multitudes of Christians devoted to fulfilling the Great Commission, few complaints run deeper than that, in their unrivaled mass-media opportunities, ecumenists tend to obscure the singular truth of revealed religion and the good news of the Gospel. This dilution of historic Christian beliefs, whether in deference to modern theological alternatives or to socio-political activism, has nurtured widespread skepticism among the laity about the theological outlook of the institutional church. Ecumenical enthusiasm has been almost irreparably damaged among many laymen.

It is not that these laymen think the learned clergy are lacking in candor, or are given to fabrication and deception and to winning followers by pretense. Yet the ambivalence of many churchmen toward New Testament commitments has convinced numerous churchgoers that a cadre of contemporary religious leaders have acquired unwarranted influence, whereby they control religious information and, perhaps unintentionally, mislead the masses. Many lay leaders suspect that ecumenical bureaucrats have lost the sense of final truth.

The baffled multitudes have a right to know the truth about God. That truth is not nearly so inaccessible to the man in the street as theologians would have us believe. Nor is it dependent upon the ingenuity of modern-minded religious entrepreneurs. Any remarkably modern gospel is sure to be a false gospel. In earlier centuries, a powerful Catholic Church suppressed the Bible and shackled the people to the ecclesiastical hierarchy for their religious concepts. Neo-Protestant theologians suspend the Bible's special meaning for modern man on their own cryptic "Key to the Scriptures." In some places today Catholic leaders more energetically dispense the Scriptures (with the Apocrypha for excess measure) than do neo-Protestant radicals who are less sure of JHWH than JEPD.

Much of the new religious literature is greeted with such skepticism and suspicion that the religious book market is notably on the decline. The widespread loss of confidence and trust reflects a costly sacrifice of religious credibility. Now that God has been sensationally proclaimed to be dead, church members abreast of this information are not morbidly curious about the religious undertakers' progress reports on the supposedly disintegrating corpse.

Indeed, the theologians of modernity are no longer widely viewed as the best source of information about God. While many radical clergymen have inherited what theology they have, or have had, from these theological mentors, there is a growing feeling among the masses that, if special information about God is available, neo-Protestant theologians are not the dispensers of it.

Carl F. H. Henry, "Footnotes: The Fortunes of Theology," *Christianity Today* 16, no. 22 (August 11, 1972): 30–31.

Part III

EVANGELICALS AND EDUCATION

Chapter 17

CHRISTIAN RESPONSIBILITY IN EDUCATION

We should be roused from slumber by the specter of a society where every school may become an instrument of state policy, every classroom a center for inculcating a totalitarian creed, every lecture an occasion for delineating truth and goodness as personal prejudices instead of durable distinctions. The world still outside the communist orbit has cause to ponder the perils of education gone wholly secular and godless, and to consider afresh the influences which stand guard against irresponsibility in education.

Because of the indispensability of an enlightened public opinion in a democracy, the United States has special reason for vigilance in the sphere of education. Our republic has sought to insure an informed citizenry through the provision of public education for our youth. Today some observers insist that we had a better democracy before our national reliance on public education, and moreover, that we have had less freedom since. Be that as it may, the time has come to take a new look at American education, and to raise anew the question of Christian responsibility; indeed, to fail to do so would be a mark of our neglect.

Loss of Christian Ideals

Is there a way to bring together the concern for truth in private and public education without intruding a schismatic bias contrary to the American spirit but also without despising the Christian motifs whose dynamic once rescued the West from its pagan past and the loss of which is now sinking us into a pagan future?

In his treatment of *The Development of Modern Education*, Professor Frederick Eby sketches the rising "revolt against authority" that has "invalidated the imperatives of beauty, morality, and religion." In a chapter on "Educational Progress in the 20th Century," he reminds us: "Life has levelled off; art, intelligence, and spirit no longer aspire to the sublime. ... The very suggestion of the universal, conceptual, perfect, or the infinite induces a shudder of revulsion down the spine of the sophisticated" (*ibid.*, p. 679). Professor Eby writes not alone of the revolt against the past and against external authority; he writes as well of the increase of crime, of the exaltation of immorality, of the widespread cynicism of our times. And I cannot abstain from quoting: "Never have sex perversions; unscrupulous disregard of the evil effect of liquor, narcotics and tobacco upon children; divorce; rape; murder; political chicanery; debauchery; gambling; corrupt athletics; and contempt for law and order been so rampant and unblushing as they are today. The revolting sexual perversion extending from multiple divorce to criminal assault upon women and even little girls, frequently ending with the brutal murder of the victim; the increase in sexual relations of high school students; the heartless killings by youth of high IQ out of sheer moral idiocy; all such behavior testifies to the deterioration of public and private morality and sanity. ... One conclusion is certain: the strong claims of a century ago that a system of public schools would do away with crime now look absurd. ... Not only has public education failed to eliminate crime but it is in some measure responsible for the increase of these various evils. ... Down to the end of the last century, educational leaders were college graduates who had studied ethics and the Evidences of Christianity, and the teachers were the products of an education which respected law and reverenced moral principles and religious sanction. All this was changed at about the end of the century" (*ibid.*, p. 679 ff). So writes the Professor of History and Philosophy of Education at the University of Texas. And who need meditate long on the facts he relates without an awareness that it is timely indeed to raise the subject of Christian responsibility in education with new urgency?

A Christian Incentive

The rise of popular education in the West had a measure of Christian motivation. The urge to impart to every person a core of spiritually integrating information was lacking in the speculative philosophies of the Graeco-Roman world into which Christianity came. The ancient world not only lacked interest in universal education as such, but it lacked an evangelistic concern for the masses which might have stimulated and reinforced this. The ideal of mass education enlarged through the Middle Ages, through the Reformation, and through the Renaissance with its fresh concern for the course of this world.

Christian interest in general education and in the democratic process, however, looked beyond a secular exposition of man and society; it incorporated from the very first a concern for life on this planet fit also for the world to come. In the early American colonies, all education was Christian. When public schools emerged after the Revolution, the famed McGuffey readers preserved this sense of citizenship in two worlds. The Christian churches, moreover, likewise established higher education in America. Harvard was the first of a large number of colleges founded by the churches, with the special aim of an educated ministry. Two out of three of the colleges existing in the United States this very day were established by the churches.

The Tragic Decline

By the time of the first World War, the character of many of these colleges was only formally Christian. Until they were stabbed awake by the intellectual shock of the Second World War, they were not much interested in re-examining the Christian heritage. Harvard, bearing the Christian motto *Christo et Ecclesiae*, had gone Unitarian, and its Professor of Theology (J. A. C. F. Auer) was a humanist. Columbia, founded as King's College in colonial times by Anglicans who chose its motto from the Psalms—"In Thy light shall we see light"—became through John Dewey's influence at Teachers' College the fountain of pragmatic naturalism in American primary and secondary education. Chicago, established with Rockefeller funds as a Christian university with a Baptist divinity school, declined into an essentially humanistic and functional center for the so-called "Chicago School of Theology."

At the turn of the century, many universities still concealed their defection from Christianity by harboring idealistic philosophies of one sort or another. This idealistic speculation spurned the miraculous supernaturalism of the Bible, while at the same time over against naturalism it championed the reality of the supernatural world, the dignity of man, and the givenness of truth and morality. But idealism lost touch with the self-revealing God; it neglected the Law and the Prophets; it did not bow before the Incarnation, Atonement and Resurrection of Christ. It substituted for the word of Scripture the word of Hegel and Lotze and Royce and Bowne and Hocking and Flewelling. And, cut off from Christ and his redeeming work in the lives of men, it was important to halt the tidal waves of naturalism. John Dewey set the intellectual spirit of the new century by saying: "Faith in the divine authority in which western civilization confided, inherited ideas of the soul and its destiny, of fixed revelations ... have been made impossible for the cultivated mind of the western world." Although naturalism has not won the enthusiasm of the majority of the people in any nation, the enterprise of education in America, except for a few interdenominational colleges and a remnant of the church-related institutions, came to cast its weight against the theology and ethics of revealed religion.

Christianity Goes Underground

This became true in the public schools, through the infiltration of Dewey's educational philosophy; it became true in private colleges and universities, through their disregard of Christian philosophy; it was true in public-supported universities, which had difficulty in defining the place of religion in the curriculum because of the American emphasis on separation of church and state. In all these centers of academic influence, biblical Christianity became subterranean. In the centers of intellectual life, the Christian tradition was regarded, however politely, with disdain and despite.

Nowhere in this pattern of things did there arise another President Timothy Dwight who, a century and a half ago, mindful of the apostasy of the campus, entered the chapel at Yale with a sense of missionary urgency and planted the seed of faith anew in the hearts of the students.

The Definition of Deity

Today some educators are struggling against the secular surge that inundates all the spheres of learning. Yet even men of influence fail to sense that the rising tide of religiosity is no clear victory for the cause of pure religion, and that it may signify instead a resurgence of shallow superstitions in the realm of the spirit. There is pious talk of moral and spiritual values even by some educators who reject God and the supernatural; indeed, who do not even believe that any values are fixed and final. Men seem concerned to define a policy, while cautiously avoiding any definition of God.

A year ago, during extended high-level correspondence, educators began evolving a public school policy to emphasize that belief in God is inherent in American ideals and institutions. This, however, is a vague, cryptic and disappointing way of stating the facts. For the term God has now gained so many diverse definitions from American professors that the bare word is little more than a fetish.

Recently wide publicity was given the president of a university in the District of Columbia when he declared that no atheist would be approved on his teaching faculty. Asked what, specifically, was meant by an approved belief in God, the president replied: "I made no definition of 'final cause' or 'God' in my words." Thus latitude over the real identity of God gains academic respectability, while a bare belief in the existence of an undefined god presumably provides an acceptable frame for religion and virtue on the campus. In actuality, however, this nebulosity brings us to the threshold of cynicism. For an undefined god is merely a word, and no god at all. It is no mere touch of irony, but a turn of logic, that in their defection from the Logos modern men speak no longer of the Word, but simply of a word (and that an unintelligible word) when they worship. In a post-Christian society, this altar to an unknown god supplies the transition, if I may say so, to the worship of antichrist.

Values and the Living God

A genuine concern for religious values in the classroom dare not make the definition of deity a matter of indifference. Whatever comfort theological vagueness may supply to professional circles, the doubt of our demoralized decade is not likely to be dispelled by the introduction into the curriculum of an emphasis on belief in a god who may or may not be supernatural, who may or may not be personal and who may or may not be living.

Since the bare notion of "faith in god" does not specifically share the emphasis of the Declaration of Independence that a supernatural Creator endows and preserves all men with unalienable rights, I pleaded that in the teaching of moral and spiritual values in the public schools the supreme being at least be designated as the Living God. The reply was that any such qualification would be partisan and sectarian; that the doctrine of separation of church and state excludes any definition of God. I would not have thought that separation of church and state requires a platform of spiritual and ethical values indifferent to the question whether God is living or not. In fact, I rather think the founding fathers would have warned us that the loss of the Creator would sooner or later involve us—by the most rigorous logic—in the loss also of unalienable rights, and of enduring moral and spiritual values.

The Regeneration of Education

Sometimes I quite despair of our existing institutions—and in this touch of pessimism I am not alone—and wonder whether they retain any longer the spiritual courage and vision to reverse the present order of things. I do not say God has utterly cast them off, but I am unsure whether there remains any deep desire for the regeneration of education. I am not here to upbraid. And I am quite aware that even the Middle Ages produced no university fully permeated with the Christian ideal. I ask for no uncritical return to the past. But I rather fear the West has been too long adrift from its sacred moorings to cherish the prospect of a university in which an Augustine might hold the chair of philosophy; in which Calvin would teach philosophy of religion, and Zwingli comparative religions; with a Gladstone in law, a Handel in music, a Milton in literature, and a Kepler in astronomy. The virtual absence of Christians from our public faculties today almost inevitably raises the question whether contemporary education perhaps discriminates especially against them.

The Bible would not, indeed, be the only textbook in a program of education genuinely concerned with moral and spiritual values, but the students would feel the shock and sting of its sacred presuppositions. Is it not almost incredible, and yet at the same time quite natural from the standpoint of secular counterattack, that this Book from which our profoundest Western ideas and ideals are derived, and to which the dynamic for general education is itself somewhat indebted, should be increasingly banned from our public schools and bypassed by our colleges and universities? Does not history have a strange way of exacting retribution? The Bible is a bulwark of freedom; it sketches man's rights and duties, and it states facts about both true and false religion. Is it not a remarkable commentary on our century that, when they were exposed to reactionary pressures that opposed teaching the facts of Communism in the public schools, teachers who had suppressed teaching the facts of Christianity were driven to invoke the privilege of teaching the facts of naturalistic irreligion as an evidence of academic liberty?

Neglect of Higher Learning

The church, no less than the university, in our century has tended to restrict the relevance of Christian confession to religion. This limitation explains Protestantism's failure to establish a university in the large and thorough sense, which penetrates all the schools of advanced instruction from the Christo-centric point of view, thereby fitting men for the professions—medicine, law, teaching, science, as well as the ministry—with a full-orbed sense of divine vocation. We have great universities, some with an appended postgraduate school of religion, or with an appended divinity school, but we do not have a Christian university permeated by the vision of God. We have a remnant of Christian colleges, many of them weak and struggling, and a few for whom the title "university" is a misnomer. If we really face the larger problem of Christian responsibility in education we shall soon see that the effectiveness of the faith nurtured in our homes and churches, and by those Christian influences that now survive in education, is fragmented and, moreover, is constantly threatened and depressed from above. What fractional concepts and convictions survive the teaching of the lower schools remain unelevated, unsupplemented and unsupported at the higher level, and tend instead to become blurred. Advanced and professional instruction, therefore, instead of nourishing faith, impoverishes it, and the higher strategic grades of vocation are placed largely in the hands of an intelligentsia in revolt against the Christian heritage.

Christian believers in earlier centuries anticipated this danger with greater wisdom than evangelical forces today. They founded their universities first—Oxford and Cambridge, Harvard and Yale; the colleges and public schools were their offspring. The universities supplied the faculties which in turn influenced every village and hamlet of the nation. The plain fact is that if Christianity does not shape the university world, the university world will always frustrate the climaxing influences of Christian social ethics; if education at the top is hostile or indifferent to the Christian outlook, the expansion of Christian doctrine and life through all the gradations of society is hindered. This will be increasingly true in the coming generation when collegiate and university enrollment will be greatly multiplied.

Evasion of the Facts

Modern education is evasive about the facts of the history of religion. It not only shies away from spiritual decision, but it evades the teaching of the facts of religion and morality. Faith has everything to lose, doubt has everything to gain, by the suppression of those facts. Faith has everything to gain, doubt has everything to lose, by the impartation of those facts. I do not say that the public schoolroom should be used to enlist students in this or that church or denomination or religion; the wall of separation between church and state is too precious a heritage of democracy to see it thus endangered. But the students will come from our classrooms with one creed or another, or they have not been challenged much. And an American classroom that yields irreligious students, and ignores the facts of the Hebrew-Christian religion and its heritage, is neither the friend of democracy nor the foe of totalitarianism.

Our Christian Duty

What do we say then of Christian duty—of the responsibility of devoutly committed believers—in education? We must bear our witness in this as in all spheres of life and culture, even if the penetrations are but partial. We must remember that the vision for private colleges and universities has been predominantly spiritual and Christian. We must remember, too, that public education in this land does not belong to the secularists. And while the Living God doubtless chooses a remnant, he is not on that account the private property of some one church or denomination; he has a word for the public, and for public education as well. We do not deny the secularists their right to found and support secular schools, but we do challenge their right to capture the public schools of the nation for their partisan ends. The Harvard Report confessed that public education today has no unity, no goal. We must sound the alternative of a unified and purposive education in the school districts in which we pay taxes, for it is to the people, and not to the educators alone, that our public schools are answerable. We must not surrender our public schools needlessly to the spirit of the age. If we establish parochial schools, it will be as Protestants, not because public education free of ecclesiastical control is to be condemned, but because education with no concept of enduring truth and of fixed goals perverts our children; it cannot even vindicate the permanent validity of democracy. And we must train our youth for the professions, particularly for the teaching profession, whose sense of mission seems now on the wane. We do not covet for them an artificial confession of Jesus Christ that narrows the human intellect and the range of knowledge, for true faith is expansive and integrative of the whole of life. For life in this time of tyranny and trouble they require an education that not only plumbs the doubts, but emerges to a faith and resultant philosophy of life that focuses and sharpens the perspective of man and society on the eternal polestar of history—the Living God.

Carl F. H. Henry, "Christian Responsibility in Education," *Christianity Today* 1, no. 17 (May 27, 1957): 11–14.

Chapter 18

THE NEED FOR A CHRISTIAN UNIVERSITY

Ever since the post-apostolic age, the Christian revelation of God and of the world has won the attention of secular thinkers. Even scholars not captivated by its unique power to explain life and reality have recognized in biblical supernaturalism an option that must be openly met and debated. This confrontation has been made all the more necessary because exponents of Christianity have advanced the case for revelational theism within the framework of Western philosophy, and not simply in the tradition of sacred theology.

Moreover, the Christian movement has confidently sponsored schools at all levels of human interest and learning. The religion of the Bible became, in fact, the mother of general education; it boldly established universities and then also kindergartens and Sunday schools. Wherever men have delved into the nature of existence, there Christian thinkers have upheld the scriptural revelation of God as the one coherent explanation of the whole of experience.

But the Christian stake in higher learning has now come upon hard times. The disrepute of Christian perspectives in American public education is shown by the widespread disregard of the Christian world-life view in the classroom. True, people remain sympathetic to the churches, and school administrators and teachers still count church affiliation an asset. But in most public elementary and high schools, teachers seldom expound the governing ideas of the Judeo-Christian revelation and rarely offer the biblical view as a serious option for understanding either God or man. Assembly exercises and devotional programs once served to draw attention to the biblical view; now Supreme Court rulings have stifled even these remnants of revealed religion. So little continuity remains between school instruction and religious instruction that churches and synagogues have become filling stations for doing weekend emergency repair jobs on students whose shaky outlook depends increasingly on naturalistic supports.

At the university level, the assault on the scriptural understanding of life becomes more energetic and explicit. Religion departments are almost invariably slanted against the orthodox biblical heritage. Only a minority of philosophy departments include any competent champion of supernatural perspectives, and many are dominated by exponents of logical positivism or naturalism. Many of the professors who do claim to hold the Christian view misrepresent it in the anti-intellectual mood of liberalism, Barthianism, existentialism, and linguistic theology. Some united campus ministries now provide a platform for death-of-God theologians in order to attract attention to the claims of religion.

There are some significant exceptions. On many campuses one can find in various departments articulate professors who expound the Christian option alongside rival views and who objectively state the merits of the biblical position. In a few situations, they even provide the nucleus of a Christian college within the university.

However, it is virtually impossible for students to base their study programs on these offerings and, within the pluralistic framework of the campus, coordinate the various disciplines of liberal learning with an exposure to Christian views. On most campuses, moreover, the perceptive Christian faculty members are seldom found teaching subjects that especially shape the student mind. Often they are lonely men whose biblical convictions are assailed in university pulpits and by faculty colleagues who regard unitarianism and humanism as pristine expressions of Christianity and disparage evangelical theism as offbeat. What one Christian professor achieves through the objective presentation of scriptural views his colleagues often destroy through distortion and ridicule.

Larger opportunities for Christian influence come outside the classroom when professors identify themselves with evangelical student groups or give their witness within the inclusive context of ecumenical campus agencies. But the effectiveness of this evangelical leaven, even on campuses where a few outstanding professors lend their presence and influence to student causes, need not be a matter of speculation; statistics show that only a very few students are actually confronted by a Christian witness. Still more significant intellectually is the fact that evangelical students are denied the privilege of a comprehensive exposure to the Christian world-life view as it bears upon the disciplines of learning.

Never has a great Christian university been more needed. Our premise here is simply that such a university is necessary; we are not primarily concerned with its feasibility or possibility. It must be noted, however, that some educators who grant that it is feasible still doubt that it is desirable. Why? Their contention, briefly, is that the Christian task force should be completely engaged in penetrating the secular world of learning; to isolate evangelical scholars in a Christian university, they say, would virtually preclude an evangelical influence on secular higher education.

If this were the probable outcome, proposals for a Christian university should indeed be abandoned. But before conceding the point, we would do well to consider some facts.

Does Penetration Work?

Among my own academic acquaintances, a Christian university has been talked about for at least thirty years; almost ten years ago it was considered and debated in earnest. Now, for almost a decade the advocates of "penetration" have had the field to themselves. In a few places (the universities of Michigan and Iowa, for example) a small nucleus of able Christian scholars has emerged—and that is all to the good. But most campuses, even those that have added new courses in religion, still neglect the evangelical option.

Is this situation an effective alternative to a Christian university? Would it be so even if these gains of the past ten years were doubled in the next ten? Does the pluralistic state of higher education today really offer unlimited opportunities for Christian penetration—even if much more can be (and ought to be) achieved? And, if these opportunities do exist, would not a Christian university, whose graduates took doctoral degrees at prestigious state universities as well as at their alma mater, equip an admirable task force to have a greater effect upon secular learning? Is the ideal that motivated the founders of schools like Harvard, Yale, and Princeton outmoded today? Or has the miscarriage of their ideal created a new need for a university committed to goals these founders cherished?

We ought not to expect non-Christian scholars to show any great enthusiasm over proposals for a Christian university. Whatever significance these scholars assign to Christianity they find in the emotional or volitional aspects of man's experience, or in considerations of cultural heritage, rather than in its contemporary intellectual relevance. For them, biblical religion as a system of revealed thought has no durable or decisive bearing on academic learning.

To explain secular disinterest in the Christian view as a matter of hostility of biblical supernaturalism is too simple. Admittedly, a naturalistic bias pervades modern philosophy and permeates much of the campus; the humanities, social sciences, and physical sciences widely reflect this mood. Yet the academic community welcomes pious Christian scholars as faculty colleagues. Moreover, the university seldom attacks the church as a community agency but instead often commends it as a center for promoting humanitarian ideals, or as an emerging instrument of social revolution.

The secular university mind and the Christian mind no longer divide mainly over the problem of miracle, or even over the larger question of the reality of the supernatural. In part this is because of the readiness of influential members of the Christian community to compromise many cardinal tenets of the historic faith. Many university churches have shown a prolonged tolerance of humanism; teachers in church-related colleges have ranged themselves on various sides of most doctrinal issues; and some seminary administrators have brought naturalists into their faculties under the misleading label of "empirical theists."

Facing Fragmentation

Today a deeper cleavage divides non-Christian from historic Christian thought patterns. A generation ago, important surveys of leading American universities lamented the lack of moral and religious certainties on campus, and deplored the academic non-realization of the ideal of rationally integrated learning. Studies of the state of university learning, such as the Minnesota report and the Amherst and Columbia reports, readily admitted the need for a comprehensive correlation of the fragmented elements of classroom study. But today many secular scholars question the very possibility of a rationally consistent world-and-life view. They surrender in advance any hope of embracing man's knowledge of reality in a single explanatory whole. In fact, the very effort to present a rationale for life and being is often disparaged as an evidence of human pride.

Underlying this depreciation of the ultimate significance of reason are numerous forces that shape modern history and thought. Evolutionary naturalism, the theory that reason is a late evolutionary emergent rather than the constitutive principle of reality, has encouraged the view that life is "deeper" than logic and that experience is "profounder" than consciousness. Recent existentialist philosophy assails the effort to comprehend reality rationally. That man has no cognitive knowledge of the supernatural world, and that such knowledge is unattainable because of the nature of reality or of human experience (or both)—these are controlling tenets of the modern mind.

It is at this level that a Christian university—if it took seriously the ontological nature of reason, man as a creature uniquely lighted by the Logos, the reality of intelligible divine revelation, and the possibility of a logically consistent view of God and the world—would pose a direct threat to the orientation of modern learning. For most secular educators today believe that intellectual synthesis is an excessive goal inherited from the medieval universities, and that the price exacted by scholasticism to achieve it included an arid rationalism and an undue restriction of academic freedom. In higher education today, there is a widespread notion that academic liberty is preserved only when nothing is taken for granted and everything is subject to doubt; as a result, any affirmation of finalities—let alone the quest for intellectual synthesis—seems highly presumptuous.

Regrettably, the church-related or so-called Christian college today often tends to reinforce these objections. Roman Catholic colleges and universities are usually regarded as defender-of-the-faith institutions. (And it must be admitted that they have succeeded better than Protestant colleges in avoiding secularization.) But because of a polemic and defensive classroom spirit, Protestant institutions that have maintained their theological heritage seldom fulfill the alternative image they covet: that of faith-affirming institutions. When able professors leave some of the larger evangelical schools for secular universities, often at little salary increase, many of them are protesting against an intellectually restrictive climate. Proposals for a Christian university therefore raise the specter of medieval scholasticism, with its rationalistic pretensions on the one hand and its restrictions on human inquiry on the other.

It is not easy to show the difference between the spirit of a nonexistent Christian university and the impressions of evangelical education that secular observers get from some church-related colleges and universities (often those least respectable academically). The failure of established evangelical colleges to penetrate the secular milieu raises the moot question whether a Christian university would not follow the same pattern of cultural isolation or withdrawal. Some of our evangelical colleges, even with a century of history behind them and faculty members now numbering in the hundreds, have produced almost no textbooks that find a place in the mainstream of secular education. For that matter, they have not produced a comprehensive apologetic statement of the Christian view of God and the world for the evangelical constituency. In the main, they have provided a sanctuary from secular ideas and ideals rather than confronting and disputing the tide of contemporary unbelief or giving modern man an explanation of his predicament based on biblical premises.

If a Christian university simply perpetuated this pattern on a grand scale, it would compound the element of tragedy in evangelical higher education. Such a university can be justified only if it will train young intellectuals to introduce Christian ideas and ideals into all areas of dialogue, reflection, and work.

In from the Periphery

Perhaps the most significant note in current discussions of advanced Christian education is the acknowledgment (implicit in the many proposals of alternatives to a Christian university) of the urgent need that something new be done to show the relevance of Judeo-Christian truth to the pressing problems of modern thought and life. The Christian colleges are filling an important role in preventing an easy surrender by evangelical youth to the reigning tenets of modernity. And some faculty members in the secular universities effectively present Christian perspectives in academic dialogue. But they are an inconspicuous minority. Evangelical effort persists mainly on the periphery of instruction and does not hold a place as a competitor in the pluralistic situation. University instruction is largely oriented to non-Christian, if not anti-Christian, theory; this fact has created interest in the possibility of a Christian college within a federated campus complex, or, at least, of a group of Christian faculty members within a larger pluralistic context. These proposals hold an advantage over the more modest suggestion of establishing evangelical houses similar to those now functioning in Oxford and Cambridge, each directed by a competent scholar in residence: the advantage is that they make Christian perspectives an integral part of serious academic discussion within a university. It is questionable whether, in a pluralistic situation, a small body of Christian professors can achieve, either for themselves or for their students, the ideal of unified liberal learning in the light of the Judeo-Christian revelation.

Yet neither the proposal for a Christian faculty group nor that for evangelical houses ought to be dismissed summarily because of apparent limitations. Evangelicals must learn not to expect all ends from any one means. They have much to gain from investigating a variety of possibilities and putting into operation the pilot projects that show promise. Even the offering of a master's degree, and possibly of a doctorate, by every accredited evangelical liberal arts college in the one academic area in which it can best serve the Christian constituency, is overdue. It would be a great gain if one school were to specialize in advanced graduate offerings in philosophy, another in political science, another in music and the arts, another in journalism, and so on.

But these possibilities ought not to be confused with the matter of a Christian university. Such an institution would give Christian scholars at the graduate level a chance to expound all the insights of liberal arts learning in relation to the truth of revelation; this task is not adequately performed by any existing evangelical college or university on either the graduate or the undergraduate level. The proposal of a national Christian university composed of cooperating regionally accredited evangelical liberal arts colleges has the merit of endorsing the need of a Christian university in principle, and of recognizing that no comparable education is now available. But although the ideas of leased lines, coaxial cables, shared library resources, and some mobile faculty personnel should all be creatively explored in an effort to improve existing institutions, the correlation of graduate offerings on half a dozen campuses cannot produce the equivalent of a Christian university. This proposal to pool disparate resources raises some difficult questions: How effectively can a university function without a campus of its own? How can professors who have never instructed students for the doctorate suddenly become eligible to do so? How can libraries that are inadequate for doctoral studies become adequate by an expansion of undergraduate holdings or of minimal graduate holdings? Which institution will offer the degree under state charter and will thus inherit alumni loyalties?

Only with a Christian university can we now hope to fill the need. In a century that esteems education, unshaken by the fact that its terrible world wars were unleashed by two of the most literate modern nations, a Christian university can set an example of human energy in the service of the true, the good, and the beautiful—in short, of man intelligently devoted to God and his revealed will.

A Christian university would pursue scientific interests, adding to man's curiosity and desire to control nature the further motivations of glorifying God and advancing human well-being. It would study history, not simply for a knowledge of events, but in quest of the revelation of God in history. It would revive the forsaken study of metaphysics, and it would bring theology to bear on all the disciplines of learning. It would be devoted to the whole truth—nothing less. It would offer the academic world a fresh and authentic statement of the Christian option. It would relate all the assured results of learning—both the wisdom of the ages and the discoveries of our own time—to the Christian revelation, and exhibit as a coherent whole the body of truth we possess. It would train scholars and teachers for service in Christian and secular institutions and for a role of intellectual leadership in all areas of work. It would give substance to an apologetic literature for our generation.

Never has the evangelical community had a better opportunity to present a rationally persuasive case for the religion of the Bible. The secular stream of speculation has emptied into the mudbanks of intellectual confusion; the mediating religious options have run the course of anti-intellectualism and are lacking in intellectual power to persuade. This can be a new day for evangelical theism if we merge the fullest and highest resources in the service of truth.

What the Choice Implies

In deciding for or against a Christian university, we do not decide merely whether or not modern learning will concern itself with the whole truth, including the Judeo-Christian revelation. The issue is deeper.

The alternatives are either the permanent loss or the hopeful recovery of intellectually integrated learning. The loss of a unifying frame in liberal arts studies is now acknowledged not only on secular campuses but in many church-related colleges as well. The primary issue, therefore, is whether liberal learning will be permanently abandoned to its present chaotic plight, or whether the Christian rationale will be openly and convincingly asserted in the academic arena.

It is no exaggeration to say that today the case for the ontological significance of reason—the confidence that reality is rationally intelligible—survives among Protestants almost exclusively as an evangelical option. Modernist, dialectical, and existential movements in modern theology have progressively retarded the role of reason in religious experience and have abandoned interest in a Christian view that gathers into one explanatory whole all aspects of human knowledge and experience. Loss of the biblical principle of intelligible divine revelation, based on the creation of the universe by the Logos and of man in the divine image, has immersed theological studies in subjectivism and deprived liberal learning of direct confrontation by the Christian world-life view.

Those who share the vision of a Christian university do not insist that, like Melchizedek, it must appear on the scene of history all at once without apparent parentage. An Institute for Advanced Christian Studies, justifiable on its own merits, could be an ideal intermediate venture. If such an institute were to succeed, it might well open the way for a Christian university; if it were to fail, the case for a Christian university would probably collapse with it.

Carl F. H. Henry, "The Need for a Christian University," *Christianity Today* 11, no. 10 (February 17, 1967): 5–8.

Chapter 19

THE RATIONALE FOR THE CHRISTIAN COLLEGE

The deepest problems of secular liberal-arts education today stem from the theory that truth and values are relative, a fallout of this generation's commitment to evolutionary perspectives. The loss of authoritative norms explains, in part, the strident student shift from reason and persuasion to mob pressure and compulsion. An evolutionary perspective provides no basis for universal and enduring human rights or responsibilities, nor can it fix normative limits of escalation or de-escalation of protest and disruption. It cannot, in fact, supply any fixed norms of ethics whatever, or any unchanging truths.

Amid lost confidence in liberal learning on secular campuses, evangelical students have—and yet neglect—a tremendous opportunity to counter radical assaults on liberal education by their own kind of demonstrations. To face the reality of the supernatural, the objectivity of truth and values, and the moral and spiritual significance of Jesus of Nazareth is crucial to any honest system of education and culture. Yet few issues are more evaded, and more arbitrarily prejudged, than these.

Nowhere, apparently, has a vanguard of evangelical students raised the pivotal questions bypassed in most modern classrooms, by pinpointing the failure of secular faculties to wrestle with the ever critical problems of the history of thought that are decisive for human dignity and the role of reason in society. *Who is God if he is? What is moral?—and so what? Is any truth final? Is Christ just a "four-letter word"?* These are great issues that believing collegians should be demonstrating for. However much some of us might cringe at placards and banners, they are an in-thing that bespeaks the importance of symbols in a mass-media age, and they can be appropriated to bring visibility to the really important questions of life.

Why do evangelical students by and large take less initiative for the triumph of truth than for the triumph of grace? Our evangelical colleges champion the Christocentric view of life. But they often fail to dissect the life-situations and thought-struggles that inundate most people today. Amid basic efforts to preserve and herald the truth of the Gospel, they forgo a direct confrontation over the truth of truth and the meaning of meaning. Too easily evangelical dialogue bounces within personal and pietistic dimensions when, in fact, it ought to grapple with the very survival of civilization.

The image that evangelical colleges present to the world must embrace truth, justice, and grace as concerns indispensable to Christian education. We are debtors not simply to the evangelical community but to the whole modern world in which we live. Evangelical schools bear this global duty in respect to truth no less than evangelical missions bear a world-wide task in respect to grace.

Over half the world population is sealed against overt evangelical proclamation. But the other half is locked up far more than we realize to American evangelical resources for its impressions of the credibility of Christianity. As never before our global burden in these harried years is one of intellectually responsible formulation and communication of the truth. Classrooms where teachers and students use reason to face the agenda of the world, grapple with ideas in the context of the truth of revelation, and apply the test of coherence to every truth-claim are the launch-pads of this witness. Valid ideas presented precisely and attractively through every available means can and must be the stock-in-trade of evangelical education.

The mission of the evangelical college is nothing less than to make known *the whole truth for the whole man for new life in a new world.* Only a comprehensive perspective like this can undermine the presumptive definitions of human nature and destiny posed by utopian ideologies, speculative rationalisms, and self-fulfillment theories, and can illumine the vision of the ideal man and society by the truth of revelation. This banner maintains, moreover, the indispensable and indissoluble bond linking truth, justice, and grace, and by claiming this present world for God's spiritual purpose in creation, reopens man's soul to the eternal transcendent world.

Unveiling the reality of the supernatural and expounding the special method whereby God and his ways are to be known demand an intellectual precision that draws the world of unbelief and doubt inescapably into the crossfire of ideas. For this engagement Bible departments must be keen and exciting, philosophy classes powerful and relevant. Campus achievements exhibited to donors and alumni must involve victories of Christian thought and truth more than physical expansion, athletic prowess, even evangelistic endeavor.

To say, as some do, that the distinctive contribution of Christianity to the world of learning and life is one of perspective, is not enough. To be sure, the Christian view of God and the cosmos and man does involve a unique perspective on the whole of reality. But so, for that matter, does Buddhism, or any other *ism* one cares to mention. The unique contribution of biblical religion is the truth of revelation and its implications for human redemption and destiny.

Only if—as we believe—revelational truth is of one and the same order as all other truth, or, as Christians also contend, if the validity of any and all truth depends ultimately on the truth of God and his revelation, have we a platform for integrated learning in the context of Judeo-Christian revelation. Christian education that overstresses the uniqueness of the Christian perspective without attending seriously also to the final truth of the Christian revelation faces rough going in the seething world of thought. Nor is it enough simply to affirm the validity of the Christian revelation; nothing less than lucid marshalling of intellectual evidence will make plain why evangelicals are convinced that they have meshed mind with the eternal world.

If, on the other hand, the truth of revelation is truth of a different order, truth whose validity and authority rest simply on subjective preference or internal decision, then we ought to conserve our time and energy and explore the possibilities of merger with Zen Buddhism.

The world we seek to confront is precommitted to evolution as the ultimate explanatory principle, and the limitation of knowledge to the horizons of human history. Unless we grapple with these prejudices, what seem to us to be bold and brave claims for faith will appear to others as tender-minded credulity. It will not do, therefore, to portray the evangelical campus to the world simply as an institution that believes in the inerrancy of the Bible. To be sure, the Word of God cannot be broken, and the authority and plenary inspiration of Scripture is a foundational affirmation. But our day of intellectual relativism and moral nothingness (even amid notable social concern) requires more than formulas that are mainly intended to reassure apprehensive evangelical donors.

In a 1965 statement, spokesmen for faith-affirming colleges concurred that "the over-all purpose of the evangelical college, as a distinct type of institution, is to present the whole truth, with a view to the rational integration of learning in the context of the 'Judeo-Christian' revelation, and to promote the realization of Christian values in student character."

Only if evangelical learning highlights and vindicates the pre-suppositions of this umbrella-statement will this comprehensive purpose become significant. For the contemporary mind neither concedes nor comprehends that knowledge is a unitary whole; that integration is ideally rational; that divine revelation supplies the ideal context for integration; that "Judeo-Christian" revelation is incomparably unique; that academic learning has inescapable implications for a student's moral outlook and behavior. Because the academic mood on many campuses is implicitly if not overtly naturalistic and relativistic, demonstrating the viability of evangelical alternatives requires an earnest wrestling with undergirding convictions. As the 1965 statement put it, our faith-affirming colleges are called to exhibit "the rational integration of the major fields of learning in the context of the 'Judeo-Christian' revelation." Without a fulfillment of this intellectual priority, non-theistic views, however weak, will remain pervasively influential, while Christian theism, however superior, remains notably unimpressive.

If we take seriously the biblical correlation of learning and values, knowledge and piety, then our schools will strive to graduate men and women who not only know the truth of revelation

but also live the real life. We are not in the business of produc-
ing *Übermenschen* or philosopher-kings, but students for whom
Jesus Christ is Logos and Light and Life. No one in the moral
history of the West has been more unjustifiably reduced to a foot-
note in modern texts on ethics than Jesus of Nazareth; in an age
suffocating with moral pollution, evangelical colleges have the
opportunity to rectify this injustice in word and deed.

Christian education needs to recapture the ethical excitement of this dimension of Christian learning and witness. Forged
mainly in terms of negations, as often happens, Christian ethical
concern soon loses its critically important role of illuminating
the line between morality and immorality in terms of the truth
of revelation and scriptural principles of conduct. To say this is
not to decry campus rules, nor to imply that the alcohol traffic,
the tobacco industry, and the cinema no longer pose any moral
issues. Indeed, it is ironical that some evangelical schools relaxed
rules on movie attendance precisely at a time when X-rated films
began to deluge the theaters; and on smoking just when medical research convinced even government agencies to discourage
the cigarette habit. Evangelical colleges could become a moral
force in our drifting society by training disciplined, dedicated
young people who are able to discuss intelligently the issues of
our time—from abortion to vivisection and voodoo and Zen. If
recent American politics has failed to inspire youth to anything
higher than opting out of the system and its commitments, then
evangelical education has the special opportunity of integrating the issues of truth, righteousness, and justice in a claim from
which no human being can drop out and still remain human.

We should note, moreover, that in expounding "the whole
truth, with a view to rational integration ... in the context of
'Judeo-Christian revelation,'" the faith-affirming colleges in the
1965 declaration consider the Bible to be "an integrating force"

and "not merely ... an additive." The Christian Apostle to the Gentiles set even the atoning sacrifice and bodily resurrection of the crucified Jesus in this scriptural context; fundamentally important to the Christian message, he avers, is "that Christ died for our sins according to the scriptures, and that he was buried, and that he was raised the third day according to the scriptures ..." (1 Cor. 15:3, 4).

This rationale for human life and destiny seems as alien to the modern mind as it did to the Athenians when Paul first proclaimed it. The most conspicuous difference between the first and the twentieth centuries is not that the Christian rationale as such now seems foreign. It is, rather, that for modern man, every speculative alternative has lost credibility. Another difference is that much of the Christian task force today, despite its impressive endowments and properties and libraries, its salaried personnel and small army of young followers, lacks the boldness of apostolic times to put the world on the defensive.

While Christian education centers in the manifestation of God in Christ, evangelical colleges have always sensed the need for a more explicit and articulate delineation of basic beliefs. The theological ambiguity of modern ecumenism has, in fact, unwittingly created fresh respect for succinctly stated positions; open-ended pluralistic ruminations on Christian identity are falling out of fashion if not out of favor. Once again, in a day when ecumenical institutions are more concerned with structure than with truth, the great ecumenical creeds—particularly the Apostles' and Nicene—provide a basis for stressing central articles of Christian faith. In view of its criterion of the Scriptures as the divine rule of faith and practice, a tenet reaffirmed by the Protestant Reformation, evangelical education holds the ecumenical creeds of Christendom to be proximate normative expressions of the historic Christian faith.

Totalitarianism or even tax-supported education is hampered by the interests or antagonisms of ruling forces; evangelical education, on the other hand, thrives where and because open competition prevails in the world of ideas, and can best serve where it fulfills its specific mission with competence. In a non-evangelical college, a student may easily accumulate a kaleidoscopic confusion of views gleaned from left-of-center liberals, conservatives, naturalistic philosophers, relativistic anthropologists, and Marxist economists, with one or two demonstrative burn-the-building-and-destroy-the-system activists thrown in for good measure. In such a time as this, it will be scant credit to evangelical education, however, merely to be able to label itself as unlike other education. As far back as 1945 the Harvard Report on *General Education in a Free Society* saw no possibility of a return to theistically oriented education. How much more today, then, do faith-affirming colleges have the unique responsibility of propelling a systematic theistic view into a naturalistic climate, and of delineating the unified view of life required by revelational theism.

Carl F. H. Henry, "The Rationale for the Christian College," *Christianity Today* 15, no. 17 (May 21, 1971): 7–10.

Chapter 20

DEATH OF A MODERN GOD

That American college education is in serious crisis, particularly in the liberal arts and sciences, is apparent. Far-reaching social and cultural changes sweeping our campuses are leaving behind a strange flotsam and jetsam for us to sort out.

Academic strongholds, presumably exalting rational criteria, have erupted into places of rioting and demonstration, moral deviation and permissiveness, drug addiction and youth rebellion. Once the intellectually critical fortresses of American life, colleges and universities are instead being shaken and remolded by pressures with which they may be unable to cope. As the price of staying in business, not a few college administrations have compromised the role of reason and persuasion by placating minority groups, radicals, and reactionaries.

American education as a whole is headed for far-reaching changes in the very near future. Almost all traditional notions about education are likely to be questioned by creatively critical educators. To what extent should parents determine the educational policies and procedures affecting their children? Can education be achieved, and perhaps more effectively, by alternatives to the liberal-arts college or university? Is the bachelor's degree—or any four-year program, for that matter—sacrosanct? Should new patterns of post-high-school education be projected that automatically pour every student into collegiate work? Are mass-media teaching techniques adequate substitutes for the classroom?

Questions like these may not be the fundamental ones in education, but they point to pragmatic matters that must be faced. Evangelicals, too, must face them, for Christian education can escape neither the impact nor the competition of such concerns. Indeed, a virile educational task force would take some initiative in projecting creative alternatives.

Public criticism now often leveled at the secular campus concerns the content and consequences of liberal learning more than its means and methods. Relativistic attitudes toward truth and morality, disrespect for inherited values, ready tolerance of radicalism, blatant atheism, and neglect of reflective exposition and appraisal—these are matters of mounting complaint.

But on-campus discontents strike even to deeper levels. Why have advanced liberal learning at all? we are asked. Some students contend that campuses ought to be platforms for aggressive political activity and social change, rather than towers of rational contemplation. But others ask whether—in view of its ambiguous rationale, intellectual open-endedness and lack of cohesion—a college education is any longer worth $12,000 and four years of time and energy. Why not simply accumulate this world's goods and preferred vocational status, since many business firms now devalue a college degree? Still other students welcome educational happenings that take a novel form, such as the free university. Some think that science's destructive uses—whether in war or pollution—and its massive technological depersonalization require opting out of the whole cultural enterprise.

A great and influential god is dying. On its breastplate are etched the words LIBERAL LEARNING. Its final blasphemy is its verdict that the God of the Bible is dead. The fatal cancer of liberal learning is its assumption that empirical methodology validates the only truth and reality on which man can bank his life. The more this sensate methodology is scientifically refined, the more it demeans theological and moral assertions to the level of personal preferences and excludes intelligent decision, purposive acts, and personal selves from the real world. Man no less than his Maker is reduced to insignificance. When modern philosophy sponsored "Does it work?" (or "Is it profitable?") in place of "Is it true?" as the prime question, it addressed to the world of reality its theory of knowledge that made mastering the cosmos more crucial than preserving man's soul in this life and the next.

Colleges and universities in America are in line to experience the public disfavor that has already engulfed the institutional church. Just as multitudes of disenchanted churchgoers are canceling financial support and dissociating themselves from ecclesiasticism gone fuzzily ecumenical and doctrinally nebulous, so educational institutions may plummet into disfavor among alumni who have long championed liberal education but who are now perturbed by administrative policies of schools they endow and the open rebellion of students they shelter. Some alumni will turn their educational sympathies to new educational forms and structures.

Many church-related colleges are caught in the compromises of both institutional church and secular education, and may be doubly vulnerable to alumni pressures. Financial cutbacks are already heavy.

With the rise in enrollment expected in government-subsidized institutions, evangelical colleges are likely to influence a smaller and smaller segment of the student world. In many cases they will face a strenuous fight for survival. As colleges strive to keep abreast of the times, expanding computerization, the need for increasingly sophisticated, scientific equipment, and incorporation of bigger and better communications techniques will continue to push competitive education to the hilt and often to the wall.

Carl F. H. Henry, "Footnotes: Death of a Modern God," *Christianity Today* 16, no. 3 (November 5, 1971): 36–37.

Chapter 21

COMMITTING SEMINARIES TO THE WORD

This paper was given at a symposium on "Theological Education: Freedom and Commitment" that was held at Concordia Seminary, St. Louis, Missouri, in October 1975.

Evangelical seminaries and colleges generally require their teachers to subscribe to a rather fulsome doctrinal statement. When these institutions are seeking or being reexamined for accreditation, such statements have almost routinely been challenged as possibly restrictive of academic freedom. I have served as professor or visiting professor on half a dozen evangelical campuses and have noted that accreditation inspection teams seldom fail to ask how, in view of such commitments, academic liberty can be preserved.

I well recall the founding of Fuller Theological Seminary. First we were told that no application from the school could be considered until after it had graduated its first class of seniors. Then, in the year following the first commencement ceremonies, Dr. Daniel Williams of Union Theological Seminary, New

York, paid a preliminary visit. In a meeting with faculty he asked how Fuller's official doctrinal commitments could be maintained alongside a regard for professorial freedom. Dr. Edward Carnell asked in turn whether Union Seminary would add to its faculty a professor who did not subscribe at least to some beliefs, say belief that there is a God. Williams conceded that belief in God would probably be an indispensable minimum. Carnell then remarked that the difference lay not in whether any beliefs were required but in *which* beliefs were required.

I should explain that this conversation occurred at mid-century. More recently, some nonevangelical seminaries seemed to consider the presence of a death-of-God spokesman in their faculty a doctrinal imperative. Others seemed to feel it was imperative not to have any full-time evangelical professor. It is tempting to consider others broadminded only if they are broadminded in the way in which I am broadminded.

Yet we cannot escape the imperative of ongoing intellectual appraisal of our own heritage as well as of rival views and recent innovations. To be sure, gazing at one's own navel is not an advisable classroom preoccupation. But simply taking for granted that one's vital positions are properly covered may lead to embarrassing public exposure and charges of nudity. Academic integrity is served neither by censorship of foreign views nor by an authoritarian inculcation of one's own ideology.

The temptation merely to indoctrinate is not confined to any one school of thought. The fiercest ideology in our times, Communism, does not dispute revelational theism on its own merits. Rather, it has made atheism the advance ideological commitment of national governments and university campuses alike.

Let me speak for a few moments as an evangelical journalist rather than as a professional theologian. In my experience, evangelical campuses—though they reflect the theological commitment of a majority of American churchgoers—on the whole do a fairer job than non-evangelical campuses in examining and presenting the views of opposing scholars, and in giving them personal representation. At Union Seminary's commemorative convocation for Karl Barth, Geoffrey Bromiley, who translated Barth's *Church Dogmatics*, was not even invited, let alone given a place on the program. Only last year a Nashville seminary that professes to represent all points of view in the classroom rejected a request by some of its ablest students that one course be offered based on the writings of twentieth-century evangelicals like Machen, Carnell, Clark, Ladd, Ramm, Schaeffer, and Van Til.

Some years ago, Gerald Beavan was working for a master's degree in religion on a Texas campus where the only significant classroom reference to evangelical Christianity he can recall was a professor's passing remark that "the only scholar the fundamentalists have ever had was Machen." Beavan therefore thought it strange that not even Machen was on any of his reading lists, and from the library he signed out *The Origin of Paul's Religion*. Reading it he had a conversion experience. Later he became the ablest promotion specialist that evangelist Billy Graham has ever had (after the Harringay crusade, the Advertising Council of Great Britain gave him—the first time ever to an American—its award of the year). Unofficial censorship of competing views breeds in the present student generation a reaction that outwits a narrowly protective mental custody.

The special protection of theological perspectives is not confined to any one tradition. I took a master's degree in 1940 in Illinois where Karl Barth then got about the same silent treatment as Gresham Machen in Texas.

Let me pay special tribute to the most genuinely liberal scholar under whom I have studied, Edgar Sheffield Brightman.

Brightman championed a finite god and repudiated miraculous theism. After I completed doctoral work in philosophy, we were walking together to the commencement exercises when he said in effect: "It always pleases a professor when his ablest students hold his own views. You don't share my philosophy, but you have done good work. I know how easy it is simply to parrot a professor's views, especially on the way to a degree, and you haven't done that. It's been a pleasure to have had you as one of my students." My dissertation, *The Influence of Personal Idealism on the Theology of A. H. Strong*, was a criticism of the baneful effect on evangelical theology of a philosophy like Brightman's (that of his predecessor, Bordon P. Bowne). Brightman went the added mile; when the dissertation was published, he wrote a commendatory foreword.

An academic institution that offers publicly recognized degrees should not penalize students for not subscribing to views of the faculty. The student should be expected only to master the course requirements, faithfully reproduce this content, give reasons for accepting or rejecting debatable positions, and demonstrate the ability to use his scholarly tools creatively.

I well recall the days at Northern Baptist Seminary when nonevangelical students began to attend my classes in theology. When some of them finished graduate degree work, we as an evangelically conservative faculty decided that we were not ordaining candidates to the ministry nor putting an *imprimatur* on the views of graduates but were certifying only that they had fulfilled certain academic requirements.

A great deal of attention is now being given to the subject of manipulation. While the discussion focuses upon the use of drugs, electrodes, and hypnosis for mind control, it has widened to include the education of children.

Advocates of self-sovereignty think it is deplorable for parents to impose a value-system and religious beliefs on their children. The charge of manipulation in the home is readily extended to manipulation in the schools. Educational instruction is increasingly scrutinized as an arena of compulsion in which teachers exercise subtle forms of mind and behavior control.

The issue at stake is not presuppositional versus non-presuppositional learning. No learning takes place in a presuppositional vacuum; the speaker who disavows a doctrinal stance merely masks his assumptions. But if students are given a censored or heavily biased view, or if certain positions are reduced to inarticulate manikins, a form of classroom manipulation occurs because the student is not involved at the level of dialogue that his or her intellectual maturity deserves. An academic setting becomes in these circumstances a theater for skillful mind-control. The question that an instructor needs continually to ask is, Would I want my convictions treated as I treat those of others?

The Bible exhorts us: "Train up a child in the way that he should go, and when he is old he will not depart from it" (Prov. 22:6). Need such training be considered manipulation? If training involves no appeal to self-responsibility and self-formation, it is dehumanizing in that it arbitrarily imposes beliefs and conduct, refuses discussion of the *why*, and regards the teacher as beyond all answerability to the learner.

If faculty colleagues are to remain colleagues, the bond that holds them together must be more than mutually held salary contracts and a mutually felt burden to impart individual beliefs. Ideally a theological faculty has a spiritual bond. But it would be futile to argue that such a bond is most secure where no doctrinal consensus exists. I know scholars of high excellence serving on ecumenically pluralistic campuses who have confided that they are among the loneliest of men. I also know evangelical campuses where personality differences and rivalries place faculty members at a distance despite common doctrinal loyalties.

A theological institute owes its faculty, students, supportive constituency, and the larger Christian Church an articulate statement of the principles on which it stands. No school can be a distinctive institution without some shared beliefs. Its principles should be in clear view, and should be renewed periodically. An institution committed to nothing articulate is not only intellectually unstable but also vulnerable to forfeiting whatever it considers valuable at any given time.

To many secular scholars today, any and every claim to final truth seems specious. Since the secular campus knows only opinion and not final knowledge, any community that salutes fixed beliefs appears to be restricting liberal learning. To such scholars it makes little sense if we emphasize that great philosophers and early scientists were devout Christians; to be a Christian, as they see it, is not to take seriously either science or philosophy. A faculty generation and a student generation filled with doubts about everything in the name of academic earnestness tend to be "ever learning, and never able to come to the knowledge of the truth" (2 Tim. 3:7). Neither the classic Greek philosophers nor the great Christian theologians, however, saw in relativism a commitment that poses a threat to enduring truth. What relativism threatens most of all is true freedom and any claim whatever that the relativist himself would care to make about truth or anything else.

Yet doctrinal commitment can be less than intellectually honest if it is blind commitment. The assumption regarding a seminary faculty is, of course, that invited scholars have wrestled the issues for themselves before uniting with that faculty. One lamentable feature of theological education today is that some prospective faculty members assert their intellectual concurrence when seeking a position but, after receiving tenure, disavow those commitments. The practice extends the readiness of some ministerial candidates to be ordained in accord with historic church standards and then to defect from those standards in the pulpit. I know of at least two instances in which scholars gave unqualified assurance to the president and then to faculty colleagues only to reverse those assurances after they became securely entrenched. Academic tenure than is invoked to protect theological vacillation, and administrative protest is deplored as a compromise of academic freedom. Similarly, the Church is frequently accused before the world and through the secular press of intellectual sterility if it insists that its ordained clergy be faithful to their vows.

It is always possible that a scholar may develop sincere doubts about institutional commitments after uniting with a faculty. Such doubts should not be simply deplored; they should be taken seriously by colleagues who profess to be leaders in an academic community. The issues can be discussed and debated objectively in special faculty meetings without placing the scholar in jeopardy. Serious theological discussion is regrettably at a premium, even on many conservative campuses; I was associated with one seminary for five years during which the faculty on no occasion gathered to hear and discuss a theological presentation by one of its members. The extensiveness of an institution's theological statement ought to coincide with a faculty willingness to evaluate it critically no less than to be critically governed by it.

A faculty member who has doubts about institutional commitments is either right or wrong. If he is wrong, or colleagues are convinced that he is, he should withdraw from the institution, unless his colleagues and those responsible for the institution are persuaded that the issue is no longer as important to the institution as its founders thought. In that event all faculty members should consider themselves free concerning this commitment, and the constituency should be told.

It is highly important that students not simply parrot an inherited tradition but rather win the Christian heritage for themselves. Objections to the great doctrines of the faith must be earnestly wrestled in theological college and seminary, and not merely glossed over. The very existence of God, the fact and nature of divine revelation, the precise significance of Jesus Christ, the unity and triunity of God, indeed the whole gamut of religious beliefs, is to be fully debated. A commitment based on unexamined assumptions is always weak in the next generation.

Yet not every professor has a chair whose duties center in challenging all Christian positions. The prime responsibility of the faculty is to clarify Christian claims and consistently set forth their implications. A faculty that is dominated by critical professors and that fails to communicate the content of the Christian heritage fails to fulfill the mission of theological education. Criticism has its rights, but so does the criticism of criticism; on balance, the latter has been more widely neglected in modern theology than the former. In my student days one divinity school in the Midwest was notorious for its circuitous handling of the Bible. Professors would indicate that their courses were not the ones in which the content of the Bible was taught; that would be gotten elsewhere in the curriculum. But graduates complained that they never found the course in which the content of Scripture was actually taught. Patrick Henry said: "This book [the Bible] is worth all the books which were ever printed." It is a supreme tragedy when the Bible does not appear on a seminary's required reading list and books about the Bible usurp its place.

In critically evaluating one's own heritage, it is easy in our day to challenge historic commitments in the name of current deviations. One may dispute some or all ecclesiastical positions out of professed love for the Church or out of a desire to preserve respect in an academic environment gripped by secular presuppositions; but Jesus reminded theologians of an earlier generation that it is more important to honor God than to honor man and that only if God's Word abides in us can we be preserved from deceptive loyalties to our religious communities (John 5:38, 44). Freedom to be a school respected among its peers does not require theologians to repudiate the distinctive way of knowing that is appropriate to the science of God. What it does require is the presentation of rational supports for a truth that neither empirical science nor conjectural philosophy can attain, a truth that has its basis in God's intelligible initiative and act and Word.

A theological seminary has the high duty of justifying all its doctrinal commitments in view of divine revelation. Holding the Word of God as the central referent for all theological discussion keeps doctrinal affirmation from deteriorating into a mere salute to tradition and keeps theological commitments perpetually open not to human divergence but to the Word of God. Gamaliel's counsel is not an adequate platform for theological education: even if Christianity won its way in the ancient world, the synagogues were steadily sealed against the Gospel of Christ, and those who delayed decision forfeited redemptive truth and grace. Pragmatism involves a kind of detente between the claims of God and of the devil more appropriate to political ecumenism than to theological lucidity.

———————————

The justification of theological commitments by the scriptural Word will also best preserve the vitality of theological education. Those who hold that academic excitement depends upon a diversity of viewpoints forfeit a transcendently valid norm. The intellectual force of divergent contemporary views can be preserved by other means than a theologically divided faculty. One is by required reading and critical evaluation of competitive viewpoints in courses on current religious thought. A scholar's books often present his position in a more orderly and disciplined way than do his classroom lectures. Additionally, the guest-lecture circuit, which does not involve the question of faculty tenure, can provide live contact and discussion opportunity with scholars of other viewpoints. On occasion I have invited one of the scholars whose work we have studied in a course in contemporary theological perspectives to dinner and an evening's informal dialogue with members of the seminar.

The notion that no seminary can give a fair hearing to dissenting scholars except by according them faculty status is more agreeable in principle to those committed to theological pluralism than to those adhering to revealed theology. In practice, however, nonevangelical seminaries tend to make little more room on their faculties for competent evangelical scholars than do evangelical institutions for nonevangelical scholars.

I see no prospect of transcending the divisions within Christendom by a misguided emphasis on the intellectual propriety of pluralistic and contradictory theologies and the consequent severance of divine revelation from truth. To be sure, our perceptions of divine revelation are vulnerable to the abuse of skewed perspectives. But to admit that is quite different from resigning ourselves to skewed perspectives as a victory for faith. If our traditions are answerable to no superior criterion, if they are to be viewed as fallible testimony to some inexpressible truth, to truth that depends ultimately upon individual decision, then we had better give public notice that theological truth is not openly identifiable and that truth in religion is whatever one commits himself to. We would not need to learn from each other if we already had a theology of glory, if we were sons of God wholly conformed to Christ's image, if our theological truth-claims were unscarred by evident theological contrariety and even contradiction. The designation of the Pope as antichrist by the Lutheran confessions and the Roman Catholic confession of him as Christ's unique vicegerent on earth cannot both be true; you may even excuse a Baptist for suggesting that both are wrong.

What could be real gain for the Christian witness in the modern world would be not simply to wrestle our differences but to emphasize also what we affirm in common in view of the scripturally revealed truth of God. The real issue is not whether theological commitment is compatible with academic freedom to believe whatever one prefers. It is whether, in the absence of commitment and more particularly of commitment to the intelligible revealed truth of God, we educators can long preserve sense for either freedom or academia.

Carl F. H. Henry, "Committing Seminaries to the Word," *Christianity Today* 20, no. 10 (February 13, 1976): 6–9.

Part IV

EVANGELICALS
AND SOCIETY

Chapter 22

THE CHRISTIAN-PAGAN WEST

The West once was pagan and then became Christian; historically, it is the pagan-Christian West. Today, in contrast, it has become the Christian-pagan West. No century was ever more misjudged than the twentieth by those who hailed it as the "Christian" century. For the once banished demonic spirits have returned again to inhabit the abode of Western culture, and some, indeed, seem to be securing permanent tenure.

Thinking men may scorn the phrase "the Christian-pagan West" as ill-tempered. The West is, after all, the Christian West; what specially distinguishes Occident from Orient is this Christian motif. Moreover, even the compound "Christian-pagan" may seem as artificial as "pagan West," for after all, whatever is pagan is non-Christian, even as what is Christian is assumed to be Western.

Decline of Christian Spirit

Such an evaluation of events, however, is outdated; indeed, it is actually irrelevant. It reflects the romantic overconfidence of earlier generations and of the past century. It assumes, and erroneously so, that traditional patterns of the home and work, of civilization and culture still prevail. It perpetuates the illusion of a people who took for granted that the inherited spirit of the West could not die.

Never Fully Christian

Admittedly the West has never been the totally "Christian West." At best, it has been the "Christian West plus or minus," the Christian West qualified by some limiting word, e.g., the "imperfectly Christian West." Scholars now admit, indeed, that the Dark Ages were less dark than historians once pictured them; yet the Middle Ages stood nonetheless in drastic need of the Reformation. The tradition of papacy, monasticism and scholasticism developed an hierarchical, ritualistic and legalistic religion. Superstition and legend abounded; faith was often blind and unreasoning; piety and sacrifice were common substitutes for virtue; ascetic self-denial and gross sensuality flourished side by side; and the church was drawn frequently into the current of political intrigue and immorality. As Philip Schaff remarks, "the medieval light was indeed the borrowed star and moonlight of ecclesiastical tradition, rather than the clear sun-light from the inspired pages of the New Testament; but it was such light as the eyes of the nations in their ignorance could bear, and it never ceased to shine until it disappeared in the day-light of the great Reformation" (*History of the Christian Church*, Vol. IX, p. 12).

Yet Luther and Calvin, no less than Augustine, Anselm and Aquinas, stood in hourly need of justification on the ground of Christ's death for sinners. The same applies to the early apostles Peter, Paul and John, and in our century to evangelical giants like Dwight L. Moody and Billy Graham. The smudge of sin discolors even the best Christian history.

Heritage of Greatness

Nevertheless it must be said that no other world culture has lived on the Christian side of life and history; it has had a Christian past, with a lease on Christian experience. The classic pagan mind, shaped by Graeco-Roman idealism, even at best was not good enough for the West. The old culture at its vulgar or common level was beneath the dignity of Christians. And the vices of infanticide, religious prostitution, and slavery were abhorrent and repugnant to believers. Because they revered Christ as the guardian of purity and as the champion of sexual virtue, the Christians renounced adultery, covetousness, craftiness, dishonesty, drunkenness, theft. Doubtless the New Testament exhortations, and the picture in the Revelation of the decline of the seven churches in Asia Minor, caution us against painting the first century only in the brightest colors. Yet even in wicked Corinth the apostle Paul could write the world-stained believers: "Such were some of you: but ye are washed, but ye are sanctified, but ye are justified in the name of the Lord Jesus, and by the Spirit of our God."

Virtue in Abundance

Actually, Christians were known from the very beginning more for their positive ethical and spiritual performance than for mere abstinence. Pagan observers marveled "how they love one other." An inexplicable joy irradiated the lives of these ordinary mortals; the peace that became theirs was unknown even to an age free of international hostilities; a boundless flood of kindness and benevolence was turned toward neighbors and strangers; godliness came to live in human flesh. These were a holy people, graced by the Holy Spirit. Acquaintance with the Risen Christ endowed them with a spiritual treasure so surpassingly superb that they laid down their lives rather than renounce Him. Even where totalitarian rulers brandished steel against them, they preferred martyrdom to the sin of silence. They were "called Christians first at Antioch" (Acts 11:26), and they were worthy of His Name. They had a divine commission to go to a perishing world; they were "under orders" to witness of the Redeemer to lost men. Their "conversation"—their walk as well as their words—was halo-bright. The incarnate, crucified, and risen Christ was the meeting place of their hopes and fears. Their marching orders were to confront the world in an armor the pagan empires had never worn. They eclipsed all the previous generations in their embodiment of love, of joy, of peace, of long-suffering, of gentleness, of goodness, of faith, of meekness, of temperance.

Inspiration of Christianity

All that became noblest in the West was but the lengthened shadow of such faith and life. In a world abounding with religions, biblical Christianity supplied a distinctive view of God and the universe, of man and his destiny. The life of the West came to revolve around the drama of divine incarnation and atonement. The span of human existence was related in every sphere to the God-man who died in the stead of sinners and who rose for them in triumph over death. Between the divine creation of man and the final judgment of the race, the advent of the Redeemer stood as the dominating peak of history. Time "before Christ" lacked any climax; it was a movement of events in which the redemptive promise of God waited fulfillment. "The year of our Lord" became synonymous with the age of grace, in which redeemed men and women were adopted into the family of faith, with the risen Redeemer as their living Head. Since the sixth century the West has based its calendar upon the reality of the incarnation.

While Christian monotheism furnished the lofty inspiration of religion and morality, its influence did not stop there. It shaped literature and the arts. It even furthered the confidence of the

West (although contemporary thought arbitrarily obscures this debt) in the unity and rationality of space-time existence, and hence stimulated the growth of science. Christianity upheld the ultimate significance of reason and conscience under God, and it proclaimed as well a providential universe on the basis of divine creation and preservation. Neither ancient polytheistic religion nor philosophical dualism had produced this lively sense of God and the supernatural world, and of man's awesome destiny.

A Squandered Inheritance

Today this inheritance is all but squandered. No doubt those who disparage life in the Middle Ages as measured by the purity of New Testament religion can make their case, but nonetheless the world today, in contrast with earlier centuries clothed by Christian influences, stands starkly naked in moral shame.

Call it a return to paganism or barbarism or what one will, the fact remains that in the West for three centuries Christian influences upon society, the state and culture have decreased while secular influences have increased to dominating proportions. In the eighteenth century the upper classes of society broke with Christian beliefs, and the unity of Western Christendom vanished. While phantom unity remained in the balance of power preserved by the absolute monarchies, when these fell, only the myth of the West's ongoing progress concealed its fragmenting ideals. When progress, in turn, seemed doubtful, only the rise of dictators preserved the outward illusion of unity.

Terrifying Ambiguities

Today's situation is awesome in its ambiguities. The largest strength of the Communist party, next to Russia and China, is in Italy, home of Vatican City and the organizational head of the largest body of professing Christians. Many who vote Communist still attend Roman Catholic mass in Italy (in contrast with the French).

The Italian Senate's only woman member, Senator Lina Merlin, has charged that between two and three million women live by prostitution; that in Rome houses of prostitution operate under government license "all over town, and near schools and churches." Such confusions and contradictions strike ever deeper and deeper in nominally Christian centers today; principle and piety seem ever less and less a central concern of human existence.

The Reformation warned that the Christian West had deteriorated to quasi-Christian foundations, and called for a full and swift return to biblical supports. Scholasticism had one-sidedly emphasized the intellectual element in Christianity. The community it produced repeated the Apostles' Creed, but without putting heart and soul in the opening word. For *Credo* (I believe) it tended to substitute *Credendum est* (it is believed). A generation merely mouthing the creed led to another generation that could not in good conscience even repeat it. The highest language of faith, used first by saintly men, next by carnal men, and then by unregenerate men, at last vanished entirely from the vocabulary of the modern pagan.

Medieval Compromises

The medieval compromise, in fact, reached far beyond matters of doctrine and personal virtue. It involved also a misconception of the social order and of the church's relation to culture.

In the provocative volume *Man in This World*, Hans Zehrer reaches back a thousand years to A.D. 1075 and the autocratic Pope Gregory VII's Twenty-Seven Theses, which led in 1308 to the bull *Unam Sanctum* as the pivot of the Western revolt against authority. By their own claims the papal despots began to lessen the distance between God and man, and man and God. Drawing the spiritual sword, popes presumed to rule over emperors and their subjects in place of God. "In setting himself in the place of God, the Pope gave the signal for every class to do likewise. 'Why should *you* be God and not I?' is a question before which title-deeds lose their force" (Zehrer, *op. cit.*, p. 67). Thereafter, the man who would be God becomes in swift turn the man freed from all superior authority, who loses at last not merely the image of God, but in doing so loses also the image of man, and descends to bestiality. He becomes the herd man of our era, easily led by totalitarian superiors. In the Christian-pagan West he emerges as the beast-man of evolutionary naturalism, although in actuality he is the man-beast.

Men with Half a Soul

Whatever may be said about Zehrer's thesis, the fact is that for five centuries, since the mid-fifteenth century yielded to the post-medieval era, the man of Europe and the Americas has stood increasingly confounded and mute in the presence of the Great Questions. His distant forefathers had been heirs of the classic Graeco-Roman world view and prized the Christian inheritance even above that. The death of ancient culture they counted gain because of the birth of a higher. But the modern man, by contrast, gave half his soul to the Renaissance, and was half-hearted toward the Reformation. He now gave snap answers to Ultimate Problems, answers which blurred the Christian motif, and from which all remaining biblical hues, already pallid, would soon fade.

Those who today call merely for "a new Reformation" thereby betray the fact that they judge current history unrealistically. Latin America, perhaps, is a prospect for such a duplication within history. There, as nowhere else, the smoldering revolt against a medieval temper could erupt into a war of ideas, involving Renaissance as well as Reformation claims. But elsewhere the West has already stripped human life of much of its traditional meaning. The inherited patterns of civilization are paling swiftly. Priority Answers of the past are now repudiated, and the Priority Problems along with them. The current failure to grasp the world of ultimates commits man to categories that imply the end of a rational-moral cosmos and the consequent insignificance of reason and the good. For two generations influential philosophers in the once-Christian West have ceased to ask, "Who is God?" "What is the purpose of history, and of the universe?" "How shall we define man's dignity?" "What are the permanent aspects of truth and morality?" but instead have been asking "Is there a God?" "Does purpose exist in history and the universe?" "Is man essentially unique?" and "Have reason and goodness any objective significance?"

The Drift Downstream

The chorus of intellectual giants answering these questions negatively has swelled. Paraded as the verdict of modern intellectual genius are the dogmas that the binding force of reality is not supernatural and that life and society are held together best if God be dissolved. Confused Western man has been floating downstream on the river of negation, for driftwood requires nothing in the way of spiritual decision. Today, tossed by doubt and uncertainty, modern man is wearying of this world and of himself. His day-to-day existence balances on the sharp edge of chilling questions.

The geographical frontiers of Christendom have shrunk perceptibly. The Russian Orthodox Church and the vast evangelical Stundist movement in the U.S.S.R. eke out their existence by the tolerance of a totalitarian government. The Ukraine, where Roman Catholic congregations date back a millennium, is enslaved behind the Iron Curtain. France, a half-century ago included in every list of nominally Christian great powers, has a bankrupt faith; of its 42 million inhabitants, 35 million no longer attend mass (a mortal sin for Catholics). Only European lands on which the Reformation made a strong theological impact are today virile in their resistance to Communism.

But the shriveling of the Christian claim upon modern thought and life is even more shocking than the shrinking of Christian territorial frontiers. Almost everywhere the West shows a return to pagan ways of thinking and living. Before Christ and before conscience it puts a score of substitute allegiances.

Eroding the Patience of God

First, the boundless wickedness of the Tigris-Euphrates valley, the cradle of civilization, eroded the patience of God's Spirit, and the early human enterprise was finally deluged in doom. The new beginning was grounded in revealed religion; the sacred Hebrew narratives carry forward the best of the old history from Abraham to Moses and Sinai, to David and the Hebrew temple, and through the prophets of the Old Testament. Furthermore, they light up this whole venture of faith with Messianic expectation.

Then, the decline of the proud and classic Graeco-Roman civilization ended in the tribal sack and fall of Rome. This extremity of the pagan world became the Christian believer's opportunity; the weakness of the pagan gods revealed the strength of the Lord of glory.

The third long night of human barbarism seems to have begun. To many observers, the horizon of this third night exhibits little, if any, prospect of a sunrise. Earlier and once benign cultures perished in judgment. The first civilization in the Tigris-Euphrates valley came to naught with the destruction of a generation hardened in its revolt; the glory of the Hellenic world could not withstand its later disintegration and doom. Descending from its pinnacle of lofty achievement, the Christian West in becoming pagan is headed for inevitable doom. The light men shun today is blinding, for the post-Christian era revolts against the most sacred inheritance of the race. To assume that an anti-Christ culture will escape perdition is sheer madness.

Carl F. H. Henry, "The Christian-Pagan West," *Christianity Today* 1, no. 6 (December 24, 1956): 3–6.

Chapter 23

HUMAN RIGHTS IN AN AGE OF TYRANNY

The modern era has seen the collapse of the Protestant liberal inflation of man into a divinity; now it strives against the naturalistic deflation of man into a slave of the state.

Firming up the case for human rights and responsibilities at the local level has become an imperative necessity for the vagabond West. The logic and urgency of the issues of man's dignity and duty do not grip the man in the street.

The generation of tyranny has driven many Christian churches in the free world to a fuller accent on human worth and liberty. Christianity has long stood guard against both the romantic and the pessimistic misjudgments of man. Neither a deity nor an animal, man is a creature fashioned in the divine image, fallen into sin, bearing a unique dignity and traveling to an uncommon destiny. What is the meaning of this truth for a time of tyranny?

The theme of human freedom throbbed blood-fresh in the veins of America's Founding Fathers. Alongside the titanic brutalities of our time, the tyranny they deplored as insufferable was perhaps only the shadow of sorrow. Nevertheless, they appealed to the one eternal Preserver of man's responsible existence, the almighty Guardian of the dignity of man and Definer of the powers of the state. In the words of the Declaration of Independence: "All men are ... endowed by their Creator with certain unalienable rights ..."

The Christian conformity of some signers of the Declaration of Independence is definitely debatable. There is little doubt, however, that the great majority were evangelical believers theologically at home in the doctrines of the Bible. True, they disapproved religious sectarian intolerance no less than political intolerance. Devout men, like Roger Williams, an evangelical Baptist, had espoused the cause of separation of church and state, or of religious liberty, as an essential aspect of human liberty. They were determined to spare Americans all the tortures of tyranny.

The Founding Fathers were careful, however, to separate neither the individual nor the state from an obligation to God. Nor did they leave the concept of God nebulous and undefined and wholly subject to private interpretation—contrary to a tendency thriving in American life today. Not the slightest hint can be found that by God they meant anything other than a personal supernatural being, the Creator (a distinctly theistic and biblical conception) through whose specific endowment the human race has been peculiarly endowed with inalienable dignity and with inalienable rights. Even the right of religious freedom had in their outlook a religious basis. Man's unique place in society and in the universe was guaranteed by rights supernaturally supplied and sanctioned by a sovereign Creator imposing duties which both the rulers and the ruled must everywhere respect.

Confronted by the tyrannical totalitarianism that continues to deform our world, the General Assembly of the United Nations eight years ago overwhelmingly approved the so-called Universal Declaration of Human Rights. The world still outside the spreading Soviet sphere is appropriately constrained and compelled to study anew the important issue of human liberty, lest man's freedom, taken for granted, and no longer cherished nor understood, be disassembled and dissolved.

The reasons are close at hand, therefore, why the U.S. National Commission for UNESCO, commemorating and promoting the national and local observance of Human Rights Day annually on December 10, is disappointed and even somewhat baffled because its enthusiasm has not filtered down to the community level. Even in the District of Columbia only fragmentary participation greeted the occasion.

To overcome this national lethargy to the observance of U.N. Human Rights Day, some leaders of the U.S. National Commission for UNESCO (a semi-governmental agency that serves the Department of State in an advisory capacity) have proposed a new organization, whose chairman they hope will be named by the government and functioning as a voluntary private body to solicit funds and provide guidance, a timetable of operations and materials and tools for a grass-roots nationwide observance. Under an alternate plan, the National Commission would itself seek, from the 60 voluntary organizations nominating members to that body, something beyond their present disappointing creation of interest and would secure the time of established organizations to implement the U.N. program on a local basis. By one or other of these mechanisms, it is hoped, the nation, faced by the grave world threats to human dignity and freedom, will be rallied to observance of the U.N. Day of Rights.

The effort to gain a more spontaneous dedication on the American popular level for the theme of human rights has not been limited to the U.N. thrust. The preaching of Christian churches has been increasingly alive and awake to the implications of biblical theology for the socio-political order. Confessedly, the pulpit has lacked the note of uneasy urgency essential to combat the current totalitarian devaluation of man. Why then has there not been a merging of church and civic efforts to firm up the case for human rights on the local level? At the national level, admittedly, the National Council of Churches and the National Catholic Education Association are among the movements represented on the National Commission. Yet the local churches in the hamlets and cities of America tend to show only a spotty enthusiasm for the emphasis on human rights in U.N. dimensions. Why this hesitancy?

Doubtless part of the nonparticipation in the human rights program results from the indifference of some churches to questions of social morality. They are at home in questions of Christian personal ethics, but not of Christian social ethics, except in the barest personal dimensions. Even where the relevance of Christianity to culture is not excluded, some churches tend to suspect massive movements of any kind, both political and ecclesiastical. Often their reasons are eschatological (the totalitarian world beast of Revelation 13) or anthropological (concentration of power tends to be corruptive), if not both. Those who share this forecast must always square their consciences, of course, with the complaint that whatever a given organization *may* become, Christian duty today must be judged in terms of what it *is*.

But this is hardly the whole ground for hesitancy. Many Christian leaders think, and not without reason, that an unhappy ambiguity and obscurity run through the present UNESCO handling of human rights. They fear that the American people, and that mankind as a whole, cannot be assured of real progress in the field of human rights until this equivocation is candidly exposed and confronted. Especially is this true of many evangelically minded Protestant ministers, who support an emphasis on human rights that accords with both the historic American spirit and the spirit of the Hebrew-Christian tradition, and who for that reason are less than happy with the U.N. formulation. The vagrant phantoms of totalitarianism and of anarchism, they fear, are not effectually exorcised by the U.N. Declaration of Human Rights. For the only adequate reply to the atheistic devaluation of man as they see it—and here they are on the side of the inherited tradition of the West—is an alternative that, in the spirit of the Declaration of Independence, is frankly theistic.

The very first article of the U.N. Declaration at once reflects its differences with the Declaration of Independence in clear light. That article declares: "All human beings are born free and equal in dignity and rights. They are endowed with reason and conscience and should act toward one another in a spirit of brotherhood."

The U.N. statement incorporates no references to a supernatural Creator, nor does it anywhere assert that God endows mankind with specific rights. It asserts that men are "endowed with reason and conscience," but it does not specify the source of this endowment; it goes on to specify a list of rights, but it nowhere asserts that it is the Living God who sanctions these rights. Its repeated formula is "Everyone has the right to ..." It is remarkable that the fact sheet distributed on Human Rights Day by the U.S. National Commission for UNESCO, while quoting the emphasis of the Declaration of Independence on "unalienable rights," wholly ignores the Declaration's associated emphasis that these rights are an endowment by the Creator.

The U.N. Declaration therefore leaves in doubt the crucial fact that human rights have an ultimate basis, that God Himself insists upon these rights, that man has been endowed with these rights in view of his unique dignity by creation. It erases, therefore, the emphasis that the Declaration of Independence vigilantly sustained, that the Living God is the source and sanction of human freedoms.

The consequence of this deletion is far-reaching. For one thing, the promulgation of the U.N. Declaration, in the present conflict of ideas, could leaven the confused popular mind with an inadequate and unprotected view of human rights. Furthermore, by disjoining the question of freedoms from God as their source and sanction, the U.N. Declaration shifts the whole discussion of responsibility one-sidedly to that of human rights, and neglects the equally important subject of human duties.

The observance of Human Rights Day in the Free World ought to confront the totalitarian threat to human liberties head-on. But the U.N. formula fails to do so; in fact, its very neutrality leaves human rights vulnerably exposed and endangered.

Since the U.N. Declaration does not assert that God is the source and sanction of these rights, an impression continues to gain ground that the United Nations is their source and sanction. "The U.N. guarantees these rights!"—this is the formula one overhears time and again. If that really be the case, then the individual is guarded from the tyranny of the totalitarian state only by the totalitarian superstate. For if the U.N. is the source and sanction of human rights, there can be no appeal to a source and sanction higher than the U.N., by reference to which even the positions of the U.N. are to be approved or disapproved. In that event, the conflict between the Soviet orbit and the United Nations reduces to a conflict between superstates; the only issue in the balances is, which of them has the power of the totalitarian determination of human life? Either there is a source and sanction of human rights superior to the United Nations, a supernatural exposition of man and his station in the universe, or the conflict over human rights reduces to an intramural struggle between two totalitarian powers. The framers of the Declaration of Independence saw this issue with clearer vision than our modern statesmen. And until this issue of the ultimate source and sanction of human rights is clearly faced within the U.N., those who see dim outlines of a totalitarian superstate need not be dismissed as suffering from eschatological oddity.

If the Free World is really to stand fast against the threat to human freedoms, it will find the first line of defense, and the only unassailable tower, where the Christian patriots who forged the American Declaration of Independence located it, in the fact that man bears by divine creation a unique dignity, and that the state and citizen alike are bound in a responsible way to the Living God.

Stated in this way, the issue of human liberty will not be discussed independently of the issue of human liability. What the nations of the world need, in this sixth decade in the century of tyranny, is the compelling rediscovery of human duties no less than of human rights. Why a human rights day, in disconnection from a human responsibilities day? The one-sided observance easily gives rise to expectations that are not properly bounded by obligations. If the Christian church is to give effective leadership to a world that has lost its way, it dare not detach the question of human liberties from the knowledge of the Living God who has placed all men and nations under divine command.

Carl F. H. Henry, "Human Rights in an Age of Tyranny," *Christianity Today* 1, no. 9 (February 4, 1957): 20–22.

Chapter 24

PERSPECTIVE FOR SOCIAL ACTION

Modern society no longer respects the Church as its major interpreter and guide in the social crisis. There are many reasons for this development.

Christianity on the Defensive

For one thing, the Church herself appears inundated by the World; never has she been so unmercifully challenged to justify her very right to existence. To be sure, Christianity always has been a minority movement, and the World has always confronted the Church with some degree of deliberate indifference and hostility. In our day, however, the front of opposition reveals a swaggering re-enforcement quite unknown in ancient, medieval and early modern times. In strategic Western intellectual circles, self-assured and bold philosophical naturalism has triumphantly overrun the social sciences and therefore culture itself. Moreover, the lunge of communism betrays a veritable lightning thrust of social revolution. Its world penetration and power have made the Christian impact seem embarrassingly inefficient and ineffective.

As never before, the ranks of atheism are trying to uproot and to discard Christian guidelines; their concerted drive to dominate and monopolize both intellectual and functional areas of society has anti-Christian goals. Naturalism is deaf to the Church's verdict on the social order because it considers a supernatural faith devoid of authentic credentials to survive a scientific age. It believes the Church sooner or later must simply learn to speak the language of this World.

For this misunderstanding and abuse the Church itself must accept a measure of blame, although certainly not because of failure to convert the whole World. Actually, global *conversion* has never been her God-given responsibility, although this fact in no way excuses laxity and deficiency in her primary task of evangelism and mission. Her blameworthiness, rather, rises from other considerations.

At one time, when the Church was socially significant, the effects thereof were unforgettably bad. Students of the Middle Ages can recall especially the fifteenth century in this regard.

Today the Church's ineffectiveness and disrepute stem not from her one but rather from her multiple and conflicting solutions for the social crisis. Too many answers dilute modern respect for the Church. While professing to embody and to channel the unique perspective of divine revelation, the Church has failed to convince the world of this orientation. Her many contradictions in teaching and in social action have not confirmed nor illustrated the demands of her declared frame of reference. She has therefore been pushed to "excuses" rather than to reasons for her exclusive independency. Were the Church therefore to openly identify herself as simply the vehicle of a lofty but changing ethic and not as the ordained bearer and defender of an absolute and once-for-all revelation of redemption, the secular world would embrace her as a powerful, useful, cultural dynamism. The

Church's inconsistency in regard to social issues, her incompatibility and vacillation of message while claiming to speak for the living God, surely place an intolerable and insulting strain on the World's credulity and reason.

Pessimism over Social Change

Not only from without but even from within, the professing Church manifests signs of uncertainty and pessimism today about the nature of her social responsibility. Many vigorous proponents of supernaturalism and special revelation now argue that the Church's role is simply to challenge rather than to re-create society. This logically means casting the whole ideal of Christian culture to the uncertainties and vagaries of our storm-swept social order. With no built-in controls to assure direction, the ideal of Christian culture will scarcely get into orbit, let alone chart a visible and measurable course in the world. The Christian believer is to compassionately picket the cultural order with a signboard: "Outrage to love and justice." All the while, however, the social order remains permanently aligned with the world, the flesh and the devil. To take issue with this neo-orthodox thesis of challenge, rather than re-creation, as the task of the Church brings charges of perfectionist insensitivity to the depth of sin in human life and history.

Reaction against Liberal Optimism

The present wave of pessimism must be understood as a reaction to the tide of optimism that had previously overflowed and soaked into the Christian social vision. It was this exuberance of the early twentieth century that produced the social gospel. Interestingly enough, the distinctive feature of the social gospel was neither its passion for social justice nor its conviction that Christianity has social relevance. What might by way of contrast be called social

Christianity long antedated it. Both Christianity's emphasis on justice and on the social relevance of redemptive religion throb through the pages of Scripture. Without this balanced approach, Christianity becomes anemic. The social gospel knowingly surrendered the personal gospel of Jesus Christ's substitutionary death and his supernatural redemption and regeneration of sinful men. Instead, it sought to transform the social order by grafting assertedly Christian ideals upon unregenerate human nature. This optimistic approach assumed first, that the World will steadily and progressively improve until it finally culminates in an enduring kingdom of righteousness and peace. Second, such transformation of the social order can result (perhaps even within our lifetime) by inspiring unregenerate mankind to live by Christian ethical principles. Third, such achievement does not require nor depend upon personal redemption by divine grace and supernatural sanctification.

A Forfeited Opportunity

Perhaps at no time in modern history was American Protestantism so propitiously situated as at the early twentieth century for a world impact. The age of discovery and invention was thriving. Their interest in each other warmed by the revival flames of the previous generation, the scattered churches were already being united in a formal way by ecumenical efforts. Idealistic philosophy—a speculative supernaturalism of many shades—dominated the university centers while naturalism was still on the periphery. Furthermore, the Communist Party was merely an oddity. Consequently the masses (at least in America if not in Europe) still looked to the churches for constructive social guidance. Most intellectuals, too, were sufficiently versed in Western history to acknowledge Christianity as a vital force with which sociological thinkers must reckon.

Sad to say, Protestantism dissipated this great opportunity and certain dire consequences followed hard upon its growing deference to the social gospel:

The social gospel became an *alternative* to the Gospel of supernatural grace and redemption. This divergence became more and more obvious after 1910. Rauschenbusch, who supplied *A Theology for the Social Gospel* (1917) at the point where the movement had lost spiritual moorings and direction, still propounded the importance of the supernatural regeneration of sinners. At the same time, he shared Washington Gladden's explanation of evil mainly in terms of man's environment rather than of the traditional doctrine of depravity. Protestant liberal spokesmen soon enlarged the revolt against traditional theology, and fashioned their optimistic view of history and man from evolutionary theory rather than from the biblical sources of revealed religion. Seminaries training the young clergy took pains to define the antithesis. Popular books like Sheldon's *In His Steps* annulled the need of Christ's vicarious death for sinners. Through the social gospel churches were given a task unstipulated by the Great Commission. The new preoccupation perhaps came through neglect and at the expense of the Church's divinely appointed mission.

From then on, many churches in the major denominations espoused a nonsupernaturalistic interpretation of the Christian religion, or even dissolved its unique elements in the solvents of idealistic speculation. At its historic moment of world opportunity, Protestant Christianity, since the Reformation happily freed it from man-made traditions and accretions, now surrendered many of its great pulpits to the theological and social fabrications of the modern mind.

As the ecclesiastical relationships of the regular churches tightened, many churches mirrored the policies of denominational leaders aggressively dedicated to the social gospel. The independent churches, which repudiated the social gospel and therefore carried the full burden of supernatural evangelism and missions, were often embroiled in fervent criticism of denominational churches and of ecumenical activities. Even to this day more than half the foreign missionaries remain deliberately unaffiliated with world ecumenical effort. Instead, they have aligned themselves with strictly evangelical agencies. Within Protestantism itself, therefore, tensions mounted because of controversy over the nature and content of the Christian imperative.

In its reaction against the social gospel, the fundamentalist movement became socially indifferent, and even made the inevitability of social decline a part of its credo. To some extent, pessimism resulted from dispensational views which taught that world-wide spiritual apostasy must precede the second coming of Jesus Christ. So intense was fundamentalist social pessimism, in fact, that even any sign of spiritual revival was often considered suspect. The drift of Protestantism in the twentieth century, particularly widespread apostasy within the professing church, contributed significantly to this fundamentalist negativism. With organized Christianity replacing the good tidings of the death and resurrection of Jesus Christ for sinners with promotion of the social gospel instead, world doom seemed inevitable. Christ's return glowed as the only bright prospect at this time.

The Reformation Heritage

By such evangelical Protestant evasion of the larger problems of social justice, except as social betterment indirectly followed the regeneration of individuals, contemporary evangelicals contrast sharply with their Reformation heritage. Despite its closely guarded and cherished reliance upon biblical authority for the Church's message, the Protestant Reformation concerned itself no less with Christianity as a world-life view than did medieval Catholicism. The social perspective of fundamentalism may be described as a reaction. Its revolt against the social gospel deflected evangelical Protestantism from the spiritual vision of a Christian culture to an attitude of social isolationism.

Evangelical Social Passion

Admittedly not all evangelical traditions have been interested in a Christian social thrust. Social withdrawal had been the attitude of the Anabaptist-Mennonite movement. Such withdrawal, however, was not historically the normal temper of evangelical Protestants, neither in the age of the Reformation nor in the revival eras of eighteenth century England and nineteenth century America. Indeed, in his Brewer prize essay *Revivalism and Social Reform* (1957), Timothy L. Smith observes that the social passion of evangelicals in the post-Civil War period "merged without a break into what came to be called the social gospel" (p. 235). Twentieth century Protestant humanitarianism is therefore inestimably indebted to bygone evangelicals who made and maintained Protestantism as a mighty social force in America. In this sense the evangelical revival movements furrowed the ground from which the social gospel sprang. As Dr. Smith comments in another connection (*Christianity Today,* Sept. 29, 1958), the seizure by liberalism of the proprietorship of the Good Samaritan is "one of the great ironies—and falsehoods—of our time."

Fundamentalist Disinterest

The fundamentalist lack of social vision must therefore be seen primarily as a reaction against Protestant liberalism. The twentieth century "gospel" of social betterment and the first century "good news" for the individual seemed two irreconcilable statements of the Christian task and hope. Fundamentalism came to regard this antithesis of man and society not simply as accidental in view of liberalism's unfortunate defection from biblical theology, but as necessary in view of the nature of the Gospel and its course in the World. The movement of fallen history is downward; entrance to the kingdom of God comes only through individual rebirth. The primary task of the Church is evangelism and missions. Alongside these sound convictions, fundamentalism, unfortunately, neglected the Christian criticism of the social order and the task of sheltering the whole range of human freedoms and duties under the self-revealing God.

Recovering Lost Ground

During the past 20 years evangelical Protestantism has steadily sought to recover lost ground in the realm of social concern. The tiny book *The Uneasy Conscience of Modern Fundamentalism* (1947) reflected the private conviction of a growing bloc of evangelical leaders that Christianity makes imperative the declaration of the social relevance of biblical religion and ethics in all spheres of life. The six brief chapters of that book were first prepared upon request as essays for *Religious Digest*, but the magazine's editors were fearful that the series, scheduled over a period of months, would arouse misunderstanding unless published as a unit. Hence they appeared from the first in book form. Since mid-century, evangelical social concern has steadily mounted. More and more it became obvious that the evangelical failure to proclaim Christ as Lord of the whole life allowed secular and sub-biblical agencies to pre-empt the spheres of culture for alien points of view. At the present time the influence of extreme dispensational views is on the wane in interdenominational colleges and even in some Bible institutes.

New Juncture of Forces

The appearance of the fortnightly magazine, *Christianity Today*, marked a new contemporary juncture of evangelical forces with the Reformation emphasis on Christianity as a world-life view and with the insistence of nineteenth century American revivalism on the social significance of the Gospel. Other agencies contributed in a somewhat preliminary way to this confluence of conviction. For more than 15 years Reformed and fundamentalist clergy had served together on various commissions within the National Association of Evangelicals. Today the evangelical movement recognizes in a new way not only the propriety but the necessity of a social application of the Gospel. Those rejecting the concern for social justice as an illegitimate facet of evangelical interest, vocal though they may be, more and more represent a retreating minority.

———————

Given the contemporary renewal of evangelical social interest, the problem now confronting conservative Protestantism is the definition of a sound evangelical social thrust.

To answer, "Not the social gospel," is at once too simple and too full of risk. For one thing, while the old optimistic liberal *theology* is now dead, the optimistic *ethic* it generated in practice remains a very lively corpse. One need only consider government policy in the U. S. State Department. American foreign policy remains predominantly keyed to optimistic liberal assumptions about human nature and history. It is easy to detect still the lingering influence of liberal Protestant ministers whose sons

———————

Carl F. H. Henry, "Perspective for Social Action (Part I)," *Christianity Today* 3, no. 8 (January 19, 1959): 9–11.

and converts were attracted to government service as a form of Christian activity through the romantic vision of the social gospel. American strategy within the United Nations and her dealings with foreign powers often reflect the moralistic expectation (and naive trust in unregenerate human nature) that Christian principles must inevitably acquire self-evident compulsion in the thought and action of men everywhere. But naively to expect that just and durable peace can be spawned on purely natural foundations simply by the vision of righteousness (or simply to rely on the dread of mutual destruction, to add a mid-century modification based on an appeal to self-interest) is to underestimate the depth of depravity in human life and history and to disregard the indispensability of divine regeneration if the human heart is to grasp and pursue the course of righteousness.

Danger of Liberal Inheritance

Ironically, fundamentalists, in their new eagerness to correct their past social neglect, at times themselves imbibe certain errors of the social gospel. They have happily avoided the popular tendency to embrace left-wing philosophies of the day, which many liberal reformers mistook for authentic expressions of Christian ethics. (Certain American evangelical enthusiasts in the nineteenth century confessedly already had fallen into this same error, and, like some British evangelicals sympathetic to socialism in our century, thereby disclosed their failure to discern the basic clash between Christian libertarianism and collectivism.) The social gospel came to be prominently identified with collectivistic theory because Protestant liberalism has surrendered Christianity's historic confidence both in a revealed theology and in a revealed ethic. The formative philosophies of the modern era were therefore easily confused with a creative Christian social morality. Its defection from revealed doctrines and principles enabled Protestant modernism to confer Christian blessing upon contemporary programs whose basic principles sometimes contradicted the revealed social philosophy of the Church. While evangelical circles by contrast have clung fast to a biblically revealed theology and ethic, and through this fidelity have largely escaped enthusiasm for collectivistic theories of social life, evangelicals in their rediscovery of social concern stand in danger of being drawn, as Protestant liberalism was, into an arbitrary identification of current social movements and programs as intrinsically Christian. Liberal Protestantism openly equated Christian social concern with support for specific modern enterprises and goals such as the League of Nations, the United Nations, giant labor unions, and integration. During the First World War the program embraced pacifism as well. Some contemporary evangelicals newly concerned with the problems of social justice naively imply that the social gospel is acceptable enough provided only that the requirements of personal redemption and regeneration appear as its preface. But if evangelical conscience grasps basic presuppositions, it cannot regard the social gospel as an acceptable vehicle and exposition of biblical social ethics, much as the Gospel of redemption has both personal and social implications.

We do not say that the evangelical is called upon in advance to reject and repudiate everything that the social gospel espoused. But even the social gospel's constructive elements must be brought for their justification within the orbit of divinely revealed principles, and related properly to the biblical view of life and history. Moreover, social gospel insistence that only by the approval of specific contemporary agencies and programs as authentically Christian does Christian ethics become relevant must be challenged. All "isms and ists" must be brought constantly under the scrutinizing Lordship of Christ and tested by his revealed will.

Neo-Orthodox Dissent

Although the social gospel approach is still influential, the evangelical attack upon it is today assisted by neo-orthodox critics who now hold a virile grip upon many Protestant intellectual centers. Both conservative and neo-orthodox theologians scorn the optimistic portrait of a universe progressively evolving to perfection, and doubt the sufficiency of Christian idealism alone to inspire an age of dedication to truth and justice. Both movements insist that the universe is fallen and desperately wicked, and that supernatural redemption is its lone hope. Pronouncements of neo-orthodox thinkers often diverge and conflict, but certain elements nonetheless set apart the American articulation of its view of social ethics from both the classic liberal approach crystallized in the social gospel and the historic outlines of evangelical social ethic:

1. The depth-dimension of sin in human history is regarded as so determinative that the ideal of Christian culture is dismissed, all cultures being viewed simply from the standpoint of Christian criticism.

2. Social problems are regarded as not decisively responsive to personal redemption. Hence its advancement of social justice relies upon the pressure of organized opinion and the compulsion of legislation more than upon evangelism and a ministry of regeneration.

3. Although special supernatural redemption is affirmed, both revealed ethical principles and doctrines are scorned, in common with the liberal tradition in Protestant theology; social strategy is held to

be governed by "middle axioms" which, while held to be creatively and critically relevant, abandon a basis in revelation.

Now the social outlook of liberalism had sought above all else to avoid Christianity's preoccupation with the world to come in order that it might fervently address the vexing social evils of this life. The unhappy outcome was the social gospel, prone to equate the activities of unregenerate humanity at its best with authentic Christian achievements, and neglectful of the wholly proper priorities of supernatural revelation and redemption. Neo-orthodoxy is concerned to hold both worlds in view—not simply in their chronological succession of this life and that to come, but in the existential relationship of this life continually judged by Christ its exalted Lord. Yet speculative considerations bulk large in its theological and ethical positions; guiding elements already given suggest some of the unfortunate consequences accruing to its social perspective. Distrust of rational revelation leaves neo-orthodoxy without absolute basis for the ethical positions it advocates, and also with the practical problem of enlisting Christian commitment and action for temporary imperatives *as if* they were in fact the will of God. The anti-intellectual element in neo-orthodoxy thus ultimately dissipates its social dynamic and divorces its ethical declarations from an assured basis in revelation. The further reliance on factors not found in the Great Commission for the Church's special penetration into the social order tends to formulate Christian social action in terms competitive with the proclamation of the Gospel and minimizes the significance of evangelism and spiritual revival for the advancement of social morality. Moreover, the neo-orthodox disparagement of the ideal of Christian culture fails to do full justice to the power of the Holy Spirit in the life of the redeemed community.

Although a sound theology must recognize that the defilement of sin precludes both glorification in the present life of the believer and absolute perfection in history, and also that the aggregate of group behavior is likely to compound the weaknesses of individual behavior, nonetheless a distinctive social morality seems possible to the community of evangelical faith as assuredly as sanctification is normative for the regenerate person.

Evangelical Strategy

The evangelical perspective for social action is therefore sharpened by a distinctive vision of life and history inspired by the revelation of God's glory and grace.

1. Christian social leaders *set their cultural objectives in the larger framework of the Christian mission,* and do not regard themselves primarily as social reformers. They give no quarter to the illusion that Christianity is primarily an ethical idealism engaged in denouncing political and social injustice, or aiming at social reform as an end in itself. Even in the social thrust they preserve Christianity's basic nature as a religion of supernatural redemption for sinners. The Christian leaders who opposed slavery a century ago did so not simply as abolitionists, but as heralds of freedom under the Creator-Redeemer God dealing simultaneously with man's spiritual and material condition. Even well-intentioned men who regrettably turned the Scriptures to objectionable conclusions in the controversy over slavery rightly sought an *ultimate* sanction, and therefore judged slavery from the standpoint of divine approval or disapproval. The anti-slavery evangelicals saw that to undermine slavery (they would have spoken similarly of segregation and other contemporary vices), men must be led to see its intolerable contradiction of the rights dignifying all men by their creation as members of one common family, of the value attached to all men by our Lord's incarnation,

atonement and resurrection in the body, and of the temple of divinity God would make of humble believers irrespective of color and race. It would not have surprised them to learn that a citizenry that argued the question of human freedom within narrower limits would someday sense an emptiness and bondage even in the workaday world that would encourage white worker and black worker alike to reach wistfully for social redemption through the promise of a collectivistic society. They saw the interconnection of the Christian mission and human liberty.

2. Evangelical social action *throbs with the evangelistic invitation to new life in Jesus Christ.* "Ye must be born again" is the Church's unvarying message to the world. Evangelical Christianity allows the secular world no hopeful program of social solutions that renders merely optional the personal acceptance of Jesus Christ as Savior and Lord. It holds hope for the social order because it offers the prospect of personal redemption. Individual regeneration is not only a chief but an indispensable means of social reform. The kingdom of God is not to be separated from a redeemed society.

3. Reliance on the Holy Spirit to sunder the shackles of sin requires *a regard for social evils first in the light of personal wickedness.* The evangelical recognizes that social disorders are in the last analysis a commentary on the disorder of private life, and that the modern dilemma is essentially a predicament involving persons who need to be addressed individually. The hidden connection between social and private vices—as between war and lust (cf. James 4:1, "From whence come wars and fightings among you? come they not hence, even of your lusts that war in your members?")—is thus kept in conspicuous view. The spectacle of prominent social reformers indifferent to their own private vices—the divorced statesman championing international unity,

the debauched psychiatrist promising soul health to others, for example—is an absurd spectacle and an amoral luxury for the theory that decency begins at home. Deep experience of "the things of God" is thus considered the Christian reformer's best asset. The new birth restores fallen man's personality and his powers to the service of God, qualifying him with a new nature and moral dynamic.

4. Evangelicals insist that *social justice is a divine requirement for the whole human race*, not for the Church alone. The revealed commandments and rules of behavior are universally valid. All the basic laws of society begin with the divine law. Righteousness exalts a nation; a people voluntarily given over to oppression must suffer divine judgment. That man and society live on a moral basis is a requirement of both human laws and of the law of God as well. The Christian witness will stress the interdependence of revealed religion and human freedom, which is dependent on spiritual and moral foundations. Freedom is indivisible (it is not "four freedoms" nor five); man's liberties are interdependent. (Wherever freedom's spiritual foundations crumble, these liberties vanish; conversely, where freedom disappears, the propagation of Christianity is jeopardized.) Revealed religion proclaims the threat to freedom latent in collectivistic social planning and in big government. The neglect of the larger facets of freedom, and the consequent detachment of social principles from a supernatural source and sanction, have indirectly aided the socialistic and totalitarian assault on free enterprise, private property and the profit motive, as well as upon other principles approved by the biblical doctrine of human rights and responsibilities. To assail national strongholds of evil in quest of a righteous nation, to challenge institutional sin in order to widen Christian influence over human society, are essential requirements of the Christian

conscience. Both the affirmation of the Lordship of Christ and the imperative of the Great Commission provide an impetus to seek the renewal of society.

5. Despite their insistence on the spiritual and moral roots of social evil, evangelicals are aware that *personal sin often finds its occasion in the prevailing community situation.* They do not underestimate the importance of the general environment. In the task of social reform evangelical Protestantism exalts the ministry of preaching with its call to personal decision; it stresses the role of Christian preaching, evangelism and revival in weakening and overcoming community evils. The prophetic ministry of the pulpit creates a climate which moves toward effective solution of the problems of social injustice by calling out a race of renewed men bound heart to heart in devotion to the purpose of God in creation and redemption.

6. The fellowship within the churches is a mirror of the realities of a new social order. *The new order* is therefore not simply a distant dream; it *exists already in an anticipative way in the regenerate fellowship of the Church.* The neglect of a shared community experience within the fellowship of the churches is one of the lamentable facets of twentieth century Christianity. The believer's vision for a more equitable social order gains its clearest perspective and major dynamic in this circle of faith. For regenerate believers are constituted one body of which the exalted Christ—having already passed through death, judgment and resurrection for us—is the living head. Moreover, from his life in the eternal order he already mediates to the body an earnest of the powers that belong to the coming age. The Christian responsibility for a more equitable social order is thus to be fulfilled first within the life of the fellowship of faith, where the passionate concern for righteousness and love is presumably the daily burden of each and all. The mission of the Church is not simply to condemn

social injustices; it is to exhibit what can be done to transcend them in a spiritual society of redeemed persons. Men everywhere are called to obedience to the revealed will of God, summoned to repentance from sin, to personal trust in Christ, and to identification with Christ's Church.

7. By maintaining the connection between social reform and the law of love, evangelicals *face the organized evils of society with the power of sanctified compassion.* Christian holiness issues no license for the ecstatic enjoyment of the vision of God as a merely private option; rather, it insists that love of God reflects itself in love for neighbor, and enlists men of piety as sacrificial servants of their fellows. The experience of sanctification more and more socializes the individual disposition and qualifies men with new moral power to implement benevolent motives. The influence of spiritual revivals and the resultant quest for Christian holiness have therefore been a prime source of humanitarian impulses. The believer's personal debt of love to God and his passion for the lost impel him, so that Christian activity transcends the antithesis between spiritual and social service. The compassionate factor in the Christian social thrust, with its eye on the value of the individual, delivers social service from its impersonal tendency to deal with the people as merely so many cases or illustrations of a given complex of circumstances. Social compassion thus holds status as a prime motive and duty of the Church. He who withholds love from another because he considers him unworthy removes himself from the love God manifested to us in the gift and death of Christ while we were yet sinners, yea, actually enemies of God.

8. *The pulpit is to proclaim the revealed will of God, including the ethical principles of the Bible.* The spoken word is to urge man's acceptance of the Crucified and Risen Christ. It prompts obedience to his will. It tests contemporary solutions by the

plumb line of these permanent guideposts. It has no franchise to invest specific contemporary parties, programs and personalities with approval in the name of divine revelation and the Church. But it has biblical authority for the courageous proclamation of the state divinely willed but limited in power, of man's inalienable freedom and duty under God, of private property as a divine stewardship, of free enterprise under God, and much else that speaks relevantly to our social crisis.

9. *The Christian influence upon society is registered most intimately through family and immediate neighbor relations, and then more broadly in the sphere of vocation* or daily work in which the believer's service of God and man is elaborated in terms of a labor of love, *and then politically as a citizen of two worlds.* In the fellowship of marriage, believers are not to be yoked with unbelievers; thus a family circle is shaped to lift the ideal of neighbor love to the most intimate and sacrificial heights. But the believer's involvement in the world of economics and the state involves necessary relations with others outside the circle of redemption. The society of the home, where children are first welcomed into the family of creation and then later into the family of faith, is a parable that quickens neighbor love and Christian witness to men in the world at large. In the realm of work, the believer blends these concerns by the way he values his daily job as a calling by which to serve God and man. In the political realm, he supports the state as an instrument of justice subordinate to the revealed will and purpose of God.

10. *Concern for righteousness and justice* throughout the social order *requires the believer as an individual to range himself for or against specific options for social reform and change.* In discriminating these he will seek in good conscience to promote above all the revealed ethical verities, bringing the contemporary

alternatives under their critical scrutiny, and approving what is good, disapproving what is objectionable.

Spared from Deviations

This frame of conviction and action not only has supplied the evangelical movement with a special orientation on social evils but has protected the community of faith in the past from many errors:

1. Indifference to the cultural situation outside the churches. They deprived "infidel" reformers of the opportunity to shame them to action because they disallowed the initiative for social renewal to pass the secular agencies which wailed the decay of Christianity. No agency more than the churches manifested a ceaseless interest in the welfare of mankind and made the elevation of degraded humanity its task.

2. The hasty imposition of Christian ideals upon the social order in the hope that their validity would be self-evident and their performance implemented by unregenerate humanity as an avenue to social stability.

3. The needless and arbitrary identification of particular social programs, sometimes quite secular in spirit, as essentially and authentically Christian.

4. An undue reliance merely on propaganda, education, and persuasion, or yet on legislation and compulsion to revolutionize society, rather than on the spiritual weapon of a regenerate morality. They suffer no illusion that society can be coerced into the practice

of brotherly kindness and mutual devotion. Rather they recognized that conscience must be rebuked and sensitized, and the will supernaturally re-empowered in the battle against social ills.

Carl F. H. Henry, "Perspective for Social Action (Part II)," *Christianity Today* 3, no. 9 (February 2, 1959): 13–16.

Chapter 25

HAS ANYBODY
SEEN "ERAPE"?

If those invisible rebel spirits of the lower world should suddenly reorganize as socialist legions, and if one materialistic
demon then were specially assigned to our world and charged
to subvert the Christian churches, what strategy would he use?
What ideas and ideals, what particular goals, would best advance
his collectivistic cause?

Should this query seem amusing, perhaps even ludicrous, it
need not therefore be irrelevant. A bit of disciplined imagination, in fact, may prove highly instructive in appraising Protestant
social welfare programs.

A Spectacle of Love

Let us call this particular demon *Erape* (a hybrid of *eros* and
agape—a double dash of "love" as it were). Since *Erape* arrives as
a spirit of love, anyone who dares to dispute his claims would face
an immediate handicap of seeming to scorn love or to condone
lovelessness. (Strategically, the *Erape*-label would excel *Agros* as
a mark of identification, since [being three-fifths ag*ape*] it implies

honor for the biblical view, although giving priority really [*Er*ape]
to speculative traditions. Forwards or backwards, however, *Erape*
spells socialism on the move.)

In courting Christians, *Erape*'s major obstacle would be their
attachment to the notion that Christ's Church has been commis-
sioned for a specific world task, evangelism and missions (Matt.
28:19, 20). This Christian preoccupation would be weakened, of
course, could one discredit the Gospel as the message of "supernatural redemption from sin." With one eye on evolutionary
theory, and the other closed to "salvation by atonement," liberal
theologians professed to find in Jesus' teaching a "social" exposition of the kingdom of God. "Real core" Christianity was equated
with the Master's teaching about "sacrifice," while the substitutionary quality of his life and death was obscured. The "good
news" lost its ancient soul and from rational secularism gained a
modern mascara. The churches were then easily drawn to a new
world mission. But critical theories no longer convincingly effect
a revision of Christian supernaturalism. The "social gospel" no
longer sparkles with John Dewey's enthusiasm over the efficacy
of environmental changes to remake human nature.

Since *Erape*'s interest lies mainly in economic secularism, and
not in redemptive religion, his influence would register most fully
were the churches encouraged to separate their financial vision
and investment from their spiritual mission—that is, were they
no longer to identify their stewardship overtly nor symbolically
with the divine revelation of redemption. Charity would then
cease to be a *commentary* on the Gospel, since it would no longer
reflect to others the believer's own unmerited participation in
"the redemptive grace of God." Instead of its performance truly
"in Christ's name," social welfare activity would then become
simply an *appendage* to the Gospel. This ambiguous relation
of charity with redemptive love (*agape*) would also weaken its

connection with supernatural justice and justification. In short order, charity could thereafter gain a relatively independent status, and merely secular considerations could soon govern public welfare activities.

This separation could be furthered by arguing that modern life requires new economic principles not comprehended in biblical religion and that neither the temporal ethical rules nor permanent precepts of the Bible provide formulas appropriate to our modern economic situation. The Industrial Revolution (and especially automation), it might be held, has so changed modern conditions, that one can no longer expect from biblical ethics answers to contemporary social problems differing in *kind*. This emphasis even seems to take modern history "more seriously" than those who gauge the differences simply as a matter of "degree," and therefore hold that sociological changes, however extensive, do not contravene controlling biblical premises applicable still to the whole of life. The newer emphasis, that the Bible relates to only part of our social predicament, is soon combined with another: that failure to accept modern social theories in dealing with mass situations not only impairs the relevance of Christian ethics, but imperils the Christian religion itself!

Even after gaining a status independent of revealed theology and ethics, welfare work would nonetheless retain a modicum of Christian devotion because of the inherited and almost intuitive generosity of the Christian community. If enthusiasm flickers momentarily because the fires of religious particularism now burn low, the Church's enlarging participation in cooperative community programs of benevolence should soon revive the glow, until finally the Christian community experiences the warmth of a merely humanistic social vision. Mounting support for community chest and other civic programs might provide a psychological transition for the ultimate use of all church benevolences for general purposes. In the one world of "togetherness" Christian brotherhood will politely assume its place within the larger brotherhood of the human race without raising provocative and ungentlemanly distinctions.

Revising the Church's Task

Sooner or later, however, the reaffirmation of evangelism, rather than of direct social change as the immediate responsibility of the Church, may stifle ecclesiastical enthusiasm. In order really to carry the day, *Erape* must therefore popularize the notion that secular welfare *rather than* spiritual regeneration is the very heartbeat of the Christian mission. This exchange of mission calls for more than merely altering the nature of Christian charity. It requires the substituted notion that the economic imbalances of society are inherently sinful, that it is wrong for one person to have less than another, and that it is wicked for some people to have more than others. Of course all people believe in *democracy;* hence, economic democracy! The thesis that Christian love requires the human leveling of material possessions therefore supplies *Erape's* strategic propaganda weapon.

How may this economic doctrine be introduced most compellingly? By stressing that poverty is obviously an evil, and by citing cases of destitution that—in the *post*-Christian era—would stir even a pagan conscience. Next, churches are called to condemn, not only the misuse of riches and the exploitation and neglect of the poor, but the very idea of economic disproportion. The clergy are urged to badger the wealthy into sharing their possessions voluntarily with the poor, or to promote the multiplication of their tax burdens as a means of involuntary equalization.

To establish this economic mission as legitimate and as indispensable, a ringing appeal is made to the "social indignation" of the ancient prophets, and then—to vindicate the details—a further appeal is made to "modern social insights." The prophets assuredly were concerned about man's exploitation and neglect of the poor; they stressed that wealth is a divine entrustment to be responsibly used; they even implied God's special awareness of the needy (the rich so often think they are self-sufficient). The Old Testament clearly teaches love for neighbor, and Jesus lifted love for stranger, even for enemy, to new importance. There are prophetic warnings against plundering the poor (cf. Isa. 3:14, 15), apostolic judgments against the oppressive rich (cf. James 5:1–6), biblical denunciations of social injustice. *And although they nowhere espouse equalization of possessions, or community of property, as a divine ideal, the sacred writers are invoked propagandawise to provide leverage for modern redistribution of wealth.* A ministry to the poor that levels earthly riches, while neglecting the supernatural gifts of revealed religion, is thereby advanced as a Christian economic duty.

What of the Heritage?

Any attempt to vindicate the universal elimination of poverty as an authentic Christian mission indubitably faces troublesome obstacles in the biblical data. The first century Jew is not the problem; like some twentieth century Gentiles, he had become possession-minded, and interpreted personal poverty as implying God's rejection, and personal riches as implying God's special favor. Hence it seemed incredible to him that Jesus actually addressed "good news" to the poor. It would, of course, be easy for us, though unjustifiable, to distort Jesus' words, "The poor ye have always with you" (John 12:8), into a controlling principle to justify social indifference to material needs—although the statement indicates that poverty is part of the risk, if not of the structure, of our present state of life. Yet the Gospel was not essentially a message of economic readjustments. Jesus' own acts and deeds imply that *universal elimination of poverty is an objective extraneous to the Christian mission.*

For one thing, the disciples of Christ gained no reputation for handouts of their material belongings and redistribution of wealth. Jesus assuredly fed the five thousand, but he expressly repudiated the multitude's clamor for a bread-and-butter ruler. Instead, he identified himself as "the Living Bread," that is, as the Redeemer who assuages man's spiritual hunger. Nor do the Gospels depict Jesus as preoccupied with physical wants of the poor. He did, indeed, heal the sick and raise the dead—but only a few, comparatively speaking (cf. John 5:3, 8), and these only in connection with forgiveness of sins. He gave alms to the needy, and that consistently—but it would be difficult even for many good Bible students to supply chapter and verse to support the fact. So unobtrusive were his gifts to the poor (he would instruct Judas on occasion to reach into the moneybag and contribute to some needy person) that the fact itself stands only in the shadows of the record. On one occasion, the disciples mistakenly think he is aiding the poor, and from this misreading of his intentions we learn of his custom (John 13:27–29). The sacred records reveal Jesus' almsgiving to the needy as voluntary and private, in contrast with that ostentatious almsgiving of the Pharisees condemned in his Sermon on the Mount (Matt. 6:1–4), and they simply leave us to infer that he made frequent distributions to the poor. Equally important, they nowhere erect the redistribution of wealth into a motif of Jesus' ministry.

To ground an "equalize the wealth program" in the example of the apostles is fully as difficult. The so-called "communist experiment" in Acts—apart from the fact of its failure—was voluntary. It sought to implement a spiritual ministry, not the universal leveling of individual belongings. Nowhere do the apostolic letters view equality of possessions as something non-Christians have a right to expect; nowhere do they enjoin Christians to demand from society the communizing of property. As the apostolic age opens, Peter, in the company of John the apostle of love, greets the long-crippled beggar seeking charity at the temple gate with these words: "Silver and gold have I none, but such as I have give I thee: in the name of Jesus of Nazareth rise up and walk" (Acts 3:6). Although the memory of Jesus' words, "It is more blessed to give than to receive" (Acts 20:35), rings fresh in their minds, the apostles nowhere recall any doctrine that riches are wicked and that elimination of economic inequalities is a primary, indispensable, or authentic task of the Church.

The Bible and Economic Vices

The Bible grades as *vices* all inordinate use of riches, exploitation of the poor, and indifference to destitution (privation which reduces men to hunger and beggary). But neither man's possession of wealth nor the predicament of poverty is viewed as intrinsically sinful. Doubtless many of the Church Fathers view riches with suspicion. They regard the wealthy as spiritually obliged to justify their use of their possessions, and they criticize luxury or extravagance beyond one's station in life. Although viewing the rich as under special moral and spiritual obligation, neither the Bible nor Christian tradition condemns riches as such, and neither supports equality of wealth or of income as an ethical ideal.

The fact, moreover, that Jesus Christ in his advent renounced "the riches of glory" voluntarily to become poor for our sakes held striking fascination for the Middle Ages. Instead of the modern notion that wealth is wicked, however, this great drama yielded the medieval discovery that poverty can mediate special spiritual values. The Church Fathers regarded poverty as within God's particular providence, as covered by special promises of divine solicitude, and as carrying both possibilities of eternal reward in the future (recall the Communist caricature of "pie in the sky") and of spiritual consolations and compensations in this present life. These spiritual rewards were not simply negative benefits—such as the poor man's freedom (alongside his exposure to the sin of covetousness which he shares with the wealthy) from the temptations peculiar to the rich (recall 1 Tim. 6:10 on the love of money, and the numerous passages on greed). Jesus' beatitudes, *"Blessed* are the poor ... *Blessed* are the poor in spirit," if not suggesting actual virtue in poverty, at least imply its contribution toward a virtuous attitude more difficult of attainment in the climate of abundance.

Modern churchmen may scorn the idea of "holy poverty in an opulent society," but the Middle Ages did not hold poverty in such contempt. Indeed, Christian leaders found spiritual value not simply in involuntary poverty, but even in voluntary poverty. Doubtless medieval ecclesiasticism carried its vindication of the propriety and spirituality of poverty to unjustifiable extremes, at times seeming to idealize poverty as a state, but it avoided the fallacious modern equation of poverty with sin.

This strangely unmodern view of poverty did not imply, however, that biblical religion regards the plight of the destitute with indifference nor that it silently condones the sins of the wealthy. Indebted to the biblical outlook, the Middle Ages came to view benevolences to the poor as a loan to the Lord. The rich, moreover, were obligated to justify spiritually, by way of accounting to the Lord, both their possessions and their use of wealth. The rich are stewards, guardians of God's wealth, especially in relation to the poor, particularly to brethren in Christ. While the Bible views poverty neither as a blessing nor an evil, it commends relief of poverty as a virtue, and deplores indifference to destitution as a vice.

Materialism and Modern Discontents

Before the influence of Karl Marx and John Dewey, who shared the romantic notion that human nature can be intrinsically revised by environmental changes, the modern Christian movement reflected the traditional understanding of its mission in economic affairs. Universal removal of poverty was no announced objective of the corporate Church. The doctrine of redistribution of wealth as a social imperative was not part of the biblical heritage. Was not Job the richest man of his day? Although Eliphaz rebukes Job for economic injustices to others, none of his philosopher "friends" traces his affliction to a failure to level his wealth. Were not Abraham, Jacob, Solomon, and David wealthy, and does not the Scripture say that God loved them? Nor do the Christian writings advocate or look for the effectual elimination of poverty in the present course of history. In fact, poverty was not, as by Marx, regarded as immoral. The modern condemnation of riches and of poverty depends upon a prior assumption of an ideal equality of possessions which historic Christianity does not share. It is part and parcel of a philosophy of "equality of condition" that any sound Christian theology must recognize as working inevitably, through its radical alterations, a great injustice upon society. For the spiritual vision of righteousness and redemption sustained by the Christian religion, it substitutes the illusion of a terrestrial Utopia, nourished by the dream of universal prosperity, and promoted by material means and earthly weapons. Seldom, if ever, is the warning of the Christian moralists heard that "the world is too much with us" and that, virtuous as it is to satisfy legitimate needs, it is also virtuous to reduce our wants. Equally, it betrays an unspiritual philosophy of possessions, one sure to arouse man's desire for material possessions by catering to the false notion that true happiness lies in a stipulated quantity of things. Contemporary American life, in which the scope of poverty is much reduced, bears full testimony by its personal discontents—its drunkards, divorcees, drug addicts, and neurotics—that plenty no less than poverty corrupts the spirit in the absence of a spiritual vision of life. In these dimensions, the prevalent philosophy of poverty serves to inflame the passions of avarice, and its implication that no life can be blessed in the absence of a proportionate share of this world's goods makes a basic concession to materialistic views of life.

Dr. Russell Kirk, editor of *Modern Age*, recently remarked—and with pointed relevance—that no era has held poverty in more contempt than ours, and that the twentieth century, having discarded the decency and respectability of poverty, has sought to abolish it. Needless to say, it has sought to abolish wealth also. Both "leveling" movements—although sometimes piously promoted under the canopy of "Christian social ethics"—may well prove destructive of Christian charity also.

Christianity and Charity

Does Christian charity then idealize poverty, and does it then regard human suffering and pain with indifference? The total impact of Christian humanitarianism through two thousand years condemns the thought. From the beginning the Christian churches have distributed material alms as a function of the churches, and devout leaders in all ages have emphasized that not only do the needy suffer, but the Church herself declines spiritually whenever this responsibility is neglected. Whoever would impugn Christian missions and extol Communist revolution is blind to the past history of the West and to the signs of our age. If anything characterizes Christianity but not communism, as Evangelist Bob Pierce often reminds Christians throughout the Orient, it is *compassion*. In the Western world today, welfare work is carried on in larger proportion than in any earlier age; in a sense, ours is the century of philanthropy. Whatever may be said of the method and motive of modern almsgiving, there can be little doubt but that its historic inspiration and impetus have come mainly through the evangelical Christian religion.[1]

————————

Christianity faces the world with *agape*, not merely with *eros*, nor with some sentimental amalgam ("erape"). Wherever professing Christians lack *agape* as a distinguishing virtue, they detach themselves in principle from the mercy God has shown undeserving sinners in his great gift, Jesus Christ. No religion like Christianity has dramatized, by the fact of divine incarnation and atonement for sinners, the high virtue of rescuing persons overwhelmed by need. Charity becomes evangelical when it reflects the drama of redemption through genuine sacrifice on the part of the donor, and when it extends not only to the "deserving" (whose need springs from no fault of their own) but to the "undeserving" (whose ignorance, folly, or perversity has worsened their plight).

The Christian approach to almsgiving is *1.* regenerative, *2.* personal, *3.* voluntary. Respect for these fundamental criteria will avoid misconceptions of the nature of Christian charity.

Charity as Testimony

Christian welfare work is *regenerative* because it seeks by its witness to restore men to God and to their true destiny. Evangelical charity is a commentary on the Gospel of God's undeserved redemption of fallen man, a vehicle for lifting needy persons to

————————

Carl F. H. Henry, "Has Anybody Seen 'Erape'? (Part I)," *Christianity Today* 4, no. 7 (January 4, 1960): 13–23.

the Savior and Lord of the whole personality. The Christian feeds the hungry to distinguish the Bread of Life. To shape a new outlook on life while relieving destitution is a legitimate and desirable Christian aim.

Whenever this witness is suppressed, charity's Christian status is blurred, and its vitality threatened. Unless *agape* is lighted by divine justice and justification, its authentic evangelical character is lost. Charity that does not confront men with Christ may as readily desert them to Marx.

Christian charity unquestionably embraces human destitution even where its witness cannot be directly given, and where the deed must speak for itself. *Agape* doubtless *works* whether associated with proclamation or not, although, as Dr. Oswald C. J. Hoffmann of The Lutheran Hour reminds us, *diakonia* without *kerygma* leaves man's deepest needs unmet. *Agape* even reaches to men who reject its witness to Christ (as God's goodness now extends to just and unjust alike). When "rice Christians" multiply, invoking the "name of Christ" merely for the sake of material aid, Christian institutions must not only recall the natural perversity of men, but resist the temptation to narrow their welfare vision to "the faithful" exclusively, thus giving other unfortunates the misimpression that they are outside the pale of Christian interest.

But *agape* never voluntarily conceals its willing witness to the Lord of love. Lifting almsgiving into the orbit of divine concern for man and his fellows, Christian charity points beyond humanitarian pity in the relief of suffering. It relates the human predicament to the divine command, exhibiting charity (and the recipient's benefactions) as a matter of obedience to God's gracious will. Thus the *testimony*-aspect of charity guards against the religious impulse's replacement by motivations of self-glorification and pride, or its decline to utility and other sinister forms of self-interest. Altruism shaped by such humanitarian formulas swiftly shades into egoism in seasons of stress and passion.

Charity as Personal

Christian participation in welfare work, moreover, is essentially *personal*. In relieving the misfortunes of others, it seeks to restore the sense of spiritual community, of family oneness by creation, while dramatizing the spirit of neighborliness as that is grasped within the family of the redeemed. Welfare work on this basis not only helps to overcome an "atomistic" view of society, but it escapes the secular humanitarian tendency to view the needy as so many "case studies" indexed by a given file number. Skilled administrators are needed in welfare agencies and some social workers, assuredly, seem better able than ministers to preserve the self-respect of individuals and families in need. But much contemporary social work has in fact deteriorated to a mere body of techniques. Real skill in social activity will preserve rather than obscure the personal dimensions of life.

Doubtless the institutionalizing of charity jeopardizes this personal touch. But it need not wholly destroy it. Even in the New Testament, collections for relief of the poor were administered in the name of the local churches by the apostles, who thus supply an early precedent for a collective form (but not for a public or state form) of charitable administration. So their spiritual ministry would not suffer neglect, the apostles themselves, after first personally handling all distributions to the poor, soon named deacons—thereby introducing a third-party relationship—to distribute to material needs. They did not consider the organization of welfare activity to be intrinsically objectionable.

These precedents do not of themselves, however, legitimate a larger view of the Church engaged in massive almsgiving as a corporate earthly institution. In much modern church welfare work, the Good Samaritan and the man in need are actually many steps removed from each other; seldom do donor and receiver meet face to face. The Church neglects to encourage charity in this dimension of direct neighbor-relations at great cost to the effectiveness of her witness. Ecclesiastical pleas for unified denominational budgets, as well as projections of welfare work along presbyterial and episcopal rather than congregational patterns of administration—almsgiving being regarded as the duty of the corporate Church acting as a group (as by the Episcopal Prayer Book)—tend to minimize the personal relationships in stewardship. Yet, it must be acknowledged, even churches whose ecclesiology stresses local autonomy (as in the case of Baptists) have felt constrained to organize large conventions to promote efficiency and effectiveness in their corporate witness. And one congregation can seldom support an orphanage. But the fact remains that the complaint most often aimed at ecclesiastical leadership is its loss of personal and local sensitivities. Does not the Church need to guard the virility of Christian charity by preserving not only its witness-character, but its sense of a vital personal relationship between benefactor and recipient?

A dissipation of the personal factor takes place in many great private foundations established for charitable purposes. In most cases such foundations arise to assure the perpetuation of ideals that are too often blurred by established agencies which welcome the funds but corrode the convictions. After safeguarding this legitimate personal interest, however, foundation charities frequently drift into impersonal stewardship through their reliance on professional administrators. The result is the concentration of charitable power in the hands of men who did not bring these foundations into being, and who may then dispense gifts without the warmth and vision of the founders.

The most extreme form of impersonalism, largely destructive of the very concept of stewardship, however, occurs through the surrender of charity to the state as a tax-supported activity. The routine and impersonal government administration of homes for the aged and public poorhouses often stands in sharp contrast to the alms houses motivated by personal charity. As the churches abandon the responsibility for welfare to the state and rely more and more upon unspiritual methods of relieving human misery, they indirectly, if unwittingly, support a theory of state charity that, ultimately, may tolerate even the Church's welfare activities only as an arm or agency of the state's program. When the limits of state power are in doubt, and when government programs of benevolence are urged as much for the purpose of equalizing wealth as for the relief of human misery, then charity is easily subverted by an alien ideology and becomes a means of implementing schemes hostile to Christian sanctions, to Christian methods, and to Christian virtues.

Charity as Voluntary

Perhaps in narrowing the opportunities for voluntarism in the sphere of stewardship, the modern philosophies betray most pointedly their clash with the biblical view of benevolences. Christian almsgiving is, as we have stated, not only regenerative and personal, but *voluntary*.

While charity confers a temporary material benefit upon the recipient, expositors of Christian morality have long stressed that charity also yields a moral benefit to the giver. In modern social welfare work, however, the volitional element is often narrowed to the vanishing point. This need not be the case—even in state welfare programs—since charity as a collective effort through government is possible, as Dr. Russell Kirk points out, where tax levies are in fact, and not only in theory, a voluntary grant (taxation reflecting a free act of those who vote the taxes for the common welfare). But representative government today tends too often to reflect representative pressure blocs more than the people. And tax-supported welfare remains involuntary on the part of those who vote against these measures.

Voluntary community agencies provide some check upon the transfer of welfare responsibility to government, and hence also serve to check the development of the welfare state. But in times of depression and hardship, supporters of these congregate services are not likely—in the absence of the sanction and dynamic of revealed religion—to pay heavy compulsory welfare taxes to the state and in addition to give voluntarily to community charities. Hence taxation tends to stifle charity.

Students of government remind us that as government moves from county to state and Federal levels the voluntary element is progressively weakened. Those who pay the taxes often do not clearly understand their purpose. Moreover, the prospect enlarges that those who pay the taxes will be outvoted by those who get them, and by those who administer them. The government's growing grab for tax monies therefore provokes counter-efforts to preserve the remnants of voluntary stewardship. Avoidance of taxes sometimes becomes a prime consideration in establishing a foundation, and charity resting on this motive is obviously not purely benevolent. But government welfare, established on a permanent basis, soon destroys the opportunity for voluntarism and the very idea of charity.

Nowhere is this dissipation of voluntarism more important than in its bearing on the churches. From the early days of the Christian movement the function of the churches has included material aid to needy persons. Neglect of this duty has always meant that the churches themselves would suffer spiritually. But today the penalty of such neglect means the removal of almsgiving from the Church to government as the authorized welfare agency. The voluntary element is, of course, already lessened whenever gifts are made, even to the churches, by donors who tithe simply as a legal routine, or because of unrelenting pressure of a finance committee, or because of fear of public opinion, so that charity becomes a matter of somebody else's expectation or insistence. But voluntarism virtually disappears when that third party is the state. If the benefit of the relief of poverty, viewed as a work of virtue, accrues to the donor more than to the recipient, the substitution of state compulsion for voluntarism dissolves this benefit.

In this transition, moreover, something more has happened. Not only has almsgiving ceased to be voluntary on the donor's part, but it becomes obligatory also in the recipient's view. The government dole is looked upon as a *right* rather than as a love-gift. Indeed, the state's welfare allotment is so much regarded as a right that some recipients even prefer subsistence aid to work.

State Monopoly of Welfare

That the churches are given the opportunity of cooperating in a massive program in which the state virtually takes over *diakonia*, that the growing government monopoly of welfare activity is hailed as a valid expression of Christian love for neighbor, that the denominations, moreover, virtually become agencies of this state program, calls for earnest soul-searching. The Church will always pay a high price for giving to Caesar what belongs to God.

How, from the parable of the Good Samaritan, and the designation of deacons in the Acts, does the Church arrive at institutional agencies for meeting a neighbor's need? Or at the voluntary agency's necessary cooperation with the welfare program of the state? Or at confusion of the welfare state with the kingdom of God, so that the former is heralded as an authentic fulfillment of Christian love for neighbor?

And what remains in this of Christian *testimony*, of the *personal* element, and of *voluntarism*? Where is *agape*? Perhaps *erape* can already report "mission accomplished," while we comfort ourselves with the delusion that he does not really exist.

Carl F. H. Henry, "Has Anybody Seen 'Erape'? (Part II)," *Christianity Today* 4, no. 8 (January 18, 1960): 12–14.

Chapter 26

THE "NEW MORALITY" AND PREMARITAL SEX

Now and then we read *Playboy*—not often, confessedly, but when Hugh Hefner, its editor, occasionally sends a copy hoping *Christianity Today* will debate his philosophy of sex and give him free promotion. There seems to be only one aspect of grammar that interests Mr. Hefner as an editor—gender, the feminine particularly, so exposed as to suggest a maternal attachment that Mr. Hefner hasn't yet outgrown. Some of his magazine's enthusiasts, ministers included, have the gall to commend *Playboy* for an interpretation of sex more authentically Christian than that given in the churches.

Today new currents of opinion are gaining force. This is not necessarily bad. Some man-made codes have too long been invested with divine status—for example, the Roman Catholic rule that sex is only for the procreation of children and that any other intention is wicked. The tardy revision of such misconceptions often raises doubts that would have been avoided had the authority of Scripture always been respected.

In the *Republic*, Plato asks whether one can accumulate all the benefits of being just by merely appearing to be just. If one could make himself invisible, would he hold up a bank or ravish a beautiful girl? Is the fear of being found out what really keeps us straight? This issue is raised in a new way by the scientists' discovery of "the pill." For the pill promises intercourse without physical consequences. What it does not promise is ideas without consequences.

The "new morality" asserts that love alone justifies intercourse and that, if two persons intend to marry, love is the only other precondition for sex relations. Christianity does not say "No" to sex; it says "Yes" on the basis of divine creation. But it says "No" to premarital sex on the basis of divine commandment. The Christian view is that sex relations are legitimate only within the marital institution.

As a protest against marriage without love (of which there is little deficiency in our time), or against marital intercourse without love, or, for that matter, against prostitution as a relationship in which both marriage and love are lacking, the plea for the centrality of love is wholesome and necessary. The Christian emphasis on personal love in the very nature of God and on Christ's love for his bride carries an implicit protest against the discounting of *agape* in the sexual life of the modern world. Our confused generation has lost the profoundly Christian meaning both of monogamous marriage and of love. It needs the example and guidance a generation of evangelical young lovers and young married couples can bring it at this moment in history. Any generation that prizes intercourse above all other intimacies and thinks that through physical love alone, apart from any transcendent relationship, the sex act unlocks life's deepest secrets and exhausts its mysteries, is doomed to deadly superficiality. What the world needs is couples capable of such a tremendous love that they want love as God gave it before Adam and Eve lost it, couples aware that in accepting the new morality one is in danger of falling, not into love, but into sin, and that love is something that one stands up for, reaching for the stars rather than the spirit of the age.

The proposition that intercourse is validated by love, not by marriage, is simply not true. Ideally, romantic love, monogamous marriage, and sexual intercourse are all bound together, and intercourse is last in order. No marriage is legal and binding until the conjugal act is performed; the courts will annul a marriage incapable of sexual consummation. Intercourse validates marriage but does not always reflect love. Outside marriage, intercourse *always* violates love, since it shatters the divine framework of sexual morality. Any person who loves self-indulgence more than obedience to God is ready neither for marriage nor for intercourse. Someone has aptly described mature love as "union under the conditions of preserving ... integrity." If love in the New Testament sense is present in the intention to marry, it will insist on marriage before the conjugal act.

To justify sexual indulgence before marriage by identifying modern engagement with biblical betrothal has three weaknesses. First, it obscures the fact that modern engagement is neither so formal nor so binding as biblical betrothal. Betrothal included payment of the dowry (Gen. 24:58 ff.) and hence involved parental consent. After the betrothal, the parties were legally in the position of a married couple, and unfaithfulness was adultery (Deut. 22:23, 24). Second, the identification of modern engagement with biblical betrothal lacks direct scriptural support; for its assumption that intercourse is permissible during betrothal depends upon the argument from silence. Finally, the comparison fails to stress the scriptural view that intercourse belongs to the divine institution of marriage.

If the unmarried cannot wait, there remains only one way to please the Lord—that is, to marry. The apostle says of the unmarried: "If they cannot contain, let them marry; for it is better to marry than to burn" (1 Cor. 7:9). Nowhere does he approve marital privileges without marital obligations; he insists on the very opposite. It is to the husband that the wife is to give the conjugal due, not to the intended husband; it is to the wife that the husband is to give the conjugal due, not to the intended wife.

The woman who indulges in premarital intercourse because she intends to marry may not be a prostitute, but she is neither wife nor virgin (1 Cor. 7:34, 35). The man too is a fornicator (v. 1). Although a wife cannot claim her body as her own, the wife-to-be can and ought to do so. The single girl is to give her husband-to-be only what is due the husband-to-be, not what is due the husband. Paul differentiates "the wife and the virgin" (v. 34); nowhere does he refer normatively to premarital loss of virginity.

In the same context Paul clearly states that fornicators, adulterers, and sodomites, along with drunkards, thieves, and idolaters, shall have no part in God's kingdom (6:9–10), and that professing Christians must put such sinful works to death or fail to inherit that kingdom. Both fornication and adultery detach intercourse from the institution of marriage, whether the offenders intend to marry each other or not. Fornication is used figuratively in the Bible in the sense of idolatry—of "whoring after" false gods.

If intention to marry justifies sexual intercourse and the actual fulfillment of that intention (or marriage itself) is not immediately relevant, then how is such intention distinguishable from emotional passion only? Recently the writer spoke at the junior-senior banquet of a large Christian college in Oklahoma. Twenty couples publicly announced their engagements that evening. The class adviser, asked for a fair estimate across the years of how many would go through with it, said 25 per cent would not. On that basis, the percentage of engagements of evangelical college students that are broken is higher than the percentage of worldly marriages that end in divorce—quite apart from the issue of premarital intercourse. This estimate is based only on formally announced engagements, and these at the college level.

The notion that two persons are free to follow their desires as long as they love each other is an invitation to exploit passionate impulses irrespective of moral restraints. Love is not self-defining; in this twentieth century it has been equated with pacifism, with socialism, and now with sexual license. A few years ago, when a divinity student at Howard University killed a young Washington woman, he said he did it because he "loved her" so much. Love that spurns the commandments of God always destroys and kills. In the nature of God, love and righteousness are equally ultimate, and *agape* is self-defining; but in the nature of man—finite, fallen, not yet fully conformed to the divine image even in redemption—*agape* is not self-defining. If our love of God and our love of neighbor are sullied and need divine direction, why do we think that the ideal direction of sexual love is self-determinable? "If ye love me," said Jesus, "keep my commandments." And some of his most serious indictments bore upon the failure even of the religious leaders of his day to understand the depth of God's claim in the area of sex. "Whosoever looketh upon a woman to lust after her ..."—how seriously do we take that? There is considerably more temptation to look and leer today than in the past, and the line between appreciation and lust is getting more difficult to draw.

Love is responsible to the commandments; it is responsible also to family, to society, and to the state. Its requirements are not exhausted by the private life of two persons. The lovers are to leave father and mother and cleave to each other, becoming one flesh. There is to be no cleaving before leaving. The family is the basic unit of society; young lovers who destroy the claim of the family are indirectly destroying themselves. Love does not overlook responsibility to parents, and those under eighteen or twenty-one are under the guardianship of their parents and should secure parental consent for marriage—or, if they prefer, for premarital intercourse! Moreover, the state is divinely willed to preserve order and justice in a sinful society, and marriage includes a responsibility to the community. Marriage is established by God and confirmed by the state; it is not dissolved by the absence of love (1 Cor. 7:10, 11) nor constituted solely by the presence of love (7:8–9). The bonding element between man and wife is not simply their private love and sexual privilege. ("Art thou bound to a wife?" asks Paul. "Seek not to be loosed" [7:27].) The couple are "bound by the law," Paul says (7:39). Private intention is not the same as a public ceremony; the connection of sex with marriage attests its answerability to both love and justice. A liberal theology, which telescopes God's wrath and God's justice into his love, has produced a liberal ethics, which artificially narrows the moral claim to *agape* alone, and in so doing falsifies the content of *agape*.

Assume now that not marriage but preferential love justifies intercourse, and that marriage is built on this prior premise. What happens if—in some hard hour—love evaporates in the home, even for a season, and the wedding expectations turn for the "worse" rather than for the "better"? And if one of the partners then loves a third party (assuming that intercourse-approving love is love for one at a time)? If marriage is really binding, then intercourse with other than one's wife is spiritually and legally excluded. But if love is the only bonding factor, the implications of this view will swiftly undermine the social order. If marriage binds in a way that preferential love does not, then the unmarried—for all their intentions—simply are not maritally bound. The revealed will of God sanctions monogamous marriage, but it nowhere sanctions extra-marital intercourse. The fact that such a relationship is pursued outside wedlock with one person at a time and continues over a long period with but one person does not sanctify it; what is wrong once is no less wrong through a process of multiplication or addition, even by the addition of the wedding ceremony.

Assume again that preferential love, not marriage, justifies intercourse—and that professors and students are free to act in this way, and unmarried ministers in their congregations. Assume that a Christian would be quite willing to tell his sister or daughter that she ought to let some young man possess her, even if the prospect of marriage is years off (remember, the intention is decisive), so long as they wave the banner of love and carry the pill. If, in fact, the connection of courtship and intercourse is permissible and proper, normative and ideal, then no lover ought to withhold this relationship from the loved one; in that case it is morally and spiritually due, so long as unmarried couples make it clear that they are courting each other, and for as long as they prefer courtship to marriage.

We can assure the Church that no doctrine it has ever propagated will be as welcome as this one. For in a single stroke what has been regarded as gross sexual immorality down through the Christian ages will be protected and promoted as an ideal fulfillment of a moral and spiritual imperative. The world will hail this late twentieth-century "insight," and the Church may count upon an innumerable host of "converts" to this notion—in fact, many unregenerates were already "converted" to it before the church's discovery, and almost every young couple in the churches will now want to follow suit.

But any such development will mark the day when the Church has gone out of the business of morality and defected from her role in the world. By maintaining the morality of sex, the Christian community fulfills a divinely given role in the world— not simply of proclaiming the standards by which God will judge the world, but of illustrating the blessings of obedience.

The new doctrine is simply a by-product of the existential spirit of our times, which has lost contact with objective norms and standards and, above all, with divinely revealed truths and precepts. In the name of *agape* it destroys *agape,* because it transgresses the Word of God. In the name of personal love it violates Christian personality, because it impairs the divine image in man by neglecting the will of God. In the name of sacramental love, it forfeits the sacredness of marriage in exchange for a few months of premature self-indulgence.

Since God is the opener of the womb and man may prevent life but only God can create it, the next step will be to honor children born outside wedlock as the fruit of *agape.* When that happens, little or nothing will be left for marriage to add. And, in the eyes of a Sodom and Gomorrah generation, marriage will appear as the enemy of love. But the devout believer will recognize this trend for what it is—a rationalization of human passions, which one man applies in the world of sex, another in the world of economics, and another in the world of international affairs, in an age whose heart is set against objective moral standards.

Carl F. H. Henry, "The 'New Morality' and Premarital Sex," *Christianity Today* 9, no. 29 (July 2, 1965): 21–22.

Chapter 27

A QUESTION OF IDENTITY

Today an emerging evangelical vanguard of state university graduates (and a smaller number from evangelical campuses) who are disenchanted with modern culture are calling, in the name of the Gospel, for a radical faith and a revolutionary commitment. Their discontents include not only secular society but also institutional Christianity. If they reproach the contemporary worldview for its technocratic depersonalization of human values, no less do they fault the ecumenical churches for secularizing the supernatural Gospel, and the evangelical churches for spiritualizing man's material needs. On the edge of the Vietnamese war, most of them question the legitimacy and effectiveness of violence in settling international differences, though not all are pacifists.

Some of these young people have emerged from the youth counter-cultural revolt to a thoroughgoing Christian commitment. While they share the evangelistic concern of the Jesus people, they are not content simply to withdraw from the world they once knew, nor do they think Christianity can long survive in free-floating patterns not theologically informed. And they are determined to bear Christian witness at socio-cultural frontiers.

Not a few are attending evangelical seminaries for an exposure to dogmatics and apologetics. They do not question the validity of the gathered church, though some question the legitimacy of the ministry, as it is presently conceived, as a Christian profession. Few of them think the pulpit ministry is their thing; most are unsure just what their vocation is. Some hopefully contemplate exploratory careers in mass communications, free university or community student centers, and the like.

A dozen or so of their number attending Trinity Evangelical Divinity School plan soon to mount their witness through a sub-culture newspaper. They hope to champion a Christian faith matched to the contemporary mind-set. They insist that what Christians offer must be intellectually satisfying, ethically sensitive, and experientially adequate. In the modern context, their message is radical. The supernatural, not society, is the decisive setting for human life; sin, not environmental deformity, is man's basic problem; Christ and catastrophe are life's only enduring options. God's offer of new life through Jesus Christ crucified and risen is their good news. They are committed to an authoritative Bible.

To this point many evangelical churches will approve. However, an establishment imprimatur means little to the new vanguard. Many evangelicals, they complain, uncritically espouse a two-car materialistic faith and a pro-American Gospel; their social and political values, moreover, are not derived from the Bible. Thousands of such evangelical churches, they say, concentrate on microethics (personal legalisms) to the neglect of macroethics (war, race, and poverty are most frequently mentioned). The student world, we are told, has largely gained the impression that Christian identification involves at least a neglect of the issues of social justice if not the negation of any commitment to it.

The questions that the young intellectuals feel they must answer are pressed upon them by non-Christians whose primary focus is the reality of the body, of society, of this world. In this milieu the worst of all options open to the evangelical is to be silent and tolerant toward social wrongs, for this adds up to implicit participation in them. A biblical faith alive to social ethics and energetically addressed to the multitudes in captivity to American culture is indispensable.

Most of these aroused intellectuals shun not only the traditional pulpit ministry but also a career in the military or in corporate business. As they see it, if the "just war" ethic is applied to Viet Nam, they want none of it. And if capitalism is to be identified with freedom to pollute the earth or to promote cigarette addiction through the mass media until government interferes, or with buy-at-your-own-risk manufacturing, they want some moral alternative. Modern America little senses how much of the revolt against inherited traditions has been bred and nourished by recent political and commercial compromises of those ideals.

Perhaps more evangelical churches than one might suspect will say, "Right on!" But these young intellectuals are wary of the right and are leaning toward the left. They are committed to social revolution and to eliminating social injustice. This does not mean, however, that they espouse anarchy or the forceful overthrow of government; after all, recent American presidents and leading evangelical evangelists alike have embraced the term *revolution*. Nor do these young people attach post-millennial Kingdom of God expectations to political change. What they promote is a humane society in which personal values hold the center of human existence. And because the political left is against the Vietnamese involvement and specializes in the vocabulary of values, the young evangelical vanguard finds a ready shelter and welcome there.

The left-leaning intellectuals desperately need funds for the bold, creative thrusts through which they seek new visibility for the Gospel. But because of apprehensions about the left—derived from the long-standing correlation of theological liberalism and political liberalism—the evangelical establishment has taken little interest in funding nonconformist evangelical ventures that combine biblical theology with a leftward look in socio-political affairs. Funding is more likely to be available from ecumenical agencies that will overlook a strenuous emphasis on biblical theology if evangelicals can be involved for political change. Even in an ecumenical context, evangelical intellectuals can probably be counted on not to muffle their gospel witness. But by its support or non-support of their efforts the evangelical establishment will, as many of these young people see it, confirm or disavow the charge of being socially insensitive and identified with a right-wing cultural establishment.

Evangelical churches are not alone in facing an identity crisis. The young evangelical intellectuals themselves face such a crisis, and detachment from an authentically evangelical milieu could worsen their plight. If, as they feel, fundamentalist Christianity has forgotten that all cultures remain subject to God's judgment, and that no economic system is to be regarded as identical with the Kingdom of God, then does not the new vanguard itself repeat and compound that error by uncritically supposing that the program of the political left is identifiable with the content of God's New Covenant? Should not any philosophy of society—left or right—furnish and sustain norms of commitment and action? Should evangelicals be taken in by a Marxist antithesis of personal and property values, or is property, rather, a personal right and stewardship?

The young intellectuals and the evangelical churches need each other—the one for evangelical illumination, the other for social concern. It would be the saddest of mistakes if, instead of complementing and building each other, they were to exhaust themselves in mutual destruction.

Carl F. H. Henry, "Footnotes: A Question of Identity," *Christianity Today* 15, no. 22 (August 6, 1971): 30.

Chapter 28

HAS DEMOCRACY A FUTURE?

Christianity makes loyalty to civil government a kind of religious obligation. It bases dutiful subjection to the powers—within certain limits—upon God's revealed will for man in a fallen society (Rom. 13) and thus considers civil obedience a Christian responsibility.

Because the Christian's supreme loyalty is to God alone, he must resist the temptation to make the nation and its institutions an object of religious loyalty. When exaggerated patriotism and uncritical loyalty to the state readily excuse its moral compromises and questionable power tactics, then a near-religious loyalty to one's government can, in fact, threaten loyalty to Jesus Christ.

Christians become vulnerable to misguided loyalty when they center spiritual commitment exclusively in personal piety, and interpret separation of church and state to mean that government leaders have the prerogative of formulating political commitments independently of the criticism and influence of Christian citizens. Whenever patriotism co-exists with non-participation in public affairs, it is easily correlated—as a matter of faith in the nation—with whatever policies national leaders may pursue.

When the state becomes one's object of ultimate loyalty, then authentic Christian patriotism yields to the religious cult of nationalism. And when faith results ultimately in the nation, the faith of citizens becomes essentially idolatrous. The nation's military and economic might soon become the distinctive criteria of national greatness, and special interests are able to erect patriotism as a sheltering umbrella for their ambitions. In time each national participant tends to absolutize private interest into a loyalty for which all citizens are expected to lay down their lives. And the nation as a military and economic force is easily cast in the role of world deliverer.

Pride in the prestige and power of a nation has no moral legitimacy apart from national dedication to justice; furthermore, all that is represented as justice—insofar as Christians are concerned—must be tested by the revealed commandments of God. Apart from such dedication and evaluation, national pride remains an ethical prerogative only if one suspends it on the prospect of national repentance.

Only an awareness of the majesty of the Lord can guard us from considering any nation, however great, as the providential hinge of history, and preserve us from the myth that any modern nation is the instrument of world redemption rather than a body in urgent need of Christian discipling.

Evangelical Christians have no biblical right to indulge the notion that civil government is a source of human salvation. Only when America's self-interest as a nation is conformed to the will of God can and will its fortunes as a nation be identified with the highest good.

In the recent past democracy has for many Americans functioned as a false religion, much as state absolutism functions in

Communist countries as the embodiment of political omnipo-
tence and the means to utopia. These people think that the principles and ideals of democracy are inherently and unconditionally
valid. Democracy's virtues have been extolled and defended, and
its indispensability for human freedom and hope emphasized
above the Church of Christ. American patriots dedicated themselves to the goals of democracy more than to those of the Church
as a bearer of hope for humanity, and expressed more concern
over what threatened democracy than over what imperiled the
Christian community.

We can rightly ask, however: What has happened to the
Church of Christ as a bearer of the moral fortunes of mankind,
once the ethical vitality of the nation as a political entity is
thought to surpass that of the Church as a new society, and the
moral energy of the body of Christ is considered inferior to that
of the body politic?

Surely, democracy is not the only form under which justice
might prevail, and many now think it just as potentially frus-
trating to justice as many another alternative. Around the free
world Watergate has darkened even further the shadow engulf-
ing American democracy as an ideal for other nations to emulate.
The growing refusal in democratic lands to accept government
policies is an ominous spectacle, since no society can long be vigorous without such acceptance. It nurtures the frightening fear
that before the present century ends surviving democracies may
succumb to and perish under dictatorships.

For all that, democracy still has a great deal in its favor. Those
who glamorize political dictatorships seem never to learn from
history.

But if not even the regenerate Church as a community of
believers rises—or can rise—to the moral power and curtailed
egoism of its best saints, how can we attribute to the collective

national spirit (even of a democracy) the ethical superiority and natural restraint that best exemplifies individual self-denial?

Apart from shared principles and earnest moral dedication, democracy crumbles into chaos. The positive political achievements of a democratic nation are not to be exempted from critical evaluation. Moreover, if the friends of democracy do not pursue such an evaluation, it will be left to those who commend fascist, Communist, or other forms of government as more utopian.

The only perfect reign known in the Bible centers in one absolutely sovereign Ruler, the Messiah; all self-appointed candidates for this totalitarian leadership are antichrist in spirit.

To expect more from any nation than it can give is not patriotism but political illusion. A decline of faith in democracy, or in any other form of civil government, and a critical questioning of national values and goals, is not devastating for the believer because faith in God is a very different faith from faith in democracy or in politics. For the Christian patriot, the nation reaches its highest pinnacle of prestige when it recognizes God as the sovereign source, support and sanction of all that is true and right, and makes its political institutions an instrumentality of public justice and order.

Perhaps the only way to avoid inordinate pride in thinking that the United States is indispensable to an exhibition of the final purpose of history is to provide a context in which human life best finds its temporal and ultimate meaning. That context must assuredly be more than political, although the political is inescapably important. The acme of national achievement will more properly and more surely be found when the nation rises to its true role in service to God and to man.

Carl F. H. Henry, "Footnotes: Has Democracy a Future?," *Christianity Today* 18, no. 20 (July 5, 1974): 26–27.

Chapter 29

JESUS AND POLITICAL JUSTICE

Jewish intellectuals frequently say that the continuing polit-ico-economic oppression on earth is proof that Messiah has not yet come. The meaning of messianic realization is such, they argue, that to dissociate the Gospel from an end to political oppression annuls the case for Jesus' divine sonship.

Radical activist theologians have insisted that Jesus' gospel was centrally political, that its very essence is liberation of the oppressed from socio-political injustices. But it is impossible to square this emphasis with the fact that Jesus' program involved no direct challenge to the political system of the Romans, whose oppression was the source of the social, economic, and politi-cal grievances that dominated Jewish life in his day. Moreover, Jesus' ministry was more concerned with personal spiritual relationships than with any forcible alteration of socio-political structures. Those who consider socio-political liberation to be the essence of the Gospel should ask themselves, furthermore, where and when the proclamation of their message has achieved such utopian results.

The New Testament does indeed emphasize—as in the Book of Revelation—that oppressive powers will ultimately be overthrown. But are we to infer that the real Messiah has not yet come because evil has not yet been wholly subordinated? Does Christianity proclaim messianism wholly without politico-economic liberation?

To make socio-political liberation the criterion of Messiah's presence blurs the biblical picture of Messiah. Such a criterion is too open-ended, since one can intend the cessation of exploitation and oppression—that is, an improved economic and political outlook—without intending love in community. Even where nourished by noble intentions, revolution has often begotten more revolution as projections of a better future have succumbed to human passions. Those who are economically and politically liberated, even for a season, often fail to sense how truly enslaved they remain. In the Bible, liberation has in view man's moral and spiritual plight, the need for meaningful selfhood, the problems of sin and guilt and identity and destiny. To deal with freedom only in relation to either external structures or internal considerations parochializes messianic meaning.

The Exodus story is often made paradigmatic in a way that oversimplifies the redemptive message. Political liberation is not the sole or even central theme of biblical redemption. The covenant at Sinai and God's choosing of a people stands much nearer the center. The Gospels notably mention that Jesus went to accomplish his "exodus" in Jerusalem, a text hardly congenial to the notion of a master political program. The weakness of all motif-research is that it tendentially orients the evidence and overlooks what falls outside its purview.

The Bible does indeed have a message for all the afflicted and oppressed—widows and orphans, the poor and destitute, the downtrodden and exploited. This theme is progressively reinterpreted as features of the Exodus are expanded, but without jettisoning the original elements. The message is still addressed to the poor and needy, but as R. K. Harrison notes, "the Hebrew term 'poor' took on an additional, non-economic meaning ... the poor, harassed remnant of spiritual fidelity in a vast morass of Hellenistic paganism. Thus 'the poor' also meant 'the faithful.' ... Christ used the term 'poor' in Matt. 5:3, Luke 6:20 in this same sense, promising the Kingdom to the 'spiritually loyal,' not to the economically or spiritually deprived" ("Poor" in *Baker's Dictionary of Christian Ethics*, pp. 515f.).

The New Testament does not, however, ignore the socio-political question, even if it does not begin with it. The discussion of redemption and reconciliation is put in a profounder context, however. It tolerates no total depoliticizing of the Gospel, even if it does not put Jesus Christ in the primary role of a contemporary socio-political liberator; indeed, he deliberately resisted a mob movement to make him king on a mistaken materialistic premise (John 6:15). But Jesus' followers nonetheless owned the crucified and risen one as "the blessed and only Sovereign, the King of kings and Lord of lords" (1 Tim. 6:15). Jesus had reminded Pilate that the Roman procurator's political power was a temporary divine entrustment, and he let it be known that he considered Herod a sly fox.

The New Testament teaches that at the Lord's return in power and glory all nations will be finally judged (Matt. 25:32) and government will at last rest upon Messiah's shoulders. The interim dimension is not avoided, however, even if Jesus' followers have tended to ignore it and thus have needlessly engendered questions about the relation of the crucified and risen Christ to the political scene. Church creeds have emphasized that Christ, who does not yet reign, nonetheless even now rules by his providence and governance, and the New Testament associates even the regathering of Israel with God's purpose in Christ.

The interim dimension has two prongs, and it is the great tragedy of the contemporary religious scene that they are so dulled, one by many non-evangelical Christians' misconception of the nature and task of the Church, and the other by many evangelical Christians' narrowing of their task in the world.

God's ideal order involves a new society of transformed men and women. The Church as the body of renewed humanity was and is to exemplify to the world the principles and practice of personal and social righteousness and love in community that Messiah approves. The whole point of Jesus' dialogue with Nicodemus was that the indispensable beginning of the kingdom of God is a divine regeneration of sinful selves. It was therefore a profoundly misguided venture when politicized ecclesiastics sought the kingdom of God by repoliticizing an unregenerate society.

A second consideration is equally important. Although the New Testament places a temporary "hold" on the forced messianic overthrow of world-powers during the Church age, it places no "hold" whatever on the divine demand for justice in the public order. Christ's followers are to exemplify the standards of God's kingdom, and they are to be "light" and "salt" in a dark and rotting society where God intends civil government to promote justice and restrain disorder. The New Testament locates the Christian attitude toward the political scene not only in the future eschatological context of Revelation 13 but also in the present sociological context of Romans 13.

Carl F. H. Henry, "Footnotes: Jesus and Political Justice," *Christianity Today* 19, no. 5 (December 6, 1974): 34–35.

Chapter 30

THE WEST AT MIDNIGHT

Western civilization is coming unglued. Those who seem least aware of its impending collapse are (1) politicians with vested interests in promising a better tomorrow, (2) philosophers who despite a dismal record keep drawing up blueprints of utopia, and (3) stock brokers whose livelihood depends on marketing a bright future. Scientists seem more realistic about the world's slide. They speak even of the end of human history—though their alarm centers in matters like atmospheric pollution, the prospect of nuclear destruction, limited natural resources, and possible famine in an overpopulated world.

Solzhenitsyn, on the other hand, pinpoints our problem as a lack of conscience and will in the face of totalitarian Communist expansion. Meanwhile Muggeridge stresses the mass media's promotion of the moral shallowness and spiritual superficiality of our materialistic culture.

What it all adds up to is the gloomy fact that for all its promise of bright tomorrows, scientific technology will itself crumble in the ashes of a society that abandons ethical and religious concerns. As the world in the last quarter of the twentieth century divests itself of belief in God and his revelation and in redemptive renewal, it is left without any clear understanding of the meaning of life. It therefore plummets toward pervasive melancholy and despair. A remnant that believes in God and his purpose in history will be left to carry the moral fortunes of a dispirited race.

It has not dawned on the West that, instead of being a conquered malady, Nazism is but a shadow of things to come, and that Russian Communism, which also arose in the West, is not the worst of all coming judgments. To be sure, the brutalities of twentieth-century Communism are aptly appraised by Solzhenitsyn:

> What had been acceptable under Tsar Aleksei Mikhailovich in the seventeenth century, what had already been regarded as barbarism under Peter the Great, what might have been used against ten or twenty people in all during the time of Biron in the mid-eighteenth century, what had already become totally impossible under Catherine the Great, was all being practiced during the flowering of the glorious twentieth century—in a society based on socialist principles, and at a time when airplanes were flying and the radio and talking films had already appeared—not by one scoundrel alone in one secret place only but tens of thousands of specially trained human beasts standing over millions of defenseless victims [*The Gulag Archipelego*, Harper & Row, 1973, p. 93].

Solzhenitsyn confesses, "We didn't love freedom enough" but submitted rather to the Party line and so "we purely and simply *deserved* everything that happened afterward" (p. 13, n. 5). The embarrassing question is whether the so-called Free World (the designation is less and less appropriate) truly loves freedom or whether it is not rather so motivated by a passion for private material gain that secular capitalism cries out for controls upon its avarice.

Does not infatuation with sex in a time of scientifically abetted libertarianism push aside moral principles and thereby cast to the winds the sanctity of marriage and the dignity of human personality? By its preoccupation with change and its enthronement of human creativity, does not modern academic learning become subservient to a renegade call for new norms, norms that simply substitute expediency for enduring truth and principle? We have turned freedom into license. Our professed love of freedom is increasingly shown to be a sophistry that replaces wisdom and righteousness with self-gratification.

———————

It is time we professing evangelicals speak up and move out. Solzhenitsyn says of the Russian believers who waited too long to take a stand that "like the ancient Christians, we sat there in the cage while they poured salt on our raw and bleeding tongues" (p. 498). Martyrdom may indeed become the fate of a faithful remnant, but it should hardly be considered glory for a remnant that was silent in a time of spiritual eclipse.

Evangelical tradition in and of itself is not good enough for an era of civilizational end-time. We need to plumb far deeper than this into the basic biblical heritage. There we find prophets willing to be jeered at, flogged, chained, stoned, tortured, and if need be killed by the sword. Solzhenitsyn writes of victims of Communist terror who "crawled along the path of hope on their knees, as if their legs had been amputated" (p. 449). If in a time of cultural decay evangelicals live as if their tongues were cut, and confine their light inside the churches, do they deserve a better fate than the godless?

However casually we may dismiss Jesus' warnings about some future judgment, we cannot refute Solzhenitsyn's awareness that judgment may also strike in the present: "Do not pursue what is illusory—property and position; all that is gained at the expense of your nerves decade after decade, and is confiscated in one fell night" (p. 591). Who is to say that "the end of all the ends" may not actually be upon us, that tomorrow may not be the very last day or tonight the last night?

————————

Signs of a bleak near future are unmistakable in the philosophy and practice of our time. Human life is cheap. Moral considerations are considered expendable in the passion for material gain and sexual gratification. Personal preference dictates what is right. Truth is viewed as a changing commodity subject to private redefinition. The inevitable outcome of such deceptions is a barbarism that will dwarf anything known to pagans in pre-Christian times.

We are approaching the deliberate abandonment of distinctions between good and evil espoused by Judeo-Christian revelation and along with this a surrender of the concept of human dignity that revealed religion has sustained. Neither American technology nor American democracy nor American capitalism in and of itself can spare us.

Let us not be taken in by illusions of political salvation. Politics has become the utopian metaphysics of restless twentieth-century visionaries, and the Christian—while he has no license to neglect politics—should never expect too much from it. Without shared national goals, without an enlivened public conscience, without a commitment to transcendent truth and law, without a sure dedication to moral and spiritual priorities, the national spirit on the eve of America's bicentennial marks us as pied pipers whose call to hollow ideology leads down the short road to disillusionment.

Carl F. H. Henry, "Footnotes: The West at Midnight," *Christianity Today* 20, no. 1 (October 10, 1975): 33–34.

Chapter 31

EVANGELICALS JUMP ON THE POLITICAL BANDWAGON

Their involvement may become as misguided as
was the earlier activism of liberal Christianity.

Evangelical Christians are swarming back into the public arena. After a generation of withdrawal from public concerns in the wake of the modernist social gospel, they are "going public" and getting socially involved on a grand scale.

Resurgent evangelical interest in politics is to be welcomed and commended. Yet some observers fear—and with good reason—that this involvement may eventually become as politically misguided as was the activism of liberal Christianity earlier in this century. Some even consider 1980 the fateful year of evangelical ingress into politics, a year of decisive long-term consequences both for the United States and for the future of evangelical churches.

During the present political campaign evangelical spokesmen have been more involved in political affairs, directly or indirectly, than for many decades. A colorful "Washington for Jesus" rally, which its sponsors at first hoped would draw a million participants, rallied less than half that number, but the throng nonetheless notably outnumbered the multitudes who welcomed Pope John Paul II to the national capital. Leaders in the electronic church, a euphemism for television religion, have formulated specific questions that churchgoers are expected to address to their congressmen on political positions ranging from abortion and a balanced budget to the Panama Canal treaty and SALT II. This has been deplored as a spiritual litmus test that suspends the Christian authenticity of congressmen on particular political commitments. But the nonevangelical ecumenists who have long lobbied Congress for their own approved specifics were hardly in the best position to complain.

As the presidential election draws near, some churchmen are again probing the possibility of rival "Clergy for Carter," or "Clergy for Reagan," or "Clergy for Anderson" committees. On the ground that this was not the proper role of the clergy, I myself frustrated a "Clergy for Nixon" initiative at a 1972 pre-election White House briefing, when a prominent New England pastor asked invited churchmen publicly to endorse Nixon's candidacy. In some local races Protestant ministers—usually fundamentalists and political conservatives—are running for office. Pope John Paul dampened the political aspirations of Catholic clergy recently on the ground that ordination vows commit them not to unraveling earthly political affairs but to elucidating the spiritual and moral principles of the transcendent kingdom of God. Some evangelicals advocate that only "born-again" candidates be elected to office. Most Christians would probably protest if Jews were to vote only for Zionists or Catholics only for those who believe in papal infallibility. The notion that a born-again president will solve all the nation's problems has run upon hard times since Jimmy Carter has occupied the White House. Spiritual rebirth bestows no special competence for resolving political specifics, although it should assure a high level of moral integrity. By remarkable coincidence, all three presidential candidates claim to be evangelical Christians. Yet each declares the others politically inadequate to the presidency. Politics, as Bismarck observed, is no exact science. Evangelical or nonevangelical candidates alike might add confusion to inexactitude, but the grassroots multitudes are calling for leaders of godly character and commitment in national affairs, and for an end to the erosion of biblical values.

Complicating the present election debate is the emergence of several evangelical groups professing to provide scriptural guidance for the evangelical community. Jerry Falwell's Moral Majority promotes corporate prayer in public schools, as does Leadership Foundation, whereas the Baptist Joint Public Affairs Committee along with the National Council of Churches resists it. Coalition for Christian Action, Christian Voice, Christian Embassy, and lesser known groups all actively support politically conservative candidates. Heartened by the impact of prolife forces and the Supreme Court's decision against welfare funding of abortions, evangelical groups hope to expand their campaign against liberal misperceptions of the good.

Does this evangelical surge into the political realm indicate that evangelical revival has crested to the level of significant social awakening? The great evangelistic crusades of the eighteenth and nineteenth centuries in England struck so deeply into history that they elicited the designation "evangelical awakening." Their notable impact upon public conscience and legislation precipitated a wave of prison reform and led to outlawing of slavery and of child labor, and to other political changes. Even nonbelievers more and more judged community attitudes and commitments by biblical principles: social conviction and sensitivity consequently underwent public transformation.

When *Time* magazine designated 1976 "the year of the evangelical" many of the movement's spokesmen hurriedly and prematurely spoke of "evangelical awakening." But the present expansive political thrust does not of itself mean that contemporary American evangelicals are as politically aware as were earlier evangelicals. The current evangelical return to the political arena involves no comprehensive political philosophy or program; it has a notably attenuated range of specifics. The evangelical agenda in public affairs is conspicuously narrow when set alongside ecumenical Protestant, Roman Catholic, or even Reform Jewish projections. The ecumenical reach extends comprehensively to almost all political concerns, even if it almost predictably signals a liberal or radical direction in politico-economic affairs, and notably neglects such issues as Communist oppression, inflation, and crime. Evangelical political activity in the main counters this socialistic trend and promotes a revival of voluntarism. But its social vision is fragmentary, often lacks substance and strategy, and focuses mainly on a one-issue or single-candidate approach. One troubled evangelical observer has already suggested that on the morning after election day some leading Christian magazine should carry a major article analyzing "Where the Evangelicals Went Wrong."

What troubles some observers is that many evangelical leaders leap presumptuously from prayer breakfasts or from individual spiritual rebirth to assuredly authentic and predictable public policy consequences. This expectation does great disservice, since it detours evangelicals around intellectual scrutiny of political options and from informed decisions on them. One need not disapprove of national or state prayer breakfasts to note that because they gather leaders holding divergent political (and often religious) views they can hardly be expected to yield specific public policy consequences. Discussion of political particularities would likely be considered spiritually divisive. The "Washington for Jesus" rally finally abandoned any agenda of political specifics in order merely to register the conviction by a massive throng of godly citizens that America is doomed unless it heeds the will of God in national life. Some observers remarked that for the $1 million cost of staging the rally, evangelicals could have given much sharper focus to specific changes they desire in the political arena.

Evangelical leaders themselves are asking some unflattering questions about those among them who are aggressively organizing and mobilizing evangelical political opinion and action, but who are Johnny-come-lately to political concerns. Personal prominence, patriotic image, institutional mailing lists are all involved. Moral Majority's newsletter reaches 250,000 persons, including 70,000 conservative pastors. The deeper question is whether evangelicals are getting adequate guidance as they move into the 1980 political context.

———————

Evangelical social action is in some respects a whirlpool of contemporary confusion with spokesmen divergently aligned on all sides while professing to speak the evangelical view. These leaders sometimes seem to speak past or at each other, more than to the public scene, without clarifying differences of principle.

The magazine *Sojourners,* whose point of view reflects a minority of the evangelical constituency, gives the impression of much wider representation through skillful use of symbols that encourage public media coverage. It almost never speaks on abortion, promotes military disarmament, and tends to blame America for the ills of the world much in the mood of ecumenical sociopolitical analysis. *Christianity Today*, the establishment evangelical voice, on the other hand, in its recent Gallup Poll of evangelical social attitudes, did not even probe the two questions—military disarmament and nuclear power—that an international ecumenical conference of scientists and churchmen meeting last year at Massachusetts Institute of Technology addressed with most conviction. *Eternity* magazine has tried to rise above evangelical divergence by a series of panel discussions that reflect evangelical conflicts and reach for greater understanding, but with qualified success.

Many evangelicals are intellectually unprepared for energetic social engagements. They do not discern the connections between theology and ethical theory and strategy. They wish to go beyond mere negative criticism of controversial ecumenical commitments, yet are largely cast on nonevangelical initiatives. A program whose theological basis is unsure, and whose content and strategy are debatable, provides no effective alternative either to costly social indifference or to a pernicious social ethic. Encouraged by ecumenical activists, some evangelicals are even prone to revise modernist social gospel assumptions in the realm of public policy, while others fall prey to Marxist-oriented liberation theology. The former approach assumes that socialist legislation will rectify the ills of society, and the latter view does not exclude violence as a means of advancing it.

A group of Washington-area churchmen recently identified the overall social issues that most concern evangelicals as government funding of abortion, homosexuality, church-state issues centering in IRS policy—impositions on private schools, economic concern for a balanced budget (through bureaucratic retrenchment without weakening defense commitments in resisting Communist expansionism). Concern for the poor has been expressed mainly through private agencies.

There is growing pressure to expand this agenda in order to focus on the impact of television on public attitudes and morals, the issue of secular humanism in the public schools, the assault on the family as the basic unit of society, and international concern for religious liberty. But it will be no comprehensive gain if evangelicals broaden their agenda in the absence of an overall social vision, political philosophy, and public strategy.

This does not mean that evangelical Christianity must speak with a monolithic voice in public affairs, far less that some self-appointed clerical hierarchy needs to tell evangelicals for whom to vote. Biblical revelation does not speak directly to the particularities of politics. Scripture leaves translation of revealed principles into viable political decisions to the conscience and will of mankind, and equally devout individuals may disagree over the best program for achieving common goals.

A particular issue or particular candidate may indeed at times be of paramount political importance. But if evangelicals participate only in one-issue or one-candidate politics and do not address the broader principles and party platforms, they may unwittingly eliminate competent office holders whose cumulative experience, strategic committee posts, and stance on other issues not currently in debate, ought not to be ignored. If they settle only for single-issue or fragmentary involvement, evangelicals will treat public concerns as but a marginal appendage to evangelism, and remain highly vulnerable to the more comprehensive political strategies of nonevangelical groups. A complete program of social involvement that aims to affect and mold the course of events will ask not only what issues need to be addressed, but at what stage they are most effectively addressed, and how. More important, ideal social engagement will spur evangelicals to pursue not only a protective special interest in the public arena, but those concerns also that transcend self-interest and coincide with universal human rights and duties.

———————

Evangelicals need positive guidance at a time when many agencies solicit their support for this or that special cause. More sources of helpful information are available than most churchgoers recognize. A recent essay titled "Can My Vote Be Biblical?" (see Sept. 19 issue, p. 14), issued by a number of evangelical cosigners, calls attention to the paperback *Almanac of American Politics* that presents profiles of the voting record of congressmen, evaluations by private organizations such as the League of Women Voters, and reports identifying financial contributions to candidates, which are available for a small fee from the Federal Election Commission. Competent analysis of numerous public issues has also been done by the Ethics and Public Policy Center in Washington, whose director, Ernest W. Lefever, sees a merely one-issue approach as the end of a responsible political ethic.

In moving more fully into public affairs, evangelicals need to be alert to three great overarching considerations.

1. The Bible is our guide in political affairs as well as in other areas. But the Old Testament does not superimpose its blueprint for the Hebrew theocracy on the pluralistic pattern of civil government in the New Testament. Yet God stipulates the rule of justice by which all nations will be and are now being measured and which provides the only basis for enduring world order and peace.

The New Testament teaches that, although presently unrecognized by the world, the risen Christ is even now Lord of the cosmos. His people extend his lordship by promoting in public life the justice that God stipulates and sanctions. Christian clergy and educators must therefore inculcate the biblically revealed principles of social ethics.

2. The Bible leaves to the people of God the application of revealed principles to concrete situations that call for specific laws. We are to weigh all particular options in the light of biblical principles. The Bible gives few rules, although it does give some (e.g., "pay your taxes," "pay just wages"). Specific applications are left to public determination, and those specifics, although answerable to transcendent norms, may well differ from place to place and from time to time. But Christians are to work for just laws and to protest injustice in the public realm.

3. Among biblical concerns specially relevant today are the primacy of the family as a lifelong monogamous union, the dignity and worth of fetal life, the plight of the poor and oppressed, the right and need to work, the pursuit of world peace and order, the just use of power to contain the expansionist policies of aggressor nations, and the preservation of natural resources.

From the governing principles contained in the Bible many inferences can be drawn. Legislation should benefit family structures, not penalize them. It should preserve the civil rights of all, including homosexuals, but not approve and advance immoral lifestyles. Government-subsidized extinction of fetal life on the basis of cost-benefit analysis is wicked, the more so when government also finances experiments to bring new forms of life into being. Something is seriously wrong when a hospital cannot sew up an injured teen-ager's body wounds without notifying her parents, while that same teen-ager can have an abortion without parents even knowing about it, and as easily as having her ears pierced.

Massive and annually escalating military expenditures should not be heralded as unmitigated good news, but as a tragic necessity, one that arises not by divine determination but through the shameful aggression of predator powers that invade weak neighbor nations and through an exaggerated human trust in the saving power of missiles. One of the bitter ironies of a world torn by international struggle is that we in America—arms exporter to the world—find these very same arms sometimes arrayed in battle against us after our forces abandon them or when friendly nations fall to hostile powers.

The earth is the Lord's and we are responsible stewards in our use of its treasures. Implicit in the biblical view is a mandate to preserve earth's limited resources. No nation, no century, no generation is to consume greedily or destroy what is useful to all mankind.

Yet the Bible does not directly address many specific issues being debated today—whether to develop nuclear power, whether to develop nuclear missiles, how and when to ration gasoline, and so on. But no just answers to such questions can be achieved unless biblical principles are honored. Citizens motivated by a concern for justice may make divergent inferences and different applications, but some options are clearly ruled out. None will be perfect, and most will be subject to revision. But a society that pursues justice in its commitments and acts out of a desire to honor the will of God in public affairs has the assurance of God's blessing. To receive a divine benediction upon its public engagement no less than upon its evangelistic and missionary effort should be the evangelical goal in the modern world.

Carl F. H. Henry, "Evangelicals Jump on the Political Bandwagon," *Christianity Today* 24, no. 18 (October 24, 1980): 20–25.

Chapter 32

PRIVATE SINS, PUBLIC OFFICE

Does the public have a right to snoop on its political leaders?

I was asked recently whether we really ought to snoop into the private lives of politicians. For all their private vices, my interrogator continued, haven't many wicked emperors in the past been effective national leaders? Doesn't the question of personal peccadilloes divert attention from a discussion of more legitimate political concerns?

Given the rash of media revelations about the lives of presidential candidates—dirty tricks, exaggerated résumés, plagiarism, premarital conception and extramarital liaison (and who knows what next)—it is natural to ask: Is it really all that important to focus on the personal morality of politicians?

Should evangelicals in particular concentrate on the importance of character and moral integrity in *public* life?

Yes and no.

Here are a few things to keep in mind.

1. *Sin stains the story not only of some prominent politicians and candidates, but of all their media critics, and of evangelical leaders also.* Even the so-called Moral Majority—from which liberal press and liberal politicos distanced themselves—must admit its own immoralities. The matter of choosing a president or governor or congressman is not a matter of immaculately conceived voters nominating sinless leaders. We live in a sinful society to which we are all contributing units.

2. *Not even civil government requires inner purity.* Government is concerned with justice, public conduct, and fair dealing. Legislation concerns what is lawful and unlawful. That does not mean that motivation is wholly irrelevant—the distinction between intentional murder and accidental manslaughter is important. But the courts do not decide whether defendants are moral or immoral; only whether they acted legally or illegally. A jury may now and then find a good person guilty and acquit a bad person. (Even the Christian doctrine of justification involves acquittal of a guilty sinner on the ground of Christ's substitutionary bearing of the penalty and guilt of one's sin.)

Yet respect for law is a prime requisite of an orderly society. No one given to injustice and illegality is worthy of office. Exposure of one's legal record is relevant to eligibility for election.

3. *Some matters of private conduct have no bearing on qualification for the presidency or any other public office.* The contemporary cult of personality is so deeply entrenched that there is pervasive curiosity concerning the habits and flaws of anyone in the public spotlight. Because human beings have a variety of faults, foibles, and frailties, we must distinguish persistent and consequential moral failure from lesser transgressions, noting the stage of life at which they occurred and how the offender handled them. A deviant society could hardly have been astonished that, before

he became a Christian, Pat Robertson fathered his first child out of wedlock. (Much more politically relevant, but overlooked by the press, was Robertson's comment that he considered the later civil ceremony of little importance alongside the earlier covenant relationship with his sweetheart.)

Of course, politically marginal matters may be highly important in other contexts. Before God, one's momentary lustful look, or coveting of a neighbor's property, renders one guilty of sin irrespective of whether one actually commits adultery or theft. But if brainwashing of all such private thoughts is a prerequisite for political eligibility, a great many public offices will remain permanently unfilled.

4. *Resentment of the media for its exposure of candidates' logical and ethical inconsistencies is misdirected.* The media may be double-standard prone, judging others at times by criteria reporters and editors refuse to apply to themselves. But that does not invalidate their criticisms of public officials. To be sure, the warning "judge not, lest you be judged" carries biblical legitimacy; not all the Washington womanizers and plagiarists are politicians, and not all the trivia unearthed by journalists (and eagerly repeated and sometimes exaggerated by them) are relevant or significant. Yet there may be good journalism by bad journalists who find the very conception of ethical absolutes exotic (but invoke them when they condemn others).

Nevertheless, the press is not running for public office, even if it is striving for public credibility. It has professional critics skilled in evaluating the integrity of aspirants whose main concern is not behavior but the invention of an image.

5. *The religious facets of public policy issues are often deliberately highlighted by those who champion Judeo-Christian values vis-a-vis secular humanism.* This invites closer appraisal of moral indiscretions in the lives of aspirants for office like Pat Robertson.

Much of the secular public may view evangelical religion as a strange cult, but it nonetheless expects gospel truth and moral purity from those who champion those virtues. The same observation can be made about Jesse Jackson, who makes the churches his special podium. Yet in the final analysis, the same standards of character must be applied to all candidates. Incumbents who lie to the public, and candidates who lie to their potential constituencies, encourage the conviction that they are not trustworthy. Americans expect fidelity and truth from their leaders; they deplore deception.

6. *The saddest aspect of the immorality controversy among politicians is the disposition of campaign spokesmen to regard the concentration on personal character as a sign of national unbalance and weakness.* Some of Gary Hart's supporters even championed an "unconventional candidate" as a sign of national maturity in a society in revolt against the nuclear family, and in which 40 percent of spouses are said to be unfaithful. But anyone who considers sexual infidelity an asset to political candidacy does not know the American mainstream.

7. *Although the Constitution prohibits a religious test for office, the question of one's religious views is relevant insofar as they bear upon political commitments.* The public properly wished to know the implications of Richard Nixon's Quaker roots for his stance on military preparedness. Today, some ask what the implications are for political action of Pat Robertson's insistence that he stands in a direct revelatory relationship to God. No less relevant would be the stance of a candidate committed to secular humanism and its denial of changeless truth and moral principles. Almost all legislation has moral implications, and contemporary society is in ethical turmoil. The Judeo-Christian moral imperatives are not irrelevant to the politician qua politician. A candidate who lacks a value system in personal relationships may deplore the moral

crisis in public speeches (often ghost-written). But he will be psychologically unable to resist the atrocities of others, let alone to model moral leadership for the nation. The political scene struggles in its foreign and domestic commitments for transcendent referents beyond utilitarianism and pragmatism. In their best moments, political leaders reach for a conscience superior to the press and to the state and even to the nation. They are increasingly wary of the ambition for power, of the autonomous products of liberal philosophy and religion, of a pseudo-intellectual elite uninterested in perennial truth and good. It does not speak well for American society that most of the best-educated in our nation seem to reject a religious basis for life and that, not surprisingly, they offer little in the way of moral leadership. Much as the Founding Fathers resisted any national church establishment, they would have insisted that the abolition of God means not the freedom of humanity but rather the nullification of humankind. For human rights are grounded in the Creator's endowment; deny the divine Creator, and human rights lose their foundation.

8. *What the political arena desperately needs is not merely better parties, platforms, and policies, but better persons.* The hour has struck for moral courage; without it the cultural crisis must inevitably overtake all facets of contemporary society. It is high time to stop concentrating on political immorality and to start giving tribute to our moral heroes. Paul's exhortation to the Philippians remains a comprehensive motto for those in public life: "Whatever is true, whatever is honorable, whatever is just, whatever is pure, whatever is lovely, whatever is gracious, if there is any excellence, if there is anything worthy of praise, think about these things" (4:8). No political agenda, however good, can be implemented effectively by candidates with tarnished reputations who have ceased to be symbols of hope.

9. *In the last analysis, sound political judgment requires a verdict on policy no less than on character.* That is not to say that more emphasis should be placed on concept than on candidate. But in an imperfect world the choices are more complex than whether to support a deceiver who champions flawed political policy or a saint committed to sound policy. Political and ethical realities often force us to choose the lesser of two evils. A candidate who has repented of his nonpayment of income taxes two decades ago and advocates a superior foreign policy should be preferred over a competitor who teaches Sunday school but holds a highly questionable view of foreign affairs. No doubt an ideal world will ultimately concentrate character and policy in the same person. But then, an ideal world presumably will dispense both with income taxes and with sinners, and thus exclude snoopers on political morality.

Carl F. H. Henry, "Private Sins, Public Office," *Christianity Today* 32, no. 4 (March 4, 1988): 28–29.

Chapter 33

THE NEW COALITIONS

Evangelicals can count on having to join forces with nonevangelicals before significant social change can come.

From social and political withdrawal to cobelligerency with conservative Catholics and other Americans is a long stride, but some evangelical spokesmen are eagerly encouraging this promising, if controversial venture.

Left far behind are fundamentalists of the 1930–50 era whose pessimistic view of history led them to exclude socio-political involvement and cultural engagement in favor of concentrated personal evangelism in expectation of Christ's imminent return. Their apolitical stance arose from a conviction that the end-time apostasy is now under way. The viewpoint still has support in Bob Jones circles and in an older Dallas seminary constituency. But "Amish evangelicals" and traditional fundamentalists pessimistic about historical involvement and change are now "out of it." Even many Mennonites no longer insist that the regenerate church as "a new society" must wholly avoid engagement with the world.

Most evangelicals assume we must be strenuously involved in public affairs. Some see this as a political necessity, since not to do so is to be disadvantaged by unbelievers sponsoring contrary values. Most declare it a moral duty implicit in the Christian's dual citizenship. The divine mandate is to beam light, sprinkle salt, knead leaven into an otherwise hopeless world.

This Christian ingress is championed in its most intensive form by those who commend one or another form of ecclesiastical imperialism—the theonomic movement (or Christian Reconstructionism) being the most egregious example.

In sharp contrast to recent modern fundamentalism, which confined the relevance of Mosaic legislation to a now-superseded dispensation, the current Reconstructionist movement proposes to "restore" Christian legislation to the United States and holds that theonomy—civil government that implements the Mosaic legislation—is the divinely intended norm for all times and places. This transformationist view correlates the Mosaic legislation not only with a covenant people, as did the Hebrews, but would bring all society under its rule and treat all humankind as part of one faith community. The theonomists regard a democratic or republican form of government as heretical, and seek to implement the political lordship of Christ over the modern nations.

Given the tendency of totalitarian regimes to use power despotically, many Christians have in modern times preferred republican or democratic forms of government in the interest of political self-determination. They connect a beneficent totalitarianism only with the coming millennial reign of Christ and view the concentration of absolute political power in the hands of human rulers as fraught with risk. To be sure, they do not deny that democracy may through lack of consensus fall into chaos, or that a benevolent monarchy may now and then arise in fallen history. But they do not view democracy as heretical, as do Reconstructionists; rather, they see theonomy as an illegitimate proposal for civil government in the present church age, and a republican or democratic alternative as compatible with legitimate evangelical concerns, especially in the American context of church-state separation.

Private versus Public Philosophies

The emphasis on a pluralistic republic poses a basic question for Christians: Are they in the public arena to concern themselves only or mainly with their own interests as one of the numerous faith communities? Or is their first obligation to identify and to promote the common good of society? Many evangelicals are uninterested in, or neglect, formulation of a public policy and exhaust their energies mainly in what they oppose, or in promoting single-issue special interests. Many church members are not taught that political developments are important. Emphasis on the importance of a shared evangelical view of a civic common good even seems odd to them.

The result is that evangelicals enter the political arena primarily in terms of the special interests of a particular faith community and justify their involvement solely in terms of an appeal to the revelatory authority of the Bible. Since they exhibit no concern for a public philosophy, they are readily perceived as a threat to pluralistic democracy; their civic involvement centers in a confrontational activism that promotes Christian legislation and a Christian state, if not under the banner of theonomic Reconstructionism then under that of a Moral Majority.

In this development, recent American political involvement acquired a very different identity from that of the eighteenth-century Evangelical Awakening in England. This departure of recent American political activists from a more traditional stance is a major reason for growing emphasis on the evangelical need for a public philosophy and for a strategy of cobelligerency. Earlier evangelicals were concerned for public justice, not simply for special evangelical interests. They identified themselves with the whole body politic in the effort to promote civic righteousness. They championed a public philosophy and addressed national conscience. This was not simply a matter of one's private vision of civic decency; it was a divine compulsion to speak of public affairs in the context of transcendent justice and of a universally binding social good. These convictions—and not solely an appeal to biblical considerations—pulsate through Wilberforce's plea for an end to the slave traffic.

The distinction between public interest and partisan interest is reflected by differing attitudes to religious liberty concerns. The Religious Right eagerly appealed to religious liberty and increasingly declared it to be basic to all other human freedoms. Yet it specially invoked religious liberty to protest encroachments on evangelical freedom, and to advance legitimate evangelical concerns. But a disciplined public philosophy would stress religious freedom for all persons of whatever faith, as at the same time the best guarantee of religious liberty for Christians. Had the Religious Right from the outset paid attention to this distinction, it would not so readily have been perceived by critics as a civic threat to nonevangelicals in its insistence on the relevance of religion to public affairs.

Conservative Protestants sought to transcend a misperception of religious intolerance by inviting like-minded Catholics, Jews, and Mormons—whose participation lent a pluralistic image of sorts to the movement. This somewhat diminished suspicions that they sought to impose an agenda of Christian sectarian legislation upon the state. But it stopped far short of articulating a public philosophy.

The Theological Base

The theological basis for evangelical involvement in public justice is located in God's creation-ethic and his universal revelation including the *imago Dei* that, however sullied, nonetheless survives the Fall. To be sure, Christian theologians have suggested other rationales. Some Reformed scholars appeal to *common grace* in expounding general revelation. Calvin propounded the doctrine, and Charles Hodge, Herman Bavinck, and Abraham Kuyper relied on it in expounding a philosophy of history and culture. No less than saving grace, common grace presupposes total depravity. But its role is limited to a divine restraining of the effects of sin and enablement of civil righteousness and human culture.

Some Reformed writers reject the doctrine of common grace, while others—notably Valentine Hepp, Kuyper, and Bavinck—developed it into a natural theology and apologetics based on general truths supposedly shared by all humanity. In doing so they disregarded Calvin's insistence that unregenerate humanity suppresses its own inescapable knowledge of the Deity.

Roman Catholicism appeals to *natural law*, the theory that despite the Fall there survives a universally shared body of moral truths. This doctrine the Protestant Reformers disavowed as involving an inadequate view of the consequences of original sin. Calvin spoke of "natural law," but by it he did not mean either that a universally shared body of ethical and theological truths survives the Adamic Fall, or that revealed ethics and theology can or should be superimposed on such an edifice. Yet the Reformers insisted that the light of general revelation penetrates the mind of unregenerate humankind universally and that all humans are guilty for their deflection of it. The basis for a public philosophy is therefore not located in sectarian religious tradition but in universal revelation and public reason, without disavowing the crucial importance of special revelation.

Some Roman Catholic Thomistic scholars confuse the Protestant emphasis on general revelation and/or on common grace with natural-law theory. In recent years a number of second-order Reformed scholars have controversially depicted Calvin as devoted to natural law, and have pursued an evidentialist apologetics highly compatible with empirical Thomistic theology. Whereas evangelical orthodoxy has stressed God's rational propositional revelation and the importance of biblically revealed principles of morality, some contemporary Catholics move the discussion toward natural-law theory and church tradition by questioning that the Bible does in fact give us much in the way of principial ethics. Richard John Neuhaus, a Lutheran thinker, holds that conservative evangelical cobelligerency with conservative Protestant ecumenists and conservative Catholics need not involve an implicit commitment to natural-law theory.

Chartered Pluralism

Proponents of the so-called Williamsburg Charter have recently emerged to champion "chartered pluralism." Shaped by British sociologist Os Guinness, the charter project is not predicated on shared beliefs. It assumes that American pluralism has now moved far past that possibility. Beyond traditional Christian (Catholic, Protestant, and Orthodox) and Jewish distinctions, enlarging clusters of Muslims, Buddhists, and Hindus are now emerging. The American population now also includes 4 percent who are completely irreligious—consider religion valueless and irrelevant to public affairs—and never go to church. Another 6 percent disavow any religious preference yet grant that religion can be important.

"Chartered pluralism" does not involve a general dilution of belief (Judeo-Christian theism) nor a fluctuating civil religion. Rather, it is a compact whereby pluralistic society embraces "the

3-*R*'s of religious liberty: rights, responsibilities, and respect." It is "chartered" in that it accommodates no one interest group, and it is "pluralistic" in that it is not merely majoritarian. Moral and religious consensus is not a *given*, but a *goal*. Instead of focusing on the narrow rubric of "church and state," it focuses in a pluralistic society on religion and government in a common version of religious liberty.

Since participating constituencies mean different things by rights and by responsibilities, some critics insist that such divergences weaken the stability of the compact. The charter was misrepresented by some critics as a betrayal of evangelical or Christian theological loyalties and the substitution of a heretical and pagan alternative. But it does neither. It is more formal than substantive. It affirms universal religious liberty, universally obligatory rights and duties. It leaves to the citizenry the establishment and vindication of specific content, whether on philosophical or revelatory grounds.

The charter has much in common with John Courtney Murray's emphasis that Roman Catholics should enter the political arena not through attempted ecclesiastical controls but through projection of a public philosophy. Armed with the Vatican II emphasis on religious liberty and with natural-law tradition, Catholics will, no doubt, expound the content of public justice consistently with their own tradition. Evangelical Protestants must carefully identify areas of consensus and difference.

The population of the United States will be even more pluralistic in the 1990s than it is now. Religious liberty is a great evangelical theme, and evangelicals should be foremost among its heralds, showing that the case for public justice rests not simply on special revelation, but no less upon God's moral purpose in Creation. Despite the Fall, humankind has some awareness of this, natural law or no natural law.

Cobelligerency will be a fact of political life in the decades ahead, not without both gains and losses for each participating group, and not without frequently shifting alliances for preferred ends. Nothing in scriptural revelation or in general revelation precludes an evangelical and a secular humanist from standing together against race discrimination or ecological pollution. A humanist may not want to stand with a theist any more than a theist would prefer to stand with an atheist. But if the issue at stake is human rights and duty or public pollution, not supernaturalism or naturalism, each can ignore what he or she perceives to be a shaky epistemology to jointly commend right action and public justice.

In *A Plea for Evangelical Demonstration* (1971), I stressed the importance of public evangelical identification with the body of humanity no less than with the body of Christ. Nothing precludes an interreligious or ecumenical cooperative public witness against injustice or for justice. If evangelicals were to take the initiative in setting the agenda, nonevangelicals would have to ask themselves whether they can "afford" to cooperate or not. We ask ourselves the question because we so easily forfeit the initiative to others.

Carl F. H. Henry, "The New Coalitions," *Christianity Today* 33, no. 17 (November 17, 1989): 26–28.

INVENTING EVANGELICALISM

No one was more pivotal to the emerging
movement than Carl F. H. Henry.

Timothy George

Carl Henry was ever the evangelist—though few think of the great theologian in this way. And sometimes he would go to extraordinary lengths to proclaim the message of the Bible. One of my most vivid memories of him is from an address he gave to several thousand Southern Baptist pastors. He was describing the bankruptcy of philosophical naturalism, which has no place for the handiwork of a personal God. His text was Ecclesiastes 12:5—the meaningless shuttle of a purposeless life, as almond trees blossom, mourners go about the streets, and "the grass-hopper drags itself along."

As Henry described all this in his high, wispy voice, suddenly I was astonished to see this lanky preacher-theologian leave the pulpit and begin to walk back and forth across the platform, slightly jumping as he imitated a grasshopper dragging itself through a field. This was as close as I ever saw Henry come to a charismatic display, but those who heard that message will never forget it.

Nor will the evangelical world soon forget him. Carl Ferdinand Howard Henry was born on January 22, 1913, in New York City, the son of German immigrant parents. He died on December 7, 2003, in Watertown, Wisconsin, with Helga, his beloved wife of 63 years, at his side. In the 90 years that intervened between these two events, Henry cut a wide and deep swath across the landscape of American Christianity and the world evangelical movement. Indeed, along with his Wheaton College classmate, Billy Graham, and distinguished Boston pastor Harold John Ockenga, Henry practically invented what later became known as evangelicalism.

A Youth Adrift

Although his father was a Lutheran and his mother a Roman Catholic, Henry was baptized and confirmed as an Episcopalian. But none of this really took, and Henry became a teenage drop-out from church in the Central Islip community on Long Island where he grew up. He could type 85 words per minute, and, during the Depression, he found work as a reporter and eventually editor of a major weekly near his home.

All of this changed in 1933 when Henry, a 20-year-old, received Jesus Christ as his Savior and Lord. He later said of this event: "Into the darkness of my young life, he put bright stars that still shine and sparkle. After that encounter, I walked the world with God as my Friend." He was dipped in baptism at a local Baptist church and soon was off to pursue studies at Wheaton.

At Wheaton, Henry met not only Graham but also Harold Lindsell, Kenneth Taylor, Sam Moffett, Richard Halverson, and other students destined to become luminaries in the dawning evangelical renaissance. Most important, he met Helga Bender, the beautiful daughter of Baptist missionaries to the African Cameroons. To help support himself, Henry taught typing; Helga was a student in one of his classes. He was enchanted with her hazel eyes, which sparkled, he wrote at the time, "like the light of heaven." They were married in 1940 and eventually had two children: a daughter, Carol, an expert musicologist, and a son, Paul, a United States congressman from 1984 until his death in 1993.

The most important intellectual influence on Henry was Gordon Clark, a Presbyterian theologian, who emphasized propositional truth and the rationality of belief in God. Henry went on to earn two doctorates, one in theology from Northern Baptist Theological Seminary in a Chicago suburb (where he also taught for several years), and one in philosophy from Boston University. Yet Clark remained the main influence on Henry's developing thought. From the beginning, Henry set out to think through afresh the historic Christian understanding of the God who intelligibly makes known his Word and his will. Theology, he believed, should not be done in a vacuum but in serious interaction with competing and opposing theological perspectives. "Evangelical theology," he wrote, "is heretical if it is only creative, and unworthy if it is only repetitious." Henry's theological work culminated in a massive six-volume study, *God, Revelation, and Authority,* published from 1976 to 1983. This was his *magnum opus,* and it remains the most sustained theological epistemology produced by any evangelical theologian of the 20th century.

New Bearings

God, Revelation, and Authority contains more than 3,000 pages, but a small, 75-page booklet, a tract for the times, gave impetus and direction to the fledgling evangelical movement in post-World War II America. *The Uneasy Conscience of Modern*

Fundamentalism (1947) breathes with fire—rejecting the failed theology of liberalism, discredited by the devastation of two world wars, but also calling fellow conservatives to a positive engagement with society and culture. Looking back on this manifesto years later, Henry wrote:

> What distressed the growing evangelical mainstream about the fundamentalist far right were its personal legalisms, suspicion of advanced education, disdain for biblical criticism per se, polemical orientation of theological discussion, judgmental attitudes toward those in ecumenically related denominations, and an uncritical political conservatism often defined as "Christian anticommunism' and 'Christian capitalism" that, while politicizing the Gospel on the right, deplored politicizing it on the left.

Henry had been a strong supporter of the National Association of Evangelicals since its formation in 1942, and some of the ideas in *Uneasy Conscience* first appeared in the NAE's *United Evangelical Action*. Like Ockenga—the impresario of "neoevangelicalism," as he called it—Henry promoted the ideals of unity, education, evangelism, and social ethics while maintaining the absolute truth claims of historic Christian orthodoxy. This combination would become a mark of Henry's leadership in many other evangelical ventures across the years.

Henry was in the thick of all these ventures. In 1947 he became the founding dean of Fuller Theological Seminary, a post made more important because Ockenga, the first Fuller president, was *in absentia*. In 1949 Henry joined with other scholars to promote serious academic discussion and suggested the group's name, the Evangelical Theological Society.

A major turning point for Henry came in 1955 when Graham, fresh from a crusade in Europe, traveled to Pasadena to talk with Henry about becoming the editor of a new publication, *Christianity Today*. This publication was to be "a magazine of evangelical conviction," combining an irenic spirit with theological integrity. With the aim of "articulating evangelical Christianity effectively in our generation," Henry recruited an impressive company of contributing editors for the initial 1956 issue, including F. F. Bruce, John Stott, G. C. Berkouwer, Bernard Ramm, and Clarence E. McCartney.

In a letter soliciting their support, Henry spoke of the strategic opportunity, in a climate of uncertainty, "to reorient to Christian compass-bearings." He also mentioned that the new *CT* offices would overlook the lawn of the White House, an indication of his vision for the culture-shaping prospect of this project. During his 12-year term as editor of *CT*, Henry encouraged evangelicals to move from the "rearguard" to the "vanguard" in efforts to apply Christian values and principles to every area of society. Henry also wrote about the importance of prayer and other disciplines of the spiritual life, but he rejected outright the kind of quietism and interiorized piety that left some Christians disengaged from the world and its pressing needs.

Henry was enormously successful as an evangelical networker, bringing together thinkers, activists, evangelists, and church leaders. His concern for "evangelical ecumenism" led to the 1966 World Congress on Evangelism in Berlin, an event chaired by Henry with Graham as honorary chairman. This gathering of evangelical leaders from around the world was a precursor of the even more influential International Congress on World Evangelization at Lausanne in 1974. His call for evangelicals to establish a "great metropolitan Christian university" in New York City was not successful. He worked closely with theological seminaries and colleges, encouraging them to train students to think in terms of the Christian worldview across the various intellectual disciplines.

One of Henry's favorite phrases was "to strike a blow for the faith," and this he sought to do wherever he went. Henry logged millions of miles of air travel, wearing a suit bought in Majorca, and carrying a well-worn beret bought in Spain, horn-rimmed glasses from Singapore, shoes resoled in Korea, and a Bible rebound in the Philippines. Along the way, he met countless people who scarcely suspected "what God can do for the individual whose mind and heart have been stretched by the Good News of the Gospel." He was lecturer at large for World Vision International (1974–86). He was also a theological mentor to Charles Colson and served on the board of Prison Fellowship Ministries (1981–98).

A Sure Foundation

In his later years, Henry betrayed a brooding concern that the evangelical movement, for all its success, could lose its core identity by uncritically accommodating to the culture. He criticized open theism as a theological dead end, and was wary of postmodernism with its lack of concern for the cognitive character of theological assertions. While Henry himself did not extend the project begun in *God, Revelation, and Authority* into more recent theological debates, it would be a mistake to dismiss his achievement as a relic from the past. His defense of biblical authority and his practice of Christian apologetics, not to say his commitment to Christian social ethics, continue to inform and enrich. If some of his ideas seem eclipsed today, I predict that a new generation of evangelicals, perhaps yet unborn, will find them still worthy of serious attention in the future.

The abiding validity of Henry's theology stems from the hope that is at the heart of true Christian faith. He knew that despite storms without and fears within, all of the biblical realities remain in place. God's promises have not been nullified, and a life transformed by the dynamic of the Gospel of Christ is as powerful as ever. He wrote in the last paragraph of *God, Revelation, and Authority:*

> God who stands and stoops and speaks is God who stays: He it is who preserves and governs and consummates his cosmic purpose. But the awesome wonder of the biblical revelation is not his creation and preservation of our vastly immense and complex universe. Its wonder, rather, is that he came as God-man to planet Earth in the form of the Babe of Bethlehem; he thus reminds us that no point in the universe is too remote for his presence and no speck too small for his care and love. He came as God-man to announce to a rebellious race the offer of a costly mercy grounded in the death and resurrection of his only Son and to assure his people that he who stays will remain with them forever and they with him. He is come in Christ incarnate to exhibit ideal human nature and will return in Christ glorified to fully implement the Omega-realities of the dawning future.

Beyond all of his accomplishments, two things about Carl Henry stand out in my mind. On his last visit to Beeson Divinity School, he spoke in chapel about his conversion to Christ. He never got over the sheer wonder and joy of having been chosen and rescued by God's surprising grace. He knew what it meant to be born again. The other thing that stands out was his extraordinary humility and kindness toward others. His commitment to the orthodox Christian faith was solid as a rock, but I never heard him speak in a bitter or disparaging way about anybody, not even those with whom he disagreed.

I last saw Carl several months ago, when Greg Waybright, president of Trinity International University, and I made a pilgrimage to his bedside at the little Moravian nursing home where he and Helga lived.

He could not walk, and could barely talk, but his mind was abuzz with ideas and plans and new ventures for the advance of God's kingdom. We prayed and read the Scriptures together. Even though he was in pain, his eyes still sparkled with the joy of Christ. Carl loved to quote Vance Havner's prayer, "Lord, get me safely home before dark." As we left, Helga thanked us for coming and said she thought Carl was ready to go home. And now to home he has gone, to the place where peace abides and grasshoppers limp no more.

Timothy George, "Inventing Evangelicalism: No One Was More Pivotal to the Emerging Movement than Carl F. H. Henry," *Christianity Today* 48, no. 3 (March 2004): 48–51.

CONFESSIONS OF
AN EDITOR

This editorial appeared in the spring of 1968, after Henry decided to step down as editor of Christianity Today *later that year.*

God stabbed my conscience that night and pinned me to the ground with a fiery bolt of lightning. He was calling me, but I had never dreamed he would or could call so insistently, nor so inconveniently. All through that sodden Long Island night he pursued me, joining thunder and flaming arrow to unnerve his retreating quarry.

When the fire fell I knew instinctively that the Great Archer had nailed me, as it were, to my own footsteps.

The Bible is not without a theology of thunder and lightning, one that differs notably from the familiar *Donner und Blitzen* of a gift-laden Saint Nicholas. It speaks, in truth, of God's judgment. And that night, as I trembled in the storm, I knew unmistakably that the Eternal One was coding an urgent message to my soul.

This harrowing moment, this unexpected meeting with God, was no ordinary, soon-to-be-forgotten rendezvous. To be sure, it had a past as well as a future. But now the fire kindled in my heart refused to die; its light exposed memories that conscience could not deny. Across the years I had sparred often with the Invisible One. All the while I was still a pagan—a neo-Christian pagan, as it were—born into a presumably Christian home where mother was a Roman Catholic and father a Lutheran. At the age of twelve I was confirmed in the Christian faith—in fact, on two successive Sundays, though still very much a stranger to Jesus Christ, I was baptized and confirmed by the local Episcopal priest. I shed the Church in my mid-teens. In the course of my evacuation I had managed to pilfer a Bible from the pew racks, however, and as I opened it now and then upon retiring, one segment of that Book held a special fascination for me: its narratives of the resurrection of Jesus Christ from the dead.

I did not know then—as I should have known, and as anyone having even the slightest contact with the Church ought not to be able to forget—that the Apostle Paul associates Christ's crucifixion for sinners and the bodily resurrection as central tenets of the Evangel, or God's great good news. I was a newspaperman preoccupied with man's minutiae when God tracked me down; the Word was pursuing a lost purveyor of words. In this encounter, my own semantic skill meant little. When, shortly after the Almighty One had used lightning to pierce my soul, a university graduate prodded me to pray, I found myself at a loss for words. There I was, a Long Island editor and suburban correspondent quite accustomed to interviewing the high and mighty of this world, yet wholly inept at formulating phrases for the King of Glory. Not even the dimly familiar words from the Order of the Holy Communion (some of which I now treasure deeply, e.g., "... Christ's blood was shed for thee ... be thankful") seemed to fit the sheer spontaneity of that occasion.

So my friend and I settled for the Lord's Prayer. Jesus had

said, "When thou prayest, enter into thy closet ..." My altar rail was the front seat of my automobile; we parked it beside the waters of Great South Bay, locked the doors, and knelt to pray. Phrase by phrase I repeated the words of my friend. My heart owned its abysmal depth of need. "How blest are those who know that they are poor; the kingdom of Heaven is theirs"—so the New English Bible translates Jesus' opening words in the Sermon on the Mount. My aching spirit cried out to God for the forgiveness of sins and for new life in Christ. Somewhere in the echoes of eternity I heard the pounding of hammers that marked the Savior's crucifixion in my stead.

Like a sure wind from the eternal world comes God's assurance of forgiveness to the redeemed. For me the fearsome lightning now became a fountain of light; the roll of thunder, a surge of confidence. Incomparable peace, the reality of sins forgiven, a sense of destiny and direction, and above all the awareness of a new Presence and Power at the core of life—this is rebirth. I was now on speaking terms with God, a friend of the King, a servant of the Savior.

The very next day I would have gone to the ends of the earth to do the Divine Redeemer's bidding. I would, in truth, have gone to China; instead, in his time, and after a time of training, I went to campuses, and then to *Christianity Today*.

And now where? After a span of service—whether here or there—to the eternal presence of God. That is the believer's momentous prospect. For Jesus Christ turns life right-side-up and heaven outside-in.

In our century everything seems to be changing; nothing abides. Only those who know the Living God escape this threat of universal obsolescence. God abides. The Divine Commandments abide. Christ's Gospel abides. And whoever abides in him now will forever abide with him. The cosmic process offers no enduring place to hide but God's own abiding place.

Carl F. H. Henry, "Confessions of an Editor," *Christianity Today* 12, no. 13 (March 29, 1968): 3.

SUBJECT INDEX

SCRIPTURE INDEX

Old Testament

New Testament